P9-BVC-526

P U R E

JFC 2D Graphics and Imaging

Satyaraj Pantham, Ph.D.

A Division of Macmillan USA
201 West 103rd Street, Indianapolis, Indiana 46290

Pure JFC 2D Graphics and Imaging

Copyright © 2000 by Sams Publishing

All rights reserved. No part of this book shall be reproduced, stored in a retrieval system, or transmitted by any means, electronic, mechanical, photocopying, recording, or otherwise, without written permission from the publisher. No patent liability is assumed with respect to the use of the information contained herein. Although every precaution has been taken in the preparation of this book, the publisher and author assume no responsibility for errors or omissions. Neither is any liability assumed for damages resulting from the use of the information contained herein.

International Standard Book Number: 0-672-31669-2

Library of Congress Catalog Card Number: 99-61348

Printed in the United States of America

First Printing: November 2000

01   00   99   4   3   2   1

Trademarks

All terms mentioned in this book that are known to be trademarks or service marks have been appropriately capitalized. Sams Publishing cannot attest to the accuracy of this information. Use of a term in this book should not be regarded as affecting the validity of any trademark or service mark.

Warning and Disclaimer

Every effort has been made to make this book as complete and as accurate as possible, but no warranty or fitness is implied. The information provided is on an "as is" basis. The authors and the publisher shall have neither liability nor responsibility to any person or entity with respect to any loss or damages arising from the information contained in this book.

ASSOCIATE PUBLISHER
Angela Wethington

EXECUTIVE EDITOR
Tim Ryan

DEVELOPMENT EDITOR
Tiffany Taylor

MANAGING EDITOR
Lisa Wilson

PROJECT EDITOR
Dawn Pearson

COPY EDITOR
Michael Henry

INDEXER
Johnna VanHoose Dinse

PROOFREADER
Jill Mazurczyk

TECHNICAL EDITOR
Jeff Perkins

TEAM COORDINATOR
Karen Opal

MEDIA DEVELOPER
Craig Atkins

INTERIOR DESIGN
Karen Ruggles

COVER DESIGN
Anne Jones

COPY WRITER
Eric Borgert

PRODUCTION
Stacey DeRome
Ayanna Lacey
Heather Hiattt Miller

Overview

Contents

About the Author

Dr. Satyaraj Pantham earned a Ph.D. from the Indian Institute of Science, Bangalore (India) for his research work in flight stability and control. He has worked as a professional programmer for a decade, developing software for a variety of systems that range from aircraft to email.

Dr. Pantham has been programming with Java since the beginning of the Java revolution. He works as a consultant for Sun Microsystems. This is the second book written by the author; his previous book, titled *Pure JFC: Swing,* focuses on the Swing technology provided in JFC. He currently works on a Java project to build a production control system for the manufacturing industry. His software design and developmental interests include JFC Swing, 2D and 3D graphics, design patterns and UML, and distributed computing using Java IDL.

Dedication

To the memory of my younger brothers, Prasad and Suresh.

Acknowledgments

Initially, I would like to acknowledge the pioneers who created the Java 2D API. I would also like to thank my friends Venkat and Bhaskar, and my brother Ganesh for their interest and enthusiasm on the completion of this book. Again, while working on this book, I have sacrificed my family life with my absent-minded attitude. I must surely thank my wife Pushpa and my son Saravan for the cooperation and support they have given me.

Special thanks goes to Sams executive editor Tim Ryan for his interest in creating this book. Thanks to Tiffany Taylor for the developmental help and excellent suggestions. I would also like to acknowledge Mike Henry for copy editing, and Dawn Pearson for her work as project editor. Thanks are also due to Jeff Perkins for reviewing the examples from this book.

Tell Us What You Think!

As the reader of this book, *you* are our most important critic and commentator. We value your opinion and want to know what we're doing right, what we could do better, what areas you'd like to see us publish in, and any other words of wisdom you're willing to pass our way.

As a Publisher for Sams, I welcome your comments. You can fax, email, or write me directly to let me know what you did or didn't like about this book—as well as what we can do to make our books stronger.

You can download the code associated with this book by going to **www.samspublishing.com/productsupport** and entering the ISBN for this book (0672316692).

When you write, please be sure to include this book's title and author as well as your name and phone or fax number. I will carefully review your comments and share them with the author and editors who worked on the book.

Fax: 317.581.4770

E-mail: `java@mcp.com`

Mail: Tim Ryan
Executive Editor
Sams Publishing
201 West 103rd Street
Indianapolis, IN 46290 USA

Introduction

The Java Foundation Classes (JFC) are a set of API classes for the Swing Set, Java 2D API, drag and drop, and accessibility technologies. This book covers the Java 2D API portion of the JFC. For a concise reference on the Swing Set, readers can consult *Pure JFC: Swing*, also published by Sams.

The Java 2D API is produced with the joint effort by Sun Microsystems and Adobe Systems Incorporated. The API provides advanced 2D graphics classes for comprehensive drawing, fonts, and text layouts, creating color spaces, and imaging. The API also includes support for geometric transformations, color compositing, rendering hints, and alpha channeling. The classes and interfaces in the Java 2D API are compact and simple to use, but very flexible and powerful. With their help, you can add dazzling graphics to Java programs.

The Java 2D API is also compatible with the graphics support in Abstract Windowing Toolkit (AWT). The graphics generated by using the Java 2D API are device-and resolution-independent. Of course, because the API is a core portion of Java, the programs are platform-independent, complying with the logo "Write Once and Run Anywhere."

This book is essentially a reference on Java 2D API, rather than a text book of computer graphics in general. Java developers will find the API classes and interfaces demonstrated in this book a good reference in various contexts of their programming work. The primary goal of this book is to concisely cover the Java 2D concepts to a reasonable depth and demonstrate them using suitable examples.

The demonstration examples provided form the heart of the book. The examples implement various concepts of Java 2D to demonstrate them. Most of the examples provided in this book are interactive, which means they expect the user to input actions in order to output various interesting results. Also, the snippets that build the sample programs are meant to be used in the programs written by developers. The source code files are available for download from http://www.samspublishing.com. When you reach that page, click the Product Support link. On the next page, enter this book's ISBN number (0672316692) to access the page containing the code.

The book assumes that the reader already knows the Java language. It is certainly helpful if you have a prior knowledge of AWT; however, it is not mandatory. Knowing AWT allows you to speed up the learning process. For readers who have no knowledge of AWT graphics, the first chapter in this book will provide the necessary footing. The first chapter basically discusses the fundamentals of Java 2D, and the remaining chapters will present various Java 2D topics. The following is a brief account of the chapters in this book:

- **Chapter 1**—This chapter initially focuses on various fundamental concepts of Java 2D to prepare the reader to write the first graphics program, Hello! Graphics World!. The other topics in this chapter explain the graphics model used by Java 2D, the process of rendering graphics objects, how to create graphics context, and how to modify the graphics attributes.

- **Chapter 2**—This chapter discusses the Java 2D API classes and interfaces that enhance color handling (by introducing the color spaces and transparency of colors), and allow filling various 2D shapes with different color patterns. The chapter also discusses the management of device-independent colors.
- **Chapter 3**—This chapter and the next two chapters discuss the capability to create line art using the Java 2D API. In this chapter, you will explore the API details and code examples on line segments, rectangles, and rectangles with rounded corners.
- **Chapter 4**—In this chapter, you will explore how to draw and operate on some more geometric shapes: quadratic and cubic curves; arcs of open, chord, and pie types; and circles and ellipses.
- **Chapter 5**—This chapter also discusses how to create shapes that are made up of two or more available geometric shapes by using constructive area geometry (CAG). Constructive area geometry creates custom shapes by performing addition, subtraction, intersection, and exclusive-OR operations. This chapter also presents how to create general paths that represent arbitrary shapes.
- **Chapter 6**—This chapter initially focuses on the enhanced font support to harness the fonts from the given platform. Then the text layout mechanism is discussed, along with the topics on hit testing, highlighting, and caret positioning and moving.
- **Chapter 7**—The first section in this chapter examines the anatomy of a buffered image (an image created in the accessible memory of a computer) that is based on the immediate mode model. The remaining sections in the chapter show how to create and display buffered images. Developers will also observe the advantage in storing images in a buffer through certain examples that demonstrate image replication and animation.
- **Chapter 8**—This chapter discusses the image processing filters provided in Java 2D. This chapter initially presents the information on the underlying filtering interfaces. Then the sections on various filtering operations follow, with suitable demonstration examples.
- **Chapter 9**—The Java 2D API has introduced comprehensive printing capabilities to overcome the deficiencies experienced in the printing capabilities supported in the previous releases of JDK. This chapter presents the printing concepts introduced by Java 2D and the governing interfaces and classes with suitable examples.
- **Chapter 10**—This chapter initially presents the inheritance hierarchies of classes and interfaces from various Java 2D packages. The chapter also provides the quick reference for selected classes and interfaces.

CHAPTER 1

Fundamentals of Java 2D

The Java Foundation Classes (JFC) are a set of graphics classes that enable developers to write graphics applications and build sophisticated user interfaces with drag-and-drop features. JFC is an integrated and core technology in the Java 2 platform (also code-named JDK 1.2). The Java 2D API is one of the significant components of JFC; it furnishes enhanced 2D graphics, fonts and text, and imaging features for Java. These enhancements are backward compatible with the existing graphics support available in the Abstract Windowing Toolkit (AWT).

With the advent of the Java 2D API, you—the Java developer—can build various types of applications that involve sophisticated 2D graphics, text, and image handling. Typical application areas include the following:

- *Presentation graphics*—A way of displaying certain data by means of colorful graphics representations to enhance the viewer's understanding of the phenomena represented by data. The most common representations are pie charts, bar graphs, and task-scheduling charts.
- *Computer-aided design (CAD)*—Lets the designer interactively design various electrical, mechanical, structural, and network systems in 2D and 3D spaces.
- *Scientific visualization*—Helps the viewer understand the phenomena represented by certain scientific or engineering data by using a simulated graphics model.
- *Cartography*—The schematic representation of measured data of geographical and other natural using computer graphics.
- *Commercial* a*dvertising and entertainment*—Charming applications to attract the viewer.

The Java 2D API provides support for various geometric shapes, Bezier paths, coordinate transformations, compositing, pen styles, fill styles, and rendering quality. The API enhances the AWT font support by allowing applications to utilize the available platform fonts. Java 2D also supports bidirectional text layout and rendering for two-way display of text. (Examples of bidirectional languages—languages that are read and written from right to left—include Arabic, Urdu, and Japanese.) You will also find support for buffered images and image filters.

In addition, the Java 2D API supports a sophisticated and flexible framework for device and resolution independent graphics. You can use a coordinate system called *user space* to represent data used in an application (or an applet). The final output of the program is manifested on a targeted device by transforming the data from the user space into the coordinate system of the device space. By using Java 2D API, you have support for a broad range of devices such as monitors and printers.

This chapter initially focuses on various fundamental concepts of Java 2D to prepare you to write the first graphics program, Hello! Graphics World!. To a large extent, we will follow a similar approach in the next chapters while writing more sophisticated applications involving complex geometric shapes, fonts and text, and image manipulations. The next sections in this chapter explain the graphics model used by Java 2D, the process of rendering graphics objects, how to create graphics context, and how to modify the graphics attributes.

Java 2D Graphics Model

In order to display a graphics element such as a geometric shape, text, or image on a targeted device, Java 2D adopts a model that is similar to one used to implement AWT graphics. Basically, you need to prepare a graphics context that allows the initialization of various graphic attributes to display graphics elements. The graphics context is analogous to the preparation you make to paint a drawing or portrait. The preparation might require assigning the background color of the canvas on which you paint, foreground color of the paint, brush width, stroke type, and so on.

The Java 2D API supports a graphics context class called `Graphics2D` that extends the AWT graphics context represented by the `Graphics` class (see Figure 1.1). The graphics context class contains various attributes that you can modify to control the rendering of graphics elements. With the support of `Graphics2D`, you will be able to exercise control on the greater number of graphics attributes required for Java 2D. The package `java.awt` contains the classes `Graphics2D` and `Graphics`.

After a graphics context object is created with the necessary attributes, you can call a suitable method to render the graphics elements. To apply the graphics attributes while rendering, you need to pass the graphics context object as an argument value to one of the rendering methods: `paint()`, `paintAll()`, `print()`, `printAll()`, or `update()`.

```
java.lang.Object
   └── java.awt.Graphics
          └── java.awt.Graphics2D
```

Figure 1.1
The class hierarchy of the Graphics2D class.

In order to make programs independent of the display or printing devices, the Java 2D API requires you to specify various graphics elements in a coordinate system that is independent of the end devices. The specified coordinates of the graphics elements in the program are transformed at a later stage to suitable coordinates for the end device. The next section will discuss the coordinate spaces adopted by Java 2D.

User and Device Coordinate Spaces

In order to allow the development of an application independent of various output devices, Java 2D uses two different coordinate systems: user space and device space. You can initially represent the application-input data with reference to the user space. After necessary processing for graphics manipulations, the Java 2D support automatically transforms the output data based on the target device, such as the screen or a printer.

NOTE

As an application developer, you need not perform any transformation of data from the user space to device space. Using the installed device drivers, Java 2D support can apply suitable transformation to convert data into the device space.

User Space

In Java 2D, the user space is basically a rectangular coordinate system with its origin O (0, 0) located at the intersection of the horizontal x- axis and vertical y- axis in the top-left corner (see Figure 1.2). The pixel values along the x- axis increase in the right-hand direction. The pixel values along the y-axis increase in the downward direction. Figure 1.2 depicts the location of a generic pixel P (x, y) in the two-dimensional space.

The coordinate system in the user space is independent of that of the output device. To appropriately manifest data in the targeted output device, each pixel in the user space is translated into the corresponding device space. Therefore, you can develop programs without even considering the end devices on which the results are manifested.

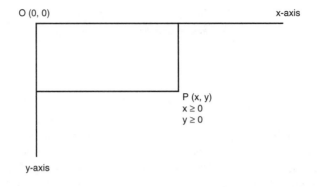

Figure 1.2

The user coordinate system used in Java 2D.

Device Space

Device space is any coordinate system that is assigned to a device by its developer. Thus, the coordinate system need not be the same as the user space. For each device, the coordinate system can be different. Often, the device driver contains the information to transform the user coordinate system to the device space. The data of the graphics elements is transformed into the device space before rendering by using a suitable transformation, as shown in Figure 1.3.

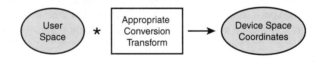

Figure 1.3

Conversion of user coordinates into device coordinates.

Creating the Graphics Context

The graphics context is an approach by which you specify or modify various graphics attributes before rendering a graphics element such as a geometric shape, text, or an image. In AWT applications, you typically create a graphics object of type `Graphics` as an argument to the method `paint()`. The `paint()` method overrides the same method from the base class `Component`.

To implement the graphics features from Java 2D, you can follow the same approach used in AWT, and cast the object of type `Graphics` to the object of type `Graphics2D`. Doing so will enable you to use more graphics attributes introduced in the `Graphics2D` class. The following are the commonly used code statements to get a reference to the graphics context in Java 2D applications or applets:

```
public void paint (Graphics g) {
    // Prepare the graphics 2D context
    Graphics2D g2D = (Graphics2D) g;

    // Rendering code comes here
    ...
}
```

Hello! Graphics World! Example

In the previous section, you saw how to prepare the graphics context to perform rendering of graphics elements. Using these rudiments, let's build a sample program that simply greets the graphics world. The code is given in Listing 1.1; its output is shown in Figure 1.4. The program also implements code to modify various graphics attributes. You will learn about these graphics attributes in the next section.

Figure 1.4

The Hello! Graphics World! greeting.

Listing 1.1   A Greeting Program Using 2D Graphics (THello.java)
```
// Demonstrates some of the fundamental concepts of Java 2D

import java.awt.*;
import java.awt.event.*;
import java.awt.font.*;
import java.awt.geom.*;
import java.awt.image.*;

// 1. Create a frame to which you can add a canvas containing text
class THello extends Frame {
    // Constructor
    public THello() {
        super("THello");
        add(new TextCanvas()); // Add the text canvas
        addWindowListener(new WindowEventHandler()); // To close the frame.
        pack(); // pack around the child component, i.e., text canvas
        show(); // display the frame
    }
```

continues

Listing 1.1   continued

```
// 2. Code to handle the closing of frame
class WindowEventHandler extends WindowAdapter {
    public void windowClosing(WindowEvent e) {
        System.exit(0);
    }
}

// 3. The main method...
public static void main(String arg[]) {
    new THello();
}
}

// 4. Canvas to paint the "Hello! Graphics World!" text
class TextCanvas extends Canvas {
    Font font;
    FontMetrics fontMetrics;

    // Constructor
    TextCanvas() {
        // Define a font and obtain its metrics
        font = new Font("Dialog", Font.BOLD, 40);
        fontMetrics = getFontMetrics(font);
        setSize(400, 150); // canvas width=400, height=150
    }

    // 5. Paint method that overrides paint() inside Component
    public void paint(Graphics g) {
        // Set up the 2D graphics context
        Graphics2D g2D = (Graphics2D) g;

        // Say Hello!
        sayHello(g2D, 30, 50);

        // Say Graphics
        sayGraphics(g2D, 30, 100);

        // Say World!
        sayWorld(g2D,
                fontMetrics.stringWidth("Graphics")+45,
                100);
    }

    // This method draws the text "Hello!" with gradient-paint
    public void sayHello(Graphics2D g2D, int x, int y) {
        // Assign font type
        g2D.setFont(font);
```

```java
    // Create a gradient paint object and assign it
    // to the 2D graphics context
    GradientPaint gp = new GradientPaint(
                        30.0f, 50.0f,
                        Color.blue,
                        fontMetrics.stringWidth("Hello!"),
                        fontMetrics.getHeight(),
                        Color.red);
    g2D.setPaint(gp);

    // Draw the string Hello!
    g2D.drawString("Hello!", x, y);
}


// 7. This method draws the text "Graphics" with texture-paint type
// fill pattern
public void sayGraphics(Graphics2D g2D, int x, int y) {
    // Create a texture paint
    BufferedImage bi = new BufferedImage(5, 5,
                        BufferedImage.TYPE_INT_RGB);
    Graphics2D big = bi.createGraphics();
    big.setColor(Color.magenta);
    big.fillRect(0,0,5,5);
    big.setColor(Color.black);
    big.fillOval(0,0,5,5);
    Rectangle r  = new Rectangle(0, 0, 5, 5);
    TexturePaint tp = new TexturePaint(bi, r);

    // Assign the texture paint and draw text
    g2D.setPaint(tp);
    g2D.drawString("Graphics", 30, 100);
}


// 8. This method draws the outline of the text "World!".
public void sayWorld(Graphics2D g2D, int x, int y) {
    AffineTransform at = new AffineTransform();
    at.setToTranslation(x, y);
    at.shear(-0.5, 0.0);
    FontRenderContext frc = new FontRenderContext(at, false, false);

    // Text representation to say World!...
    TextLayout tl = new TextLayout("World!", font, frc);

    // Obtain the outline of the text in object tl, and draw
    // it by invoking the draw() method in graphics context.
    Shape outline = tl.getOutline(null);

    // Set the outline color to blue
```

continues

Listing 1.1   continued

```
    g2D.setColor(Color.blue);

    // To control the stroke width
    BasicStroke wideStroke = new BasicStroke(2.0f);
    g2D.setStroke(wideStroke);

    // Draw the outline
    g2D.draw(outline);
  }
}
```

Code Analysis

Snippet-1 defines the application frame named THello. Inside its constructor, a text canvas is added to the frame. You will also find the code to add a window event handler and display the frame by properly packing around the text canvas. Snippet-2 defines the window event handler class. This class implements the method to exit the application on closing the window. Snippet-3 defines the main method that creates an instance of the frame THello.

Snippet-4 defines the class TextCanvas that extends the Canvas class. The constructor of this class creates a font object, obtains its font-metrics, and assigns the specified size. Snippet-5 shows the paint() method that overrides the same method inside the class Component. Notice that the method paint() contains an object g of type Graphics as its argument. In the next lines of code, this object is cast to create the graphics context g2D for rendering using 2D graphics attributes. The remaining lines of code inside the paint() method simply render different words of the greeting Hello! Graphics World! by calling three methods: sayHello(), sayGraphics(), and sayWorld(). Inside these methods, the graphics attributes are modified and rendering is performed. The details of these methods will become clear as you progress through the remaining sections in this chapter.

Modifying Graphics Attributes

The previous THello.java program uses different attributes to make the greeting more attractive. In this section, you will study various graphics attributes in detail and see how to modify them. To customize different graphics elements, you can modify these attributes before rendering.

In Java 2D, the graphics context represented by the class Graphics2D supports various rendering attributes to apply different pen strokes, fill types, fonts, transforms, rendering quality, clipping paths, compositing of overlapped colors, and so on. The following subsections will discuss these attributes. As you progress through the subsequent chapters, you will find various applications using these attributes in a sophisticated manner.

Specifying Stroke Types

Strokes are pen styles that draw graphics elements. Using Java 2D, you can choose different pen styles with varying widths, end caps, joint styles of segments, and dashed patterns. The *pen width* is the width of the stroke, measured perpendicular to the path of the pen. An *end cap* is a decorative finish at the end of a stroke segment. The *joint style* or *line join* is a decorative pattern at the point where two path segments are joined. The *dashed pattern* is a disjointed stroke.

The class `BasicStroke` represents a stroke by defining a basic set of stroke attributes. This class implements the design level interface `Stroke`. The `Stroke` interface allows a `Graphics2D` object to obtain a geometric element that has the decorated outline or stylistic representation of the outline. The outline of a geometric element is represented by the interface `Shape`. The interfaces `Stroke` and `Shape` and the class `BasicStroke` are located in the package `java.awt`.

You can call the methods `draw()`, `drawLine()`, `drawRect()`, `drawRoundRect()`, `drawOval()`, `drawArc()`, `drawPolyline()`, and `drawPolygon()` from the graphics context (`Graphics2D` or its superclass `Graphics`) to render the corresponding geometric element that implements the interface `Shape`. You can change or modify the stroke attribute by calling the following method from the graphics context class `Graphics2D`:

```
abstract  void setStroke(Stroke s)
```

WARNING

> If a `Stroke` object is modified after it is assigned in the graphics context, there is no guarantee that subsequent rendering will behave as expected.

The following sample code writes the word *World!* using a stroke width of 2.0 and dashed pattern when inserted in a program. See Figure 1.5:

```
// Modify the stroke width
float dash[] = {1.5f}; // For a simple dash pattern
BasicStroke newStroke = new BasicStroke(
                    2.0f, // Stroke width
                    BasicStroke.CAP_BUTT, //cap
                    BasicStroke.JOIN_MITER, // join
                    10.0f, // Miter limit
                    dash,
                    0.0f); //dash phase
g2D.setStroke(newStroke);


// Say World! (See the 'Hello! Graphics World!' code)
sayWorld(g2D, 15, 50)
```

Figure 1.5

The word World! with different stroke attributes.

Specifying Fill Patterns

Fills are color patterns or textures that are used to fill graphics elements. Inside text or a geometric shape, you can fill a single color uniformly, apply a gradient of one or more colors, or paint with a certain texture. Because the fill attribute is a painting pattern, it is described by the design interface java.awt.Paint. Thus, the classes such as Color, GradientPaint, and TexturePaint that serve to fill a graphics shape implement the interface Paint. These classes represent the uniform or solid color pattern, gradient pattern of colors, and texture pattern of colors, respectively. The java.awt package contains these classes.

You can assign objects of interface type Paint to the Graphics2D context using setPaint(Paint paintObject) in order to specify the color pattern to be used. The method setColor(Color c) supported in Graphics can be invoked to fill uniformly with a single color. After the fill pattern is assigned, the graphics context uses the pattern while rendering the graphics shape. Following are the typical code statements used to apply a gradient fill:

```
...
GradientPaint gp = new GradientPaint(10.0f, 10.0f,  // (x, y) of point-1
                                     Color.yellow,  // Color at point-1
                                     40.0f, 40.0f,  // (x, y) of point-2
                                     Color.red);  // Color at point-2

g2D.setPaint(gp); // Assign the fill pattern to graphics context

// Call suitable fill method as, for example,
g2D.fillOval(20, 20, 100, 100);
...
```

The following sample code applies the texture fill style to graphics elements, such as the text string "Graphics" here (see snippet-7 of Listing 1.1):

```
// Create a texture paint
BufferedImage bi = new BufferedImage(5, 5,
                        BufferedImage.TYPE_INT_RGB);
Graphics2D big = bi.createGraphics();
big.setColor(Color.magenta);
big.fillRect(0,0,5,5);
```

```
big.setColor(Color.black);
big.fillOval(0,0,5,5);
Rectangle r  = new Rectangle(0, 0, 5, 5);
TexturePaint tp = new TexturePaint(bi, r);

// Assign the texture paint and draw text
g2D.setPaint(tp);
g2D.drawString("Graphics", 30, 100);
```

The result of this code appears in the output of the program THello.java. The words Hello! and *Graphics* are filled with the gradient and texture patterns, respectively (see Figure 1.4). You can also see Chapter 2, "Color Handling," to understand how the gradient and texture paint patterns actually work.

Specifying Transforms

The Java 2D provides the necessary API to perform the following transformations:

- Translate a graphics element from one location to another
- Rotate a graphics element about a point
- Alter a graphics element's size (scaling), or shear the object along an axis
- Perform a combination of these operations

You can either assign a new *affine* transform of class type AffineTransform, or directly use the methods in the Graphics2D class to concatenate new transformations with the currently existing transform. The package java.awt.geom stores the AffineTransform class.

The class AffineTransform represents a linear transformation for the translation, rotation, shear, or scaling of a graphic element. An important property of affine transforms is that they preserve the parallelism of lines; but they may change the lengths and angles while transforming the subject to a new location (x', y') from the initial location (x, y). The following system of linear algebraic equations represents an affine transformation

```
[  x' ]     [ m00  m01  m02]  [ x ]
[  y' ]  =  [ m10  m11  m12]  [ y ]
[  1  ]     [ 0    0    1  ]  [ 1 ]

   P'    =       M         *   P
```

where P is the initial point (x, y), P' is the final point (x', y'), and M is the transformation matrix as defined. Notice that the affine transform uses the row [0 0 1] to mathematically formulate the problem as P' = M * P. (For the derivation of matrix M, you can refer the book *Computer Graphics: Principles and Practice* by James D. Foley, Andries van Dam, et al, Addison-Wesley, 1997.)

To create a suitable object of AffineTransform, you can directly invoke one of the following six static methods.

```
public static AffineTransform getTranslateInstance(double tx, double ty)
```
returns an affine transform for translation to a new location at a distance tx in the X direction and ty in the Y direction.

```
public static AffineTransform getRotateInstance(double theta)
```
returns an affine transform for rotation by theta radians about the origin (counter-clockwise is positive).

```
public static AffineTransform getRotateInstance(double theta, double x,
double y)
```
returns an affine transform that rotates coordinates around an anchor point (x, y).

```
public static AffineTransform getShearInstance(double shx, double shy)
```
returns an affine transform for a shearing transformation. The arguments shx and shy are the shear factors.

```
public static AffineTransform getScaleInstance(double sx, double sy)
```
returns an affine transform for a scaling transformation. The arguments sx and sy are the scaling factors in the X and Y directions, respectively.

```
public AffineTransform createInverse()
```
returns an AffineTransform object that represents the inverse transformation of the current transform. This operation is subject to the possibility of inverting the transform matrix. If it is not possible to invert the transform matrix, the method throws the NoninvertibleTransformException.

In addition to using the preceding methods, you can also use six of the affine transform constructors that are available in the AffineTransform class. Chapter 10, "Inheritance Hierarchies and API Quick Reference," provides a quick reference for the AffineTransform class.

From the class Graphics2D, you can directly invoke the following five methods to con-catenate the respective transformations to the current transform of the graphics context.

```
public void translate(double tx, double ty)
```
concatenates a translation transformation with the prescribed X and Y values.

```
public void rotate(double theta)
```
concatenates a rotation transformation with the current transform.

```
public void rotate(double theta, double x, double y)
```
concatenates a translated rotation transformation with the current transform.

```
public void shear(double shx, double shy)
```
concatenates the current transform of the graphics context with a shear transformation.

```
public void scale(double sx, double sy)
```
concatenates the current transform of the graphics context with a rotation transformation.

WARNING

The method `public void translate(int x, int y)` in the `Graphics2D` class is meant for translating the origin of the graphics context to a new location `(x, y)` in the existing coordinate system. It is not meant for concatenating the current transform with the translation transformation.

Specifying Clipping Shapes

Sometimes you might want to display only a portion of the total picture or geometric shape. The process of *clipping* determines which portion of the picture will be displayed. The Java 2D API enables you to perform clipping of any shape. The opposite of clipping is *shielding*, which basically covers a portion of the picture so that it is not displayed.

To perform clipping along a shape (of a graphics element) of type `Shape`, you need to invoke the following methods from the 2D graphics context object:

```
public void setClip(Shape shape)
public void setClip(int x, int y, int width, int height)
```

These methods are stored in the superclass `java.awt.Graphics`. You can use the following method from the class `Graphics2D` to intersect an already existing clip with the interior of the specified `Shape`, and set the current clip to the intersected portion:

```
public void clip(Shape shape)
```

Clipping Example

Listing 1.2 shows a simple, sample program that demonstrates clipping along a circle at the center of a canvas. Next, the program clips the already clipped portion when the radio button Clip Further is selected. If the radio button Clip is selected again, it clips the canvas as in the beginning.

The Clip Further operation is performed along a rectangle. The rectangle has its location coordinates (x, y) at the center of the canvas, and width and height (w, h) equal to half of the corresponding dimensions of the canvas. Essentially, the rectangle clips over the already clipped portion along a circle. Figures 1.6 and Figure 1.7 show the output of this program when different clipping selections are made.

Figure 1.6

The clipped circular shape.

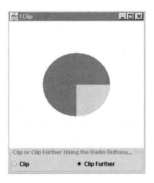

Figure 1.7

The clipping as an intersection of a clipped circle and a rectangle.

Listing 1.2   Demonstrates Clipping Operations (TClip.java)

```
import java.awt.*;
import java.awt.event.*;
import javax.swing.*;
import javax.swing.border.*;
import java.awt.geom.*;

class TClip extends JFrame {
    DisplayCanvas canvas;
    JRadioButton clipButton, clipFurButton;

    public TClip() {
        // 1. Assign a name to the frame, and retrieve the
        // content pane of the frame.
        super("TClip");
        Container contentPane = getContentPane();
```

```
// 2. Create a display canvas and add it to the frame
canvas = new DisplayCanvas();
contentPane.add(canvas);

// 3. Create a panel and add mutually exclusive radio buttons;
// then add the panel to the frame's content panel
JPanel panel = new JPanel();
panel.setBorder(new TitledBorder(
    "Clip or Clip Further Using the Radio Buttons..."));
panel.setLayout(new GridLayout(1, 2));
clipButton = new JRadioButton("Clip", true);
clipButton.addActionListener(new RadioButtonListener());
clipFurButton = new JRadioButton("Clip Further");
clipFurButton.addActionListener(new RadioButtonListener());
ButtonGroup group = new ButtonGroup();
group.add(clipButton); group.add(clipFurButton);

panel.add(clipButton);
panel.add(clipFurButton);
contentPane.add(BorderLayout.SOUTH, panel);

// 4. Add a window listener to close the frame properly.
addWindowListener(new WindowEventHandler());
pack(); // Pack the frame around its contents
show(); // Display the frame
}

// 5. Code to handle the closing of the frame
class WindowEventHandler extends WindowAdapter {
    public void windowClosing(WindowEvent e) {
        System.exit(0);
    }
}

// 6. The main method...
public static void main(String arg[]) {
    new TClip();
}

// 7. Radio button listener
class RadioButtonListener implements ActionListener {
    public void actionPerformed(ActionEvent e) {
        JRadioButton temp = (JRadioButton) e.getSource();

        if (temp.equals(clipButton)) {
            canvas.clip = true;
            canvas.clipFurther = false;
            canvas.repaint();
```

continues

Listing 1.2   continued

```
            }
            else if (temp.equals(clipFurButton)) {
                canvas.clipFurther = true;
                canvas.repaint();
            }
        }
    }
}

// 8. Canvas to display a circle and rectangle.
class DisplayCanvas extends Canvas {
    boolean clip = true;
    boolean clipFurther = false;

    DisplayCanvas() {
        setSize(300, 300);
        setBackground(Color.white);
    }

    public void paint(Graphics g) {
        // 9. Set up the 2D graphics context
        Graphics2D g2 = (Graphics2D) g;

        // 10. Retrieve the size of the canvas
        int w = getSize().width;
        int h = getSize().height;

        // 11. If the clip button is selected or when the frame is
        // initially loaded, clip along or show a circle using
        // the setClip() method.
        if (clip) {
            Ellipse2D e = new Ellipse2D.Float(w/4.0f, h/4.0f,
                                              w/2.0f, h/2.0f);
            g2.setClip;

            // Draw a filled rectangle with red color. Rectangle is
            // of the size of the canvas.
            g2.setColor(Color.red);
            g2.fillRect(0, 0, w, h);
        }

        // 12. If the clipFurther button is selected, use clip() method
        // to clip along a rectangle over the existing circle.
        if (clipFurther) {
            Rectangle r = new Rectangle(w/2, h/2, w/2, h/2);
            g2.clip(r);
```

```
        g2.setColor(Color.green);
        g2.fillRect(0, 0, w, h);
      }
    }
}
```

Code Analysis

This program is a Swing application. The class TClip is the application frame. It declares references to a display canvas and two radio buttons. The first radio button is used to perform clipping along a circle, whereas the other one helps to perform clipping along a rectangle. The rectangular clipping overlaps on the existing circular clipping.

Inside the constructor of the class, snippet-1 assigns a title to the frame and then retrieves its content pane. Snippet-2 creates a display canvas and adds it to the frame. Snippet-3 defines the radio button objects and adds them to a panel. The radio buttons are grouped to make them mutually exclusive. Next, the panel is added to the main application frame. Snippet-4 is the window listener to close the frame properly. Snippet-5 defines the corresponding window listener class. Snippet-6 is the main method where an instance of TClip is created.

Snippet-7 defines a radio button listener class. This class implements the functionality to execute appropriate code inside the paint method when a selection is made. Snippet-8 defines the display canvas class. This class defines two boolean variables to control the flow of code inside the paint method.

Snippet-9, inside the paint method, creates a 2D graphics context. Snippet-10 retrieves the dimensions of the canvas. Snippet-11 shows the if statement whose body is executed when the Clip button is selected. Here, a circle object is created and assigned to the graphic context for clipping by using the method setClip(). Next, a filled rectangle of the size of canvas is drawn with the red color. This displays only a circular portion that has been clipped.

Snippet-12 shows the code that is executed when the Clip Further button is selected. Inside the body of the corresponding if statement, a rectangle object is created and assigned to the graphics context by invoking the method clip(). This rectangle overlaps over the circular clipping portion. Next, the graphics context is set to green color and a filled rectangle is drawn over the canvas. This will display the overlapped portion between the circular clipping and the rectangular clipping in green color.

Specifying Rendering Hints

Often you cannot compromise on quality when you render graphics elements. But, on some occasions, you might be less concerned about quality and more concerned about speed while rendering. In this context, Java 2D supports the necessary control over the rendering process to achieve increased rendering speed.

Rendering hints are attributes that basically suggest to the program that it render various graphics elements with the specified quality. The class RenderingHints in the package java.awt contains a number of rendering hints as its fields. The quick reference given in Chapter 10 provides a complete list of these constants.

After a rendering hint is determined, you can invoke the method setRenderingHints(RenderingHints hints) from the class Graphics2D to assign the hint to the graphics context. The following example code shows the word *World!* with the default and modified rendering hints (see Figure 1.8 for the output):

```
// 1) Say World! (See the Hello! Graphics World! code)
sayWorld(g2D, 5, 50);  // x=5 and y=50

// This code controls the rendering quality of the word
// World. You can see the smoothing of the inclined lines.
// Create a rendering hints object and assign it to
// the graphics context.
RenderingHints qualityHints = new
    RenderingHints(RenderingHints.KEY_ANTIALIASING,
    RenderingHints.VALUE_ANTIALIAS_ON);
g2D.setRenderingHints(qualityHints);

// 2) Say World! (See the Hello! Graphics World! code)
sayWorld(g2D, 5, 100);  // x=5 and y=100
```

Figure 1.8

Demonstration of rendering hints.

WARNING

Although Java runs on various platforms, you have no assurance that the prescribed rendering-hint algorithm will be supported on all those platforms.

Specifying Composition Types

Compositing is a technique to combine graphics elements that overlap other graphics elements. A graphic element such as a geometric shape, text, or image (also referred as the *source*) can combine with an existing element (also referred as the *destination*) in a controlled manner. For example, you can overlap a red rectangle (source) on an existing yellow rectangle (destination) by controlling the red color, yellow color, or a combination of both that appears in the overlapped region.

Java 2D supports two design-level interfaces—Composite and CompositeContext—that define encapsulations for different compositing types. The java.awt package contains these interfaces. The interfaces Composite and CompositeContext work together to combine a graphics element with the underlying element. The method createContext() inside the Composite interface creates the context, represented by CompositeContext, for the compositing process. The method compose() inside CompositingContext will perform the actual mixing of the graphics elements.

To deal with blending and transparency effects in overlapped graphics elements (including images), the Java 2D API supports the class AlphaComposite. This class implements the interface Composite, and essentially provides some of the Porter-Duff rules as its fields. (These rules were initially described by T. Porter and T. Duff in their research paper "Compositing Digital Images," SIGGRAPH 84, 253-259.) The most commonly used rule is the source-*over*-destination rule. This rule is represented by the static integer field SRC_OVER. For the other fields, you can consult the quick reference provided in Chapter 10 of this book.

The class AlphaComposite does not support any constructors. However, you can create an instance AlphaComposite by calling either of two static methods.

```
public static AlphaComposite getInstance(int rule);
```
creates an instance using the specified Porter-Duff rule.

```
public static AlphaComposite getInstance(int rule, float alpha);
```
additionally allows you to specify the alpha value for the transparency control. The *alpha value* is a measure of the transparency (visibility of background objects) of overlapping colors of graphics elements. The values of alpha can range from 0.0 (totally transparent) to 1.0 (totally opaque, with no background visible).

NOTE

If any of the pixels does not contain the alpha information, all the pixels of the graphics element use a default alpha value of 1.0.

After an instance of AlphaComposite is created, you can assign the object to the graphics context of type Graphics2D by invoking the method setComposite(Composite comp).

Compositing Example

The sample program given in Listing 1.3 combines a blue ellipse (source element) with a red ellipse (destination element) using the selected rule and the alpha value. The program uses the Porter-Duff rules that are encapsulated as fields in the class AlphaComposite. Figures 1.9, 1.10, 1.11, and 1.12 show the overlapped ellipses with Clear, Source-over, Source-in, and Source-out composite rules, respectively.

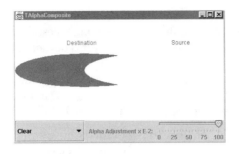

Figure 1.9

Output demonstrating the Clear composition rule.

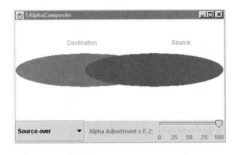

Figure 1.10

Output demonstrating the Source-over composition rule.

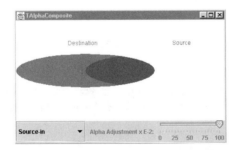

Figure 1.11

Output demonstrating the Source-in composition rule.

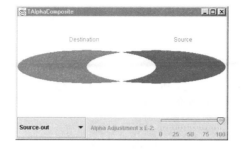

Figure 1.12

Output demonstrating the Source-out composition rule.

Listing 1.3   Illustrates Compositing Using the Porter-Duff Rules (TAlphaComposite.java)

```java
import java.awt.*;
import java.awt.event.*;
import java.awt.font.*;
import java.awt.geom.*;
import java.awt.image.*;
import javax.swing.*;
import javax.swing.event.*;


class TAlphaComposite extends JFrame {
    DrawingCanvas canvas;
    JSlider slider, sliderAlpha;
    JComboBox rulesBox;

    // Labels for Porter Duff Rules, and the corresponding fields in
    // the class AlphaComposite.
    String[] rulesLabels = {"Clear", "Source",
                            "Source-over", "Destination-over",
                            "Source-in", "Destination-in",
                            "Source-out", "Destination-out"};
    int[] rules = {AlphaComposite.CLEAR, AlphaComposite.SRC,
                AlphaComposite.SRC_OVER, AlphaComposite.DST_OVER,
                AlphaComposite.SRC_IN, AlphaComposite.DST_IN,
                AlphaComposite.SRC_OUT, AlphaComposite.DST_OUT};

    public TAlphaComposite() {
        // 1. Assign a name to the frame, and obtain its
        // content pane.
        super("TAlphaComposite");
        Container container = getContentPane();

        // 2. Create a canvas and add it to the frame
```

continues

Listing 1.3   continued

```java
canvas = new DrawingCanvas();
container.add(canvas);

// 3. Create a rules combo box, and alpha adjustment slider
// in a panel, and add the panel to the frame.
rulesBox = new JComboBox(rulesLabels);
rulesBox.setSelectedIndex(0);
rulesBox.setAlignmentX(Component.LEFT_ALIGNMENT);
rulesBox.addActionListener(new ComboBoxListener());

setSlider(0, 100, 100, 25, 5);
sliderAlpha = slider;

JPanel panel = new JPanel();
panel.setLayout(new GridLayout(1,3));
panel.add(rulesBox);
panel.add(new JLabel("Alpha Adjustment x E-2: ", JLabel.RIGHT));
panel.add(sliderAlpha);
container.add(panel, BorderLayout.SOUTH);

//4. Add a window closing listener and display frame with suitable size
addWindowListener(new WindowEventHandler());
pack();
show();
}

// 5. Class to handle the closing of the frame
class WindowEventHandler extends WindowAdapter {
    public void windowClosing(WindowEvent e) {
        System.exit(0);
    }
}

// 6. Method to create sliders with necessary configuration
public void setSlider(int min, int max, int init,
                      int mjrTkSp, int mnrTkSp) {
    slider = new JSlider(JSlider.HORIZONTAL, min, max, init);
    slider.setPaintTicks(true);
    slider.setMajorTickSpacing(mjrTkSp);
    slider.setMinorTickSpacing(mnrTkSp);
    slider.setPaintLabels(true);
    slider.addChangeListener(new SliderListener());
}

// 7. The main method...
public static void main(String arg[]) {
    new TAlphaComposite();
}
```

```
// 8. The Slider listener class
class SliderListener implements ChangeListener {
    public void stateChanged(ChangeEvent e) {
        JSlider slider = (JSlider) e.getSource();
        canvas.alphaValue = (float) slider.getValue()/100;
        canvas.repaint();
    }
}


// 9. The Combo box listener class
class ComboBoxListener implements ActionListener {
    public void actionPerformed(ActionEvent e) {
        JComboBox cb = (JComboBox) e.getSource();
        canvas.compositeRule = rules[cb.getSelectedIndex()];
        canvas.repaint();
    }
}

}


// 10. Canvas to paint the overlapped ellipses
class DrawingCanvas extends Canvas {
    float alphaValue = 1.0f;
    int compositeRule = AlphaComposite.CLEAR;
    AlphaComposite ac;

    DrawingCanvas() {
        setSize(300, 300);
        setBackground(Color.white);
    }

    public void paint(Graphics g) {
        // 11. Set up the 2D graphics context
        Graphics2D g2D = (Graphics2D) g;

        // 12. Retrieve the size of canvas
        int w = getSize().width;
        int h = getSize().height;

        // 13. Create a buffered image and obtain its graphics context
        BufferedImage bi = new BufferedImage(w, h, BufferedImage.TYPE_INT_ARGB);
        Graphics2D big = bi.createGraphics();

        // 14. Define an alpha composite instance with the selected composite
        // rule and the alpha value.
        ac = AlphaComposite.getInstance(compositeRule, alphaValue);

        // 15. Create two overlapped ellipses with red and blue colors.
```

continues

Listing 1.3   continued

```
// Draw the destination ellipse in red color.
big.setColor(Color.red);
big.drawString("Destination", w/4, h/4);
big.fill(new Ellipse2D.Double(0, h/3, 2*w/3, h/3));

// Draw the source ellipse in blue color.
big.setColor(Color.blue);
big.drawString("Source", 3*w/4, h/4);
// 16. Assign the composite object to the graphics context
big.setComposite(ac);
big.fill(new Ellipse2D.Double(w/3, h/3, 2*w/3, h/3));

// 17. Finally display the buffered image.
g2D.drawImage(bi, null, 0, 0);
    }
}
```

Code Analysis

The class `TAlphaComposite` is a Swing frame. This class declares a drawing canvas, sliders to control the alpha value, and a combo box to select a compositing rule. You can also find the Porter-Duff rules being declared as an integer array. The corresponding labels are also declared in a string type array. These labels are used in the combo box.

Inside the constructor of the class, snippet-1 assigns a name to the frame and retrieves its content pane. Snippet-2 defines the canvas object and adds it to the frame. Snippet-3 creates a combo box for selecting compositing rules and a slider to adjust the alpha value (also see snippet-6). These components are added to a panel. Next, the panel is added to the frame. Snippet-4 registers a window-closing listener to the frame and displays it with suitable size. Snippet-5 shows the code to handle closing of the frame. Snippet-6 is the method to create sliders with the required configuration. Snippet-7 is the main method that creates an instance of `TAlphaComposite`.

Snippet-8 defines the slider listener class. This class implements the functionality to update the alpha value that is declared as a field canvas. The canvas is also repainted to exercise the effect of change in the alpha value. Snippet-9 defines the combo box listener class. This class implements the functionality to assign the selected rule to the corresponding parameter of the canvas.

Snippet-10 defines the canvas class. This class declares the alpha value, compositing rule, and an alpha composite object as its fields. Inside the paint method, snippet-11 prepares the graphics context object. Snippet-12 retrieves the dimensions of canvas. Snippet-13 creates a buffered image object and retrieves its context.

NOTE

A buffered image is an image created directly in memory. It is useful to efficiently display the graphics elements whenever it is updated.

Snippet-14 defines the alpha composite instance using the selected rule and the alpha value of colors. Snippet-15 creates the source and destination ellipses in different colors. The ellipses are indicated by means of display labels. Snippet-16 assigns the composite object to the graphics context before the source ellipse is rendered. Notice that all these operations are performed over the buffered image. Snippet-17 displays the image that is stored in the buffer.

CHAPTER 2

Color Handling

The support for color handling has undergone a wide range of improvements since its introduction in the Abstract Windowing Toolkit (AWT) of JDK 1.0. Notable developments include how to harness the colors of the system windows or components, and color models to efficiently interpret the pixel data of images.

The Java 2D API enhances color handling significantly by introducing transparency of colors, the ability to fill components with different color patterns, and management for device-independent colors. When components with different colors overlap each other, the transparency of the foreground color is the extent to which it allows the background color of pixels to be visible. This property of a color is indicated by the parameter called *alpha value*.

As already introduced in Chapter 1, "Fundamentals of Java 2D," the Java 2D color system can also support gradient and texture type of patterns. These patterns can bring more attractive and realistic appearances to various graphics elements. For example, text characters can be displayed with a stone or wood type of texture.

The color management introduced in Java 2D uses color spaces to achieve device-independent color output. So far the operations of color display or printing are device dependent. Even for RGB display monitors, devices from different vendors display a particular color with some difference due to lack of standards. Similarly, different printers print a particular color differently although they use the same basic colors: cyan, magenta, yellow, and black (CMYK). Various printers proportionately blend these colors to print with a specific color. The Java 2D API aims at displaying or printing with consistent colors for graphics elements (displayed or printed) on various end devices. This chapter discusses Java 2D enhancements of color handling with suitable examples.

Colors and Color Spaces

A color is a visual effect produced by a particular wavelength of light. Interestingly, multiple colors of different wavelengths can produce a new color when they are combined. Often this phenomenon is used in practice to generate different colors from certain colors that form a basis. For example, RGB monitors use the red, green, and blue colors as the basis to generate various pixel colors in an image. Printers typically spray a combination of cyan, magenta, yellow, and black to generate the required colors for printing.

Because the basic or constituent colors can generate various colors of interest, several sets of basic colors came into practice. A *color space* essentially defines the constituent or component colors in a set of colors that forms the basis. For example, standard red-green-blue, also referred as sRGB, is a color space that has recently been proposed to be a standard.

The color space object is represented by the abstract class `ColorSpace` in the package `java.awt.color`. Specific implementations such as `ICC_ColorSpace` extend this class. The concept of color space allows developers to deal with different color-rendering procedures.

NOTE

Java 2D considers the standard RGB or sRGB space as its default color space.

You will learn more about color spaces and converting a color from one space to another while discussing the concepts of color management in Java 2D.

Creating the Instances of a Color

In Java 2D, a color is represented by the class `Color` that is stored in the package `java.awt`. This class has been made more sophisticated by allowing developers to define a wide range of colors in different color spaces. The colors can also be defined with their alpha values that specify the transparency of pixels. You can create a particular color by using the constructors presented here.

`public Color(int red, int green, int blue)`
creates a color object in the standard RGB space (sRGB) when the red, green, and blue color components are specified. The values of these component colors range from 0 to 255. The alpha value for this color object is 255. That is, the color is opaque and does not allow the background objects and their colors to be visible.

`public Color(int red, int green, int blue, int alphaValue)`
is similar to the previous constructor. However, it requires the specification of an alpha value by using the parameter `alphaValue`. This constructor helps to create a color with the specified degree of transparency.

(**NOTE**

You can specify the alpha value in the range 0 to 255, just as for the other RGB components.

```
public Color(int rgbValue)
```
creates an opaque color in the sRGB space with the specified combined RGB value. This value consists of the red component in bits 16–23, the green component in bits 8–15, and the blue component in bits 0–7 (see the program given in Listing 2.1). The transparency parameter, the alpha value, is defaulted to 255.

```
public Color(int rgbaValue, boolean hasAlpha)
```
is similar to the previous constructor; however, it additionally requires the alpha value to be combined into the RGB value. The argument `rgbaValue` should contain the alpha component in bits 24–31, the red component in bits 16–23, the green component in bits 8–15, and the blue component in bits 0–7. The `hasAlpha` parameter must be true when you specify valid alpha bits; otherwise, the alpha value is defaulted to 255 (that is, the color is opaque).

```
public Color(float red, float green, float blue)
```
creates a color object in the sRGB space with the specified values for the color components: `red`, `green`, and `blue`. The components must be specified in the normalized range (0.0–1.0). Alpha is defaulted to 1.0; that is, the color is opaque.

```
public Color(float red, float green, float blue, float alphaValue)
```
is similar to the previous constructor; however, you need to specify the alpha value explicitly to control the degree of transparency of pixels. The `alphaValue` ranges from 0.0 to 1.0.

```
public Color(ColorSpace colorSpace, float[] components, float alphaValue)
```
is the most versatile constructor. It allows you to create a color in any color space by using the components that form the basis and the alpha value. The parameter `colorSpace` is the color space object. The argument array `components` specifies the values of color components. It depends on the color space for the number of components and the colors. The `alphaValue` is the transparency parameter.

Readily Supported Colors

The `Color` class readily supports a list of colors in the standard RGB space. These colors are declared as static fields. The following is the list of these fields representing the respective colors:

```
public static final Color white
public static final Color lightGray
public static final Color gray
public static final Color darkGray
public static final Color black
public static final Color red
```

```
public static final Color pink
public static final Color orange
public static final Color yellow
public static final Color green
public static final Color magenta
public static final Color cyan
public static final Color blue
```

For example, to render the background of a canvas with any of these colors, you can use the following code:

```
...
Canvas canvas = new Canvas()
canvas.setBackground(Color.green);
...
```

Retrieving the Components of a Color

After a particular color object is created, you can retrieve the component colors in its color space and the alpha value. For this purpose, the Color class supports the necessary get methods. Note that the color class does not provide any equivalent set methods. For example, to assign a new alpha value, there is no method available—you're forced to use a suitable constructor of the Color class and create a color object with the desired alpha value. The following methods help to retrieve the components of the color:

```
public int getRed()
public int getGreen()
public int getBlue()
public int getAlpha()
```

These methods retrieve the red, green, and blue components, and the alpha value of a color object. The color components are in the sRGB space. The retrieved values of all these parameters range from 0 to 255. If you are looking for a method that retrieves the RGB values in the form of bits, the method

```
public int getRGB()
```

can do the job. This method retrieves the combined RGB value of a color object. The bits contain 0xff in 24–31, red in 16–23, green in 8–15, and blue in 0–7.

In addition to the previous methods, two more methods are supported to retrieve the color components on a floating point scale from 0 to 1.

```
public float[] getRGBColorComponents(float[] compArray)
```

returns the color components in the sRGB space. You can pass an array that can accommodate three float type color components. If the array passed is null, an array to contain three components is created and returned with the values.

```
public float[] getRGBComponents(float[] compArray)
```
returns a float array containing the color and alpha components of the color, as represented in the default sRGB color space. In case the array passed is null, an array with four elements is created to store the return value.

The following are similar to the previous methods, but these methods return the values in the ColorSpace of the Color rather than the sRGB space:

```
public float[] getComponents(float[] compArray)
public float[] getColorComponents(float[] compArray)
```

In addition to the previous methods, the methods

```
public float[] getComponents(ColorSpace cspace, float[] compArray)
public float[] getColorComponents(ColorSpace cspace, float[] compArray)
```
are supported to retrieve the components of a color in a different color space. You can specify the color space and array to store the components as argument values. The array is returned with the color components.

Retrieving Colors and Color Spaces

You can specify the string representation of a color to retrieve the corresponding color. The string is typically some system color property. The string is converted to an integer and then the representative color is returned. Three static methods support these operations.

```
public static Color getColor(String colorString)
```
returns a null object in case there is no representative color.

```
public static Color getColor(String colorString, Color defaultColor)
```
allows the specification of defaultColor that is returned in case a representative color for the colorString is not obtained.

```
public static Color getColor(String colorString, int colorInteger)
```
is similar to the second method, but it requires the specification of the default color as an integer instead of a color object.

To retrieve the color space of the current color, you can use the following method:

```
public ColorSpace getColorSpace()
```

Creating a Color from Hue, Saturation, and Brightness

If the hue, saturation, and brightness of a color are available, the following method constructs a color object and returns it:

```
public static Color getHSBColor(float hue, float saturation, float brightness)
```

In this method, note that the arguments are floating point values in the range 0 to 1.0.

Controlling the Brightness and Darkness of a Color

In an application or applet, you can control the brightness or darkness of a color by calling these respective methods

```
public Color brighter()
public Color darker()
```

that create a brighter or darker version of the current color. Note that these methods might not be exactly inverse to each other due to rounding errors. The rounding errors will magnify only when these methods are invoked several times.

RGB and HSB Color Conversions

The `Color` class supports two static methods to perform transformations between the RGB and hue-saturation-brightness (HSB) models of colors.

```
public static float[] RGBtoHSB(int red, int green, int blue,
                               float[] hsbValues)
```

transforms the components of a color specified by using the default sRGB model to an equivalent set of values for hue, saturation, and brightness. The parameter `hsbValues` is an array of float type values that will store the hue, saturation, and brightness values of the color components red, green, and blue. The method returns this array after filling it. If you substitute a null value for this array, the method creates and fills a new array, and then returns it.

Next, you can use the static method

```
public static int HSBtoRGB(float hue, float saturation, float brightness)
```

to convert the HSB components to their combined RGB value. This method transforms the components of a color, as specified by the HSB model, to an equivalent set of values for the default sRGB model. Note that the HSB values are of type float. The return value is encoded in bits and returned as an integer. The value consists of the red component in bits 16–23, the green component in bits 8–15, and the blue component in bits 0–7 (see the program given in Listing 2.1).

Demonstration of Colors Example

Listing 2.1 shows the code for an applet containing a canvas to display colors and a control panel to adjust the RGB and HSB values to create various shades of colors. The panel also provides a slider to adjust the alpha value of colors. At the bottom of the panel, the RGB value of a color is displayed. Figure 2.1 shows the output of this program.

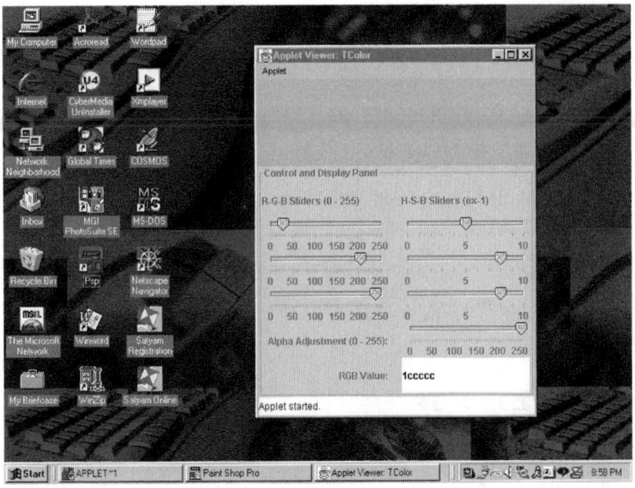

Figure 2.1

An applet to demonstrate various colors.

Listing 2.1   TColor Applet Displays and Adjusts Colors (TColor.java)

```
/*
 * <Applet code=TColor width=350 height=400>
 * </Applet>
 */

import javax.swing.*;
import javax.swing.event.*;
import java.awt.*;
import java.awt.event.*;
import javax.swing.border.*;

public class TColor extends JApplet {
    DrawingCanvas canvas; // Canvas to display colors
    JLabel rgbValue; // Label to display rgbValue of color

    // Sliders to control RGB, HSB and alpha values
    JSlider slider,
            sliderR, sliderG, sliderB,
            sliderH, sliderS, sliderBr,
            sliderAlpha;

    public void init() {
        // 1. Get the content pane
        Container container = getContentPane();

        // 2. Define the color canvas
```

continues

Listing 2.1   continued

```
canvas = new DrawingCanvas();

// 3. Create control sliders by using the method
// defined in snippet-6. The parameters of the slider
// constructors are its minimum and maximum values, current value,
// maximum and minimum tick spacings.
setSlider(0, 255, 0, 50, 5);
sliderR = slider;

setSlider(0, 255, 0, 50, 5);
sliderG = slider;

setSlider(0, 255, 0, 50, 5);
sliderB = slider;

setSlider(0, 10, 0, 5, 1);
sliderH = slider;

setSlider(0, 10, 0, 5, 1);
sliderS = slider;

setSlider(0, 10, 0, 5, 1);
sliderBr = slider;

setSlider(0, 255, 255, 50, 5); // See the integer constructor
sliderAlpha = slider;          // with alpha value of Color.

// 4. Add the labels and sliders to a panel
JPanel panel = new JPanel();
panel.setBorder(new TitledBorder("Control and Display Panel"));
panel.setLayout(new GridLayout(6,2,15,0));//6 rows, 2 cols,
                                // 15, 0 horiz&vert spacing

panel.add(new JLabel("R-G-B Sliders (0 - 255)"));
panel.add(new JLabel("H-S-B Sliders (ex-1)"));
panel.add(sliderR); panel.add(sliderH);
panel.add(sliderG); panel.add(sliderS);
panel.add(sliderB); panel.add(sliderBr);

panel.add(new JLabel("Alpha Adjustment (0 - 255): ", JLabel.RIGHT));
panel.add(sliderAlpha);

panel.add(new JLabel("RGB Value: ", JLabel.RIGHT));
rgbValue = new JLabel("");
rgbValue.setBackground(Color.white);
rgbValue.setForeground(Color.black);
rgbValue.setOpaque(true);
panel.add(rgbValue);
```

```java
// 5. Add the panel and canvas to the applet
container.add(panel, BorderLayout.SOUTH);
container.add(canvas);
}


//  6. Method to create sliders with necessary configuration
public void setSlider(int min,   // Slider minimum value
                      int max,   // Slider maximum value
                      int init,  // Slider initial value
                      int mjrTkSp, // Major tick spacing
                      int mnrTkSp) { // Minor tick spacing
    slider = new JSlider(JSlider.HORIZONTAL, min, max, init);
    slider.setPaintTicks(true);
    slider.setMajorTickSpacing(mjrTkSp);
    slider.setMinorTickSpacing(mnrTkSp);
    slider.setPaintLabels(true);
    slider.addChangeListener(new SliderListener());
}


// 7. Definition of the display canvas
class DrawingCanvas extends Canvas {
    Color color;
    int redValue, greenValue, blueValue;
    int alphaValue = 255;
    float[] hsbValues = new float[3];

    // 8. Constructor
    public DrawingCanvas() {
        // Assign a size to the canvas
        setSize(350,350); // canvas width and height

        // Assign color to the canvas
        color = new Color(0, 0, 0); // 0,0,0 = RGB values
        setBackgroundColor();
    }

    public void setBackgroundColor() {
        color = new Color(redValue, greenValue, blueValue, alphaValue);
        setBackground(color);
    }
}


// 9. Define the slider listener to alter different parameters
// of colors.
class SliderListener implements ChangeListener {
    public void stateChanged(ChangeEvent e) {
        JSlider slider = (JSlider) e.getSource();
```

continues

Listing 2.1   continued

```
        if (slider == sliderAlpha) {
            canvas.alphaValue = slider.getValue();
            canvas.setBackgroundColor();
        }
        else if (slider == sliderR) {
            canvas.redValue = slider.getValue();
            displayRGBColor();
        }
        else if (slider == sliderG) {
            canvas.greenValue = slider.getValue();
            displayRGBColor();
        }
        else if (slider == sliderB) {
            canvas.blueValue = slider.getValue();
            displayRGBColor();
        }
        else if (slider == sliderH) {
            canvas.hsbValues[0] = (float)(slider.getValue()*0.1);
            displayHSBColor();
        }
        else if (slider == sliderS) {
            canvas.hsbValues[1] = (float) (slider.getValue()*0.1);
            displayHSBColor();
        }
        else if (slider == sliderBr) {
            canvas.hsbValues[2] = (float) (slider.getValue()*0.1);
            displayHSBColor();
        }

        // Refresh canvas with new parameters
        canvas.repaint();
    }

    public void displayRGBColor() {
        canvas.setBackgroundColor();
        Color.RGBtoHSB(canvas.redValue,
                       canvas.greenValue,
                       canvas.blueValue,
                       canvas.hsbValues);
        sliderH.setValue((int)(canvas.hsbValues[0]*10));
        sliderS.setValue((int)(canvas.hsbValues[1]*10));
        sliderBr.setValue((int)(canvas.hsbValues[2]*10));

        rgbValue.setText(Integer.toString(
        canvas.color.getRGB()&0xffffff, 16));
    }

    public void displayHSBColor() {
```

```
        canvas.color = Color.getHSBColor(canvas.hsbValues[0],
                                canvas.hsbValues[1],
                                canvas.hsbValues[2]);
        // This color is not sufficient for display; we
        // need to have proper alpha value. So use this to
        // to obtain the RGB components. Anyway, they are useful
        // to adjust the values of RGB sliders.
        canvas.redValue = canvas.color.getRed();
        canvas.greenValue = canvas.color.getGreen();
        canvas.blueValue = canvas.color.getBlue();

        sliderR.setValue(canvas.redValue);
        sliderG.setValue(canvas.greenValue);
        sliderB.setValue(canvas.blueValue);

        canvas.color = new Color(canvas.redValue,
                                canvas.greenValue,
                                canvas.blueValue,
                                canvas.alphaValue);
        canvas.setBackground(canvas.color);
      }
    }
}
```

Code Analysis

The class TColor is a Swing applet. It declares a display canvas and label and a set of sliders (for controlling RGB and HSB values) as its fields. Inside the init() method, snippet-1 obtains a reference to the underlying content pane. Snippet-2 defines an object of the display canvas. Snippet-3 creates the RGB and HSB sliders. The code for this functionality is stored in a separate method, setSlider(), as given in snippet-6. Snippet-4 adds the display labels and sliders to the control panel. Snippet-5 adds the display canvas and the control panel to the applet.

Snippet-7 defines the display canvas. This canvas declares the RGB values, HSB values, alpha value, and the current color displayed as its fields. Snippet-8 is the canvas constructor. Snippet-9 defines the slider listener to receive the changes in the values of color adjustment sliders and alpha adjustment sliders. Inside the implementation method, you obtain the current value of a particular slider and assign the value to the corresponding parameter of the canvas. Then the canvas is repainted to exercise the effect of the new value. The displayRGBColor() and displayHSBColor() methods are used to display the current value of the colors.

Painting with Color Patterns

As already introduced in the previous chapter on fundamentals of Java 2D, you can fill various graphic shapes with color patterns such as gradient paint and texture paint. The gradient paint type linearly changes one color to another. The texture paint type displays a texture that is specified by an image file (x.gif or x.jpg).

Both the gradient paint and texture paint color patterns implement the interface java.awt.Paint. The Paint interface supports the method createContext() that provides the paint context object (of type PaintContext) to be used for generating a color pattern. The Paint interface extends from the interface Transparency. This interface contains the method to return one of the transparency modes: OPAQUE, BITMASK, or TRANSLUCENT. These modes are defined as fields of Transparency. OPAQUE has an alpha value of 1.0, and BITMASK represents an alpha value of 1.0 or 0.0. TRANSLUCENT represents an arbitrary alpha value between and including 0.0 and 1.0.

Working with Gradient Paint Patterns

The GradientPaint class in the java.awt package provides a way to fill a shape with a linearly changing pattern of colors. For example, if point P1 with color C1 and point P2 with color C2 are specified in the user space, the color on the line connecting P1 and P2 is linearly changed from the color C1 to C2.

Any point P' that is not exactly on the connecting line of P1 and P2, but is located to one side, possesses the color of point P, where point P is at the intersection of the connecting line and the offset dropped from point P' to the connecting line (see Figure 2.2).

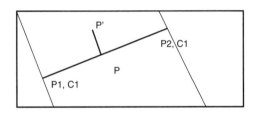

Figure 2.2

Illustration of gradient paint intricacies.

If a point lies beyond the connecting line of P1 and P2, its color is determined by the parameters cyclic and acyclic. If the color pattern is specified to be acyclic, the points before P1 possess the color C1, and the points after P2 possess the color C2 (see Figure 2.3). For the cyclic color pattern, the color pattern between P1 and P2 repeats before P1 and after P2 (see Figure 2.4). A boolean variable represents these parameters, which are opposites to each other.

Creating Gradient Paint Pattern Objects

As discussed previously, two different locations and their corresponding colors are required to define a gradient point object. A boolean parameter to specify whether the gradient paint is cyclic or acyclic is also needed. Following are the supported constructors to create gradient paint objects.

```
public GradientPaint(float x1, float y1,
                     Color color1,
                     float x2, float y2,
                     Color color2)
```

creates a simple acyclic GradientPaint object by using the (x, y) coordinates for points and the corresponding colors.

```
public GradientPaint(Point2D pt1,
                     Color color1,
                     Point2D pt2,
                     Color color2)
```

creates an acyclic GradientPaint object using the point objects and colors specified.

```
public GradientPaint(float x1, float y1,
                     Color color1,
                     float x2, float y2,
                     Color color2,
                     boolean cyclic)
```

creates either a cyclic or acyclic GradientPaint object depending on the boolean parameter. This constructor uses the (x, y) coordinates for the points.

```
public GradientPaint(Point2D pt1,
                     Color color1,
                     Point2D pt2,
                     Color color2,
                     boolean cyclic)
```

creates either a cyclic or acyclic GradientPaint object depending on the boolean parameter and the point objects.

After an instance of gradient paint is created, you can assign it to the graphics context by calling the method setPaint(). This method takes a Paint type object as its argument value.

Gradient Paint Example

Listing 2.2 demonstrates the gradient paint pattern of coloring. The program displays an application window that contains a canvas and a control panel. From the color combo box, you can choose a color; you can also select a fill mode as cyclic or acyclic. Next, by double-clicking the mouse over the canvas, you can specify the first point of the gradient pattern. Then you can choose another color from the combo box and double-click the mouse over the canvas to select the second point. Using the specified points, the program automatically renders the canvas with the gradient patterns. For testing another pattern, you can repeat the same process. Figures 2.3 and 2.4 show the output of this program in acyclic and cyclic modes.

Figure 2.3

Gradient paint pattern in acyclic mode.

Figure 2.4

Gradient paint pattern in cyclic mode.

Listing 2.2   TGradientPaint Application Displays Gradient Paint in Cyclic and Acyclic Mode (TGradientPaint.java)

```
import javax.swing.*;
import javax.swing.event.*;
import javax.swing.border.*;
```

```java
import java.awt.*;
import java.awt.event.*;
import java.awt.geom.*;

class TGradientPaint extends JFrame {
    DisplayCanvas canvas;
    String[] colorLabels = {"White", "Red", "Blue", "Green", "Yellow",
                            "Magenta", "Light Gray", "Black"};
    JRadioButton acyclicButton, cyclicButton;

    public TGradientPaint() {
        // 1. Assign a title to the frame and get a handle on
        // the frame's content pane
        super("TGradientPaint");
        Container container = getContentPane();

        // 2. Add the display canvas
        canvas = new DisplayCanvas();
        container.add(canvas);

        // 3. Create a control panel with titled border
        JPanel panel = new JPanel();
        TitledBorder border = new TitledBorder(
          "Select a Fill Mode, and Double Click Mouse"
          + " at Two Points with Different Colors...");
        panel.setBorder(border);

        // 4. Create a color combo box and the necessary radio buttons
        JComboBox comboBox = new JComboBox(colorLabels);
        comboBox.addActionListener(new ComboBoxListener());

        acyclicButton = new JRadioButton("Acyclic", true);
        acyclicButton.addActionListener(new RadioButtonListener());
        cyclicButton = new JRadioButton("Cyclic");
        cyclicButton.addActionListener(new RadioButtonListener());
        ButtonGroup group = new ButtonGroup();
        group.add(acyclicButton);
        group.add(cyclicButton);

        // 5. Add the combo box, and radio buttons to the panel
        panel.add(comboBox);
        panel.add(acyclicButton);
        panel.add(cyclicButton);

        // 6. Add the panel to the frame
        container.add(BorderLayout.SOUTH, panel);

        // 7. Add a frame closing listener and display the frame
```

continues

Listing 2.2   continued

```
        addWindowListener(new WindowEventHandler());
        pack(); // Packs around the contents with suitable size
        show(); // Display the frame
    }

    // 8. Code to handle closing of the frame
    class WindowEventHandler extends WindowAdapter {
        public void windowClosing(WindowEvent e) {
            System.exit(0);
        }
    }

    // 9. The main method...
    public static void main(String arg[]) {
        new TGradientPaint();
    }

    // 10. Canvas to draw round-cornered rectangles
    class DisplayCanvas extends Canvas {
        // 11. Points and Colors for the gradient patterns
        Point2D point1, point2;

        Color fillColor = Color.black;
        Color[] colors = {Color.white, Color.red, Color.blue, Color.green,
                          Color.yellow, Color.magenta, Color.lightGray,
                          Color.black};
        Color fillColor1, fillColor2;

        boolean cyclicMode = false;

        // Constructor
        DisplayCanvas() {
            // 12. Add the mouse listener to select points over the canvas.
            addMouseListener(new MyMouseListener());
            setBackground(Color.white);  // For canvas background color
            setSize(400, 225);  // Canvas width=400 height=225
        }


        public void paint(Graphics g) {
            // 13. Create the graphics context object and display the
            // the gradient paint in a rectangle.
            Graphics2D g2D = (Graphics2D) g;

            if (point1 != null && point2 == null)
                drawHighlightSquare(g2D, fillColor, point1);
```

```
        if (point1 != null && point2 != null) {
            Paint gp = new GradientPaint(point1, fillColor1,
                                         point2, fillColor2,
                                         cyclicMode);
            g2D.setPaint(gp);
            g2D.fill(new Rectangle2D.Double(0, 0, getWidth(), getHeight()));
        }
    }

    public void drawHighlightSquare(Graphics2D g2D, Color c, Point2D p) {
        g2D.setColor(c);
        double x = p.getX();
        double y = p.getY();
        g2D.fill(new Rectangle.Double(x-3.0, y-3.0, 6.0, 6.0));
    }
}

// 14. The mouse listener to handle double clicks over the canvas.
class MyMouseListener extends MouseAdapter {
    int clickTime = 0;

    public void mouseClicked(MouseEvent e) {
        if (e.getClickCount() == 2) {
            if (clickTime == 0) {
                clickTime++;
                canvas.fillColor1 = canvas.fillColor;
                canvas.point2 = null;
                canvas.point1 = e.getPoint();
                canvas.repaint();
            }
            else if (clickTime == 1) {
                clickTime—;
                canvas.fillColor2 = canvas.fillColor;
                canvas.point2 = e.getPoint();
                canvas.repaint();
            }
        }
    }
}

// 15. Combo box listener to handle color selections
class ComboBoxListener implements ActionListener {
    public void actionPerformed(ActionEvent e) {
        JComboBox cBox = (JComboBox) e.getSource();
        String color = (String) cBox.getSelectedItem();
        for (int i=0; i<colorLabels.length; i++) {
            if(color.equals(colorLabels[i])) {
```

continues

Listing 2.2   continued

```
                        canvas.fillColor = canvas.colors[i];
                        return;
                    }
                }
            }
        }

    // 16. Radio Button listener to select different fill modes
    // such as cyclic (true) or acyclic (false).
    class RadioButtonListener implements ActionListener {
        public void actionPerformed(ActionEvent e) {
            JRadioButton button = (JRadioButton) e.getSource();

            if (button.equals(acyclicButton)) {
                canvas.cyclicMode = false;
            }
            else if (button.equals(cyclicButton)) {
                canvas.cyclicMode = true;
            }
        }
    }
}
```

Code Analysis

The class `TGradientPaint` is an application frame that is attached to a canvas and a control panel. This class declares references to the canvas and radio buttons for fill modes as its fields. Inside the constructor, snippet-1 assigns a title to the frame and gets a reference to the underlying content pane.

Snippet-2 creates the canvas object and adds it to the main frame. Snippets-3, 4, and 5 create the control panel with a combo box to select colors, and fill modes such as cyclic or acyclic. The panel is also decorated with a titled border. The panel is added at the bottom portion of the frame, as stated in snippet-6. Snippet-7 adds a window listener to the frame to perform closing operations, and displays the frame with a suitable size. Snippet-8 defines the window listener class to implement closing of the frame. Snippet-9 is the main method where an instance of `TGradientPaint` is created.

Snippet-10 defines the display canvas class. This class declares the point objects to start and end the gradient pattern, fill color, and a boolean parameter for the fill mode, as given in snippet-11. Inside the constructor of this class, snippet-12 adds a mouse listener to the canvas, and assigns a background color and suitable size.

Inside the paint() method, snippet-13 creates a graphics context object and performs the display of the gradient pattern. The first if statement creates and displays points over the canvas when the mouse is double-clicked. The second if statement creates a gradient pattern, assigns it to the graphics context, and displays the pattern in a rectangle. The rectangle is the same size as the canvas.

Snippet-14 shows the mouse listener class. Inside the mouseClicked() method, you can find the code to implement double-clicks in a sequence. In the first double-click, the canvas displays the first point for the gradient paint. In the second double-click, the canvas displays the second double-click and then immediately displays the gradient paint. Snippets-15 and 16 show the listener classes to implement the selection of fill color and fill modes.

Working with Texture Paint Patterns

The class TexturePaint in the package java.awt represents the texture paint pattern. The texture is specified by an image of type BufferedImage. Basically, you need to store an image in a buffer that is represented by the class BufferedImage. A buffered image can then be copied efficiently inside a shape to create the corresponding texture.

A texture is anchored to the upper-left corner of a rectangle of type Rectangle2D that is specified in the user space. Then the texture is computed for locations in the device space by copying the specified rectangle infinitely in all directions in the user space.

Creating Texture Paint Pattern Objects

You can create a texture paint pattern by using the constructor

```
public TexturePaint(BufferedImage texture, Rectangle2D anchor)
```

which requires a buffered image of the given texture and a rectangle of type Rectangle2D to anchor and copy the texture image. For a texture that repeatedly fills the entire shape without any blank margins, the 2D rectangle must possess the size of the given texture image.

Texture Paint Example

Listing 2.3 presents a simple program that demonstrates various texture patterns. The texture patterns are created by using *.jpg files. The application window displays a sequence of textures as thumbnails. You can click the mouse over a thumbnail to see the texture filling the canvas that is displayed at the center of the window. Figure 2.5 shows the output when a texture has been selected.

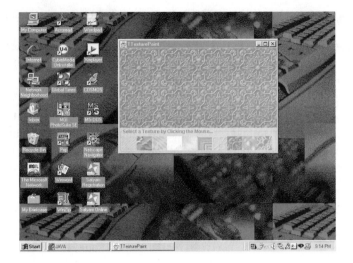

Figure 2.5

Demonstration of texture paint.

Listing 2.3   Application Demonstrates Texture Patterns Using JPEG Thumbnails (TTexturePaint.java)

```
import javax.swing.*;
import javax.swing.border.*;
import java.awt.*;
import java.awt.event.*;
import java.awt.geom.*;
import java.awt.image.*;

class TTexturePaint extends JFrame {
    DisplayCanvas canvas;

    public TTexturePaint() {
        // 1. Assign a title to the frame and get a handle on
        // the frame's content pane
        super("TTexturePaint");
        Container container = getContentPane();

        // 2. Add the canvas with rectangles
        canvas = new DisplayCanvas();
        container.add(canvas);

        // 3. Create a panel to display various textures (canvases)
        JPanel panel = new JPanel();
        panel.setLayout(new GridLayout(1,10));
        panel.setBorder(new TitledBorder(
            "Select a Texture by Clicking the Mouse..."));
```

```
    // 4. Create canvas objects displaying thumb nails of textures,
    // and add them to the panel.
    for (int i=0; i<10; i++) {
        panel.add(new SelectableCanvas(
                    "textures/texture"+(i+1)+".jpg", canvas));
    }

    // 5. Add the panel to the frame
    container.add(BorderLayout.SOUTH, panel);

    // 6. Add a frame closing listener and display the frame
    addWindowListener(new WindowEventHandler());
    pack(); // Packs around the contents with suitable size
    show(); // Display the frame
}

// 7. Code to handle closing of the frame
class WindowEventHandler extends WindowAdapter {
    public void windowClosing(WindowEvent e) {
        System.exit(0);
    }
}

// 8. The main method...
public static void main(String arg[]) {
    new TTexturePaint();
}
}

// 9. Canvas to display the selected texture
class DisplayCanvas extends Canvas {
    Image displayImage;

    // Constructor
    DisplayCanvas() {
        // Add the mouse listener to receive a rectangle selection
        setBackground(Color.white); // For canvas background color
        setSize(400, 225); // Canvas width=400 height=225
    }

    public void setImage(Image image) {
        displayImage = image;
    }

    public void paint(Graphics g) {
        // Create the graphics context object
        Graphics2D g2D = (Graphics2D) g;
```

continues

Listing 2.3   continued

```
            // Create a texture paint object and display it in a rectangle
            // by filling it.
            if (displayImage != null) {
                BufferedImage bi = new BufferedImage(
                                        displayImage.getWidth(this),
                                        displayImage.getHeight(this),
                                        BufferedImage.TYPE_INT_RGB);
                bi.createGraphics().drawImage(displayImage, 0, 0, this);

                Rectangle2D rectangle = new Rectangle2D.Float(0, 0,
                                        displayImage.getWidth(this),
                                        displayImage.getHeight(this));

                TexturePaint tp = new TexturePaint(bi, rectangle);
                g2D.setPaint(tp);
                g2D.fill(new Rectangle2D.Float(0, 0, getWidth(), getHeight()));
            }
        }
}

// 10. Class to define thumb nail objects of textures. The
// user can select a texture by clicking the mouse on the
// corresponding thumb nail.
class SelectableCanvas extends Canvas {
    Image image;
    DisplayCanvas canvas;

    SelectableCanvas(String imageFile, DisplayCanvas canvas) {
        this.image = getToolkit().getImage(imageFile);
        this.canvas = canvas;

        addMouseListener(new MouseEventHandler());
        setBackground(Color.white);
        setSize(35, 35); // width and height of a thumb nail
    }

    public void paint(Graphics g) {
        g.drawImage(image, 0, 0, this);
    }

    // 11. Class to handle mouse events that are generated
    // when the mouse is clicked on the canvas.
    class MouseEventHandler extends MouseAdapter {
        public void mouseClicked(MouseEvent evt) {
            canvas.setImage(image);
            canvas.repaint();
```

```
        }
    }
}
```

Code Analysis

The class TTexturePaint is an application frame that is attached with a canvas and thumb nails of texture patterns. The class declares a reference to the display canvas as its field. Inside its constructor, snippet-1 assigns a title to the frame and obtains a reference to the content pane of the frame.

Snippet-2 creates an instance of the display canvas and adds it to the frame. Snippets-3, 4, and 5 create a panel of thumbnails and add it to the frame. The thumbnails are essentially canvases displaying various textures. The panel also contains a title. Snippet-6 adds a listener to the frame to close the window and displays the frame with suitable size. Snippet-7 is the window listener class. Snippet-8 is the main method that creates an instance of TTexturePaint.

Snippet-9 defines the display canvas. This class declares the image to be rendered as its field. setImage() is an access method to receive an image, which will be displayed by the canvas. Inside the paint() method, a graphics context object is created. Then a buffered image of type RGB is created. The dimensions of the buffered image are specified to be those of the display image. Next, by retrieving the graphics context of the buffered image, the display image is added to the buffer.

NOTE

The display image is stored in a buffer to efficiently copy it multiple times inside a shape.

A 2D rectangle is created with the dimensions of the display image. This rectangle is used to locate and copy the specified buffered image. Then the texture object is created using the buffered image and the 2D rectangle. The texture paint is applied to the graphics context by invoking the method setPaint(). A rectangle of size canvas is drawn with the texture pattern filled inside.

Snippet-10 defines the thumbnail class that is used to create various texture objects. This class supports the functionality to allow the user to select a texture by clicking the mouse over the thumbnail.

Color Management

The RGB and CMYK color spaces used by different monitor screens and printers are device dependent. A particular brand of a monitor has its own RGB color space. Therefore, a particular color specified in the RGB space is displayed differently on different computer screens due to lack of precise standards. Similarly, a model of a printer has its own CMYK color space. The Java 2D must be able to accurately reproduce the colors specified in an application on various display and print devices.

Accurately Reproducing Colors on Output Devices

To achieve precision and accuracy in color display or printing, the International Commission on Illumination (CIE) has defined standards by introducing another color space called CIEXYZ. This color space contains three color components. When you use this color space, the device dependencies will no longer show their effects, leading to consistent colors on different end devices. The color space classes that extend the abstract class ColorSpace, such as ICC_ColorSpace, implement the methods to convert color values from and to CIEXYZ space.

Using CIEXYZ space might not always be practical due to the computational load involved. Therefore, another way to achieve device-independent colors is by describing the conversion profile between the device-dependent and device-independent spaces. The International Color Consortium (ICC) defines the color profile that is commonly used. An application using Java 2D can use an ICC profile to convert the input color (from a source such as an image) to the device-independent format, and then map from that space to the color space of the output device.

CHAPTER 3

Geometric Shapes: Lines and Rectangles

One of the most important areas of computer graphics is *modeling* of various objects. By using modeling, you can describe the geometry of an object to the computer so as to produce (or simulate) a visual display of the object. The shape of an object is created by using one or more of the *primitives* (geometric forms) that include line segments, curves, arcs, circles, ellipses, and rectangles.

In order to create complex shapes, the geometric primitives for different basic shapes must be available, and they must be easy to implement. Using the Java 2D API, you can implement standard geometric primitives and customized shapes that are independent of the display and printing devices.

In this chapter, you will explore the API details and code examples for line segments, rectangles, and rectangles with rounded corners. The code examples also demonstrate how to set up the attributes in a graphics context to render the geometric shapes. Chapter 4, "Geometric Shapes: Curves, Arcs, and Ellipses," discusses more geometric shapes.

The Shape Interface

A geometric shape in the context of Java 2D is represented by the design level interface Shape. Thus, the geometric shapes such as lines, rectangles, curves, arcs, and ellipses must implement this interface.

NOTE

Points in Java 2D do not fall under the category of shapes, and thus do not implement the Shape interface.

Iteration Objects for Boundary Data

The interface PathIterator provides a design-level abstraction for the outline of a shape. The iteration objects of type PathIterator contain the outline information of geometric shapes. The iteration objects describe the shapes using either lines or quadratic or cubic curves.

As each of the geometric shapes is discussed in this chapter, you will observe the methods to retrieve the iteration objects for the outline information of the respective shapes.

Determining Whether a Point Is Inside or Outside a Shape

The shape of an object is useful when you need to determine whether a given point lies inside or outside the boundary of the object. For a point to be inside the boundary of a given shape, Java 2D defines the following criteria:

- The point is completely inside the boundary.
- The point lies exactly on the boundary and the space immediately after the point in the increasing X direction (to the right) is completely inside the boundary.
- The point lies exactly on a horizontal boundary and the space immediately after the point in the increasing Y direction (down) is inside the boundary.

Figure 3.1 shows a shape and a collection of points P1, P2,...P10. The following discussion will evaluate whether each of these points is inside or outside the boundary of the shape.

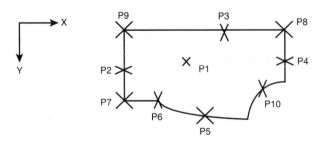

Figure 3.1

A shape whose boundary contains points P1 through P10.

Point P1 is an obvious case: You can easily conclude that it lies *inside* the boundary of the shape.

Point P2 lies *inside* the shape because it is positioned exactly on the boundary and the space immediately after the point in the increasing X direction is inside the boundary.

Point P3 also is *inside* the shape because it lies exactly on the horizontal boundary and the space immediately after the point in the increasing Y direction is inside the boundary.

Point P4 is *outside* the shape because it lies exactly on the boundary and the space immediately after the point in the increasing X direction is outside the boundary.

Point P5 lies *inside* the shape because it is positioned exactly on the boundary and the space immediately after the point in the increasing X direction is inside the boundary.

Point P6 is *outside* the shape because it lies exactly on the horizontal boundary and the space immediately after the point in the increasing Y direction is outside the boundary.

Point P7 lies *outside* the shape because it lies on the horizontal boundary and the space immediately after the point in the increasing Y direction is outside the boundary.

Point P8 is *outside* the shape because it lies on the boundary and the space immediately after the point in the increasing X direction is outside the boundary.

Point P9 is *inside* the shape because it lies on the horizontal boundary and the space immediately after the point in the increasing Y direction is inside the boundary.

Point P10 lies *outside* the shape because it is located on the boundary and the space immediately after the point in the increasing X direction is outside the boundary.

> **NOTE**
>
> For a rectangular shape, only the top-left corner point is inside the shape. The remaining corner points lie outside.

Defining Points in 2D

Points and lines are the basic building blocks of computer graphics. Lines are discussed in the next section, "Drawing Lines in 2D." Here, you will find information on how to create point objects using the Java 2D API.

A *point* is simply defined as a pair of X and Y coordinates in 2D space. Thus, you can expect these coordinates to be the fields of point objects. The abstract class `Point2D` serves as the data type for 2D points with the actual coordinate values stored in the subclass objects. The classes `Point`, `Point2D.Float`, and `Point2D.Double` extend `Point2D` and can be used to create instances of point objects.

NOTE

> The point objects in Java 2D are not considered to be geometric shapes. Thus, the point classes do not implement the interface Shape. This behavior is unlike that of 2D lines and other primitives, which are considered to be shapes. The point classes simply store the data for X and Y coordinates that may be used by other geometric shapes (see the constructors of Line2D.Float, Line2D.Double, Rectangle, and so on).

The concrete class Point represents points that are initialized with integer-type data for X and Y coordinates. The classes Point2D.Float and Point2D.Double support float and double type data. (See Chapter 10 for the related inheritance hierarchies and quick reference.)

Drawing Lines in 2D

Line segments are also fundamental to computer graphics. Java 2D API supports line segments with different precision of data values for coordinates. The abstract class Line2D represents a segment of straight line.

You can define a line segment by specifying two points or pairs of (x, y) coordinates. The concrete classes Line2D.Float and Line2D.Double extend Line2D to encapsulate the actual data values for the respective X and Y coordinates. These classes are defined as the inner classes of Line2D.

Note that the abstract class Line2D implements the interface Shape and is stored in the package java.awt.geom. Thus, the library considers line segments to be shapes. You can use the method draw(Shape shape) from the graphics context to draw different line segments.

Line2D provides many important methods (some of which are static) to perform various operations with line segments. The following sections will present the operations you can perform using the methods available in Line2D, Line2D.Float, and Line2D.Double.

Creating Line Segments

To create a line segment of type Line2D, you can use the float type or double type X and Y coordinate values for points. Each type supports three types of constructors: those that take no arguments, those that take coordinate values, and those that take points.

Constructors with no arguments create line objects that are drawn at the origin (0,0). That is, the starting point and ending point are both considered to be at the origin. These instances can be modified to represent some realistic line segments at a later stage.

Constructors that take values for x1, y1, x2, and y2 create instances of line segments that are drawn from the starting point (x1, y1) to the ending point (x2, y2). The remaining constructors that take points as their arguments create instances using the specified point objects. Here are some examples of the three constructor types:

```
public Line2D.Float()
public Line2D.Float(float x1, float y1, float x2, float y2)
public Line2D.Float(Point2D p1, Point2D p2)


public Line2D.Double()
public Line2D.Double(double x1, double y1, double x2, double y2)
public Line2D.Double(Point2D p1, Point2D p2)
```

Line Drawing Example

The sample program in Listing 3.1 demonstrates how to create a line drawing. The line drawing shows a view of a house made up of a set of line segments, as you can see in Figure 3.2. The program is an applet; it includes a number of sliders you can use to manipulate the line drawing. You can translate it along the X and Y axes and rotate it about an origin that can appear at different locations. You can also scale the drawing to magnify or reduce its size along the X and Y axes. The Width Control slider can change the width of the line segments in the line drawing.

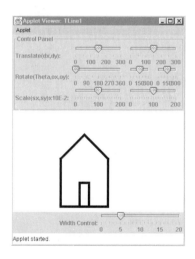

Figure 3.2

A simple drawing made up of line segments.

Listing 3.1   Line Drawing Example (TLine1.java)
```
// Demonstrates how to create a line drawing

/*
 * <Applet code=TLine1 width=350 height=400>
 * </Applet>
 */

import javax.swing.*;
import javax.swing.event.*;
import javax.swing.border.*;
import java.awt.*;
import java.awt.geom.*;

public class TLine1 extends JApplet {
    DrawingCanvas canvas;
    JSlider slider, slider1, slider2, slider3,
            slider4, slider5, slider6, slider7,
            slider8;

    // Translation distances in x- and y- directions
    double transX = 0.0;
    double transY = 0.0;

    // Rotation parameters: Theta and center of rotation.
    double rotateTheta = 0.0;
    double rotateX = 150.0;
    double rotateY = 150.0;

    // Scaling factors in the x- and y- directions
    double scaleX = 1.0;
    double scaleY = 1.0;

    // Parameters to control the width
    float width = 1.0f;

    public void init() {
        // 1. Get the content pane
        Container container = getContentPane();

        // 2. Add a control panel to the applet
        JPanel controlPanel = new JPanel();
        controlPanel.setLayout(new GridLayout(3, 3));
        container.add(controlPanel, BorderLayout.NORTH);

        // 3. Add a border
        TitledBorder border = new TitledBorder("Control Panel");
        controlPanel.setBorder(border);
```

```
// 4. Add controls to the panel
JLabel label1 = new JLabel("Translate(dx,dy): ");
JLabel label2 = new JLabel("Rotate(Theta,ox,oy): ");
JLabel label3 = new JLabel("Scale(sx,sy)x10E-2:");

// To control translation
controlPanel.add(label1);
setSlider(controlPanel, JSlider.HORIZONTAL,
          0, 300, 150, 100, 50);
slider1 = slider;
setSlider(controlPanel, JSlider.HORIZONTAL,
          0, 300, 150, 100, 50);
slider2 = slider;

// To control rotation
controlPanel.add(label2);
setSlider(controlPanel, JSlider.HORIZONTAL,
          0, 360, 0, 90, 45);
slider3 = slider;

JPanel subPanel = new JPanel();
subPanel.setLayout(new GridLayout(1, 2));

setSlider(subPanel, JSlider.HORIZONTAL,
          0, 300, 150, 150, 50);
slider4 = slider;
setSlider(subPanel, JSlider.HORIZONTAL,
          0, 300, 150, 150, 50);
slider5 = slider;
controlPanel.add(subPanel);

// To control scaling
controlPanel.add(label3);
setSlider(controlPanel, JSlider.HORIZONTAL,
          0, 200, 100, 100, 10);
slider6 = slider;
setSlider(controlPanel, JSlider.HORIZONTAL,
          0, 200, 100, 100, 10);
slider7 = slider;

// To control width of line segments
JLabel label4 = new JLabel("Width Control:", JLabel.RIGHT);
slider8 = new JSlider(JSlider.HORIZONTAL, 0, 20, 1);
slider8.setPaintTicks(true);
slider8.setMajorTickSpacing(5);
slider8.setMinorTickSpacing(1);
slider8.setPaintLabels(true);
slider8.addChangeListener(new SliderListener());
```

continues

Listing 3.1   continued

```
JPanel widthPanel = new JPanel();
widthPanel.setLayout(new GridLayout(1,2));
widthPanel.add(label4);
widthPanel.add(slider8);
container.add(widthPanel, BorderLayout.SOUTH);

// 5. Add the drawing canvas to the applet
canvas = new DrawingCanvas();
container.add(canvas);
}


// 6. Creates a slider object with the required tick marks
public void setSlider(JPanel panel, int orientation,
                      int minimumValue, int maximumValue,
                      int initValue,
                      int majorTickSpacing,
                      int minorTickSpacing) {
    slider = new JSlider(orientation,
                    minimumValue, maximumValue,
                    initValue);
    slider.setPaintTicks(true);
    slider.setMajorTickSpacing(majorTickSpacing);
    slider.setMinorTickSpacing(minorTickSpacing);
    slider.setPaintLabels(true);
    slider.addChangeListener(new SliderListener());
    panel.add(slider);
}


// 7. Slider listener class; Methods retrieve the values from
// the sliders and assign them to the respective parameters.
// These parameters are used to set up the graphics context.
// Next call the repaint() method on canvas.
class SliderListener implements ChangeListener {
    public void stateChanged(ChangeEvent e) {
        JSlider tempSlider = (JSlider) e.getSource();

        if (tempSlider.equals(slider1)) {
            transX = slider1.getValue()-150.0;
            canvas.repaint();
        }
        else if (tempSlider.equals(slider2)) {
            transY = slider2.getValue()-150.0;
            canvas.repaint();
        }
        else if (tempSlider.equals(slider3)) {
            rotateTheta = slider3.getValue()*Math.PI/180;
            canvas.repaint();
        }
```

```
        else if (tempSlider.equals(slider4)) {
            rotateX = slider4.getValue();
            canvas.repaint();
        }
        else if (tempSlider.equals(slider5)) {
            rotateY = slider5.getValue();
            canvas.repaint();
        }
        else if (tempSlider.equals(slider6)) {
            if (slider6.getValue() != 0.0) {
                scaleX = slider6.getValue()/100.0;
                canvas.repaint();
            }
        }
        else if (tempSlider.equals(slider7)) {
            if (slider7.getValue() != 0.0) {
                scaleY = slider7.getValue()/100.0;
                canvas.repaint();
            }
        }
        else if (tempSlider.equals(slider8)) {
            width = slider8.getValue();
            canvas.repaint();
        }
    }
}

// 8. Drawing canvas to draw the line segments
class DrawingCanvas extends Canvas {
    public DrawingCanvas() {
        setBackground(Color.white);
        setSize(300, 300);
    }

    public void paint(Graphics g) {
        Graphics2D g2D = (Graphics2D) g;

        // 9. Assign the translation, rotation and scaling
        // parameters to the graphics context.
        g2D.translate(transX, transY);
        g2D.rotate(rotateTheta, rotateX, rotateY);
        g2D.scale(scaleX, scaleY);

        // 10. Assign the stroke object that contains the new
        // width for line segments
        BasicStroke stroke = new BasicStroke(width);
        g2D.setStroke(stroke);
```

continues

Listing 3.1   continued

```
        // 11. Now draw the line segments that build a home view.
        drawHome(g2D);
    }

    public void drawHome(Graphics2D g2D) {
        // 12. Create line segments for home
        Line2D line1 = new Line2D.Float(100f, 200f, 200f, 200f);
        Line2D line2 = new Line2D.Float(100f, 200f, 100f, 100f);
        Line2D line3 = new Line2D.Float(100f, 100f, 150f, 50f);
        Line2D line4 = new Line2D.Float(150f, 50f,  200f, 100f);
        Line2D line5 = new Line2D.Float(200f, 100f, 200f, 200f);
        Line2D line6 = new Line2D.Float(140f, 200f, 140f, 150f);
        Line2D line7 = new Line2D.Float(140f, 150f, 160f, 150f);
        Line2D line8 = new Line2D.Float(160f, 150f, 160f, 200f);

        // 13. Now draw the line segments
        g2D.draw(line1);
        g2D.draw(line2);
        g2D.draw(line3);
        g2D.draw(line4);
        g2D.draw(line5);
        g2D.draw(line6);
        g2D.draw(line7);
        g2D.draw(line8);
    }
  }
}
```

Code Analysis

The TLine1.java program is a Swing applet, and thus the class TLine1 extends JApplet. The fields of this class include the drawing canvas to paint the line drawing, along with a set of sliders and variables to test the translation, rotation, scaling, and width control of line segments.

Inside the init() method, snippet-1 gets a handle on the applet's content pane. Note that for Swing applets you need to add the contents to the content pane of the applet or frame rather than adding them directly. Snippet-2 creates and adds a control panel to the applet. Snippet-3 furnishes a titled border around the control panel.

Snippet-4 shows various code statements. Initially, statements create a set of labels to be displayed over the control panel. Next, statements create and add a set of sliders that control the translation, rotation, and scaling; the sliders are created by invoking the method setSlider() shown in snippet-6. At the end of snippet-4, you can see the code that creates and adds a slider for controlling the width. Note that the control panel is positioned at the top of the applet, whereas the panel containing the Width Control slider is positioned at the bottom portion of the applet.

Snippet-5 shows the code to create an instance of a drawing canvas and add it to the applet. Next, snippet-6 shows the code to create a slider object with the necessary labels and tick marks. Snippet-7 is the common listener for all sliders displayed on the control panel and the slider for changing the width of line segments. The implementation method stateChanged() checks for a specific slider, retrieves the slider value, and assigns the value to the relevant variable. These variables are declared as fields of the class TLine1. Then the method repaint() is called on the canvas object.

Snippet-8 shows the class for the drawing canvas on which the line segments are drawn. The paint() method prepares the proper graphics context and draws the line segments. The program delegates the drawing of line segments in the shape of a home to another method: drawHome(), found in snippet-12 and snippet-13. This method simply creates eight instances of lines and paints them over the canvas by invoking the draw() method on the graphics context.

Working Further with Lines

In this section, you will find topics on performing various operations using lines in 2D. Essentially, these topics are based on the methods included in the classes Line2D, Line2D.Float, and Line2D.Double.

Redefining a Line Segment

There are times when the end coordinates of a line segment need to be modified to make them more accurate. Or you might need to redefine the line segment using a new set of points p1 and p2. To deal with these requirements, the abstract class Point2D supports two set methods, as follows:

```
public void setLine(Point2D p1, Point2D p2)
public void setLine(Line2D l)
```

The first method takes two point objects, p1 and p2, to redefine the line object using these points. The next one takes another line segment as its argument value to initialize the current line to the specified line.

In addition to the previous methods, the inner class Line2D.Float provides methods to change the accuracy of X and Y coordinates using double type data or to redefine the location of the line using different float type data. Here are these methods:

```
public void setLine(double x1, double y1, double x2, double y2)
public void setLine(float x1, float y1, float x2, float y2)
```

The inner class Line2D.Double also supports a method that is similar to the first method shown earlier. This method allows you to change the X and Y coordinates to a new set of data values that are of type double. Note that no method in this class allows you to reduce the precision of data by using float type argument values!

Retrieving Coordinates or Points

In a program, it is often necessary to retrieve the individual coordinate values or the point objects of the end points of a line segment. To achieve this, you can use the get methods supported in the classes Line2D.Float and Line2D.Double. Here is the list of these methods:

```
public double getX1()
public double getY1()
public double getX2()
public double getY2()
```

These methods retrieve the X and Y coordinates of the start and end points. Notice that these methods from the inner classes Line2D.Float as well as Line2D.Double retrieve the data in double precision. The following methods from these classes retrieve the point objects that represent the start point (p1) and end point (p2) of a line segment:

```
public Point2D getP1()
public Point2D getP2()
```

Distance from a Point to a Line

The abstract class Line2D supports methods to determine the distance or square of the distance from a specified point to a line segment. This distance is the shortest or perpendicular distance to the line segment. The following methods compute the distance between the point (x0, y0) and the line object on which the method is invoked:

```
public double ptLineDist(double x0, double y0)
public double ptLineDist(Point2D pt)
```

The following static method computes and returns the distance between a point (x0, y0) and a line segment with coordinate values (x1, y1) and (x2, y2):

```
public static double ptLineDist(double x1, double y1,
                                double x2, double y2,
                                double x0, double y0)
```

In a similar manner, the following methods retrieve the square of the distance:

```
public double ptLineDistSq(double x0, double y0)
public double ptLineDistSq(Point2D pt)
public static double ptLineDistSq(double x1, double y1,
                                  double x2, double x2,
                                  double x0, double y0)
```

Locating a Point Relative to a Line

While working with geometric models, sometimes you need to recognize the position of a point with reference to a line segment. It's easiest to tell whether the point is on the line or collinear. But to determine which side of the line the point exists on, you need to know whether the line must be rotated clockwise or counterclockwise about its start point at (x1, y1) to reach the point location.

The class `Line2D` supports the following methods that can be used to realize the location of a specified point with reference to the current line:

```
public int relativeCCW(double x, double y)
public int relativeCCW(Point2D p)
```

The first method takes the X and Y coordinates of the point, whereas the second method takes the point object itself as its argument value. These methods return an integer index depending on the position of the point object. If the line has to rotate about (x1, y1) in the counterclockwise direction to point to the location indicated by (x, y) or p, the method returns 1.

If the direction of rotation must be clockwise to indicate point (x, y), the method returns -1. If the point lies exactly on the line, the method returns 0. If the point is collinear with the line segment, but not between the start and endpoints, the value returned will be -1 or 1. If the point lies before the start point (x1, y1), the value returned will be -1; and if the point lies beyond (x2, y2), the value returned will be 1.

In addition to using the preceding methods, you can also invoke the following static method to locate any point (x, y) with reference to a given line segment whose coordinates (x1, y1) and (x2, y2) are specified:

```
public static int relativeCCW(double x1, double y1,
                              double x2, double y2,
                              double x,  double y)
```

This method also returns an integer index as discussed for the previous method `relativeCCW()`.

NOTE

The previous methods provide the way to ascertain whether a point lies on the line segment. The other `contain()` methods supported in the `Line2D` class always return `false` when you test whether a point is contained by this line or shape object. This result is due to the fact that a line segment has no area.

Retrieving Boundaries

For lines that are created using the class `Line2D.Float` or `Line2D.Double`, a rectangular box can provide the boundaries of the line segment. This bounding box is useful to test whether the user has performed an interactive gesture with the shape. For example, when the user clicks the mouse in the field of the shape to assign focus to it, and then drags or resizes the shape.

You can retrieve an instance of this box by invoking the following method on an object of the line segment:

```
public Rectangle2D getBounds2D()
```

For a discussion on objects of `Rectangle2D`, see the next section, "Drawing Rectangles in 2D." A rectangle object contains the top-left corner coordinate, width, and height as its data values. By applying elementary principles of geometry on this rectangle, you can easily arrive at the coordinate values (x1, y1) and (x2, y2) of the line object.

Testing Intersections

The methods in the abstract class `Line2D` also support testing the intersection of lines by returning a boolean value `true` or `false`. The methods enable you to test whether a line segment intersects another line that is specified by its end coordinates (x1, y1) and (x2, y2) or by the line object itself. You can also test whether a line segment passes through or intersects a rectangle that is specified by its top-left corner coordinates (x, y), width w, and height h, or by the rectangle object itself. The following are the respective methods:

```
public boolean intersectsLine(double x1, double y1, double x2, double y2)
public boolean intersectsLine(Line2D l)

public boolean intersects(double x, double y, double w, double h)
public boolean intersects(Rectangle2D r)
```

In addition to these methods, the following static method lets you test whether a line segment between the coordinates (x1, y1) and (x2, y2) intersects another segment specified by the coordinates (x3, y3) and (x4, y4):

```
public static boolean linesIntersect(double x1,   double y1,
                                      double x2,   double y2,
                                      double x3,   double y3,
                                      double x4,   double y4)
```

Retrieving the Shape Outline Object

The following methods from `Line2D` retrieve the iteration object that represents the outline of this shape. You need to specify the affine transform and flatness parameter of the shape as argument values for these methods:

```
public PathIterator getPathIterator(AffineTransform at)
public PathIterator getPathIterator(AffineTransform at, double flatness)
```

Testing the Equality of Lines

Sometimes in programming you must test the equality of lines, especially when two lines need to be compared. You can test the equality of two line objects by simply invoking the method `equals()` from the root class `Object`. The following is the typical code snippet that tests whether two specified lines are equal:

```
...
Line2D line1 = new Line2D.Float();
Line2D line2 = new Line2D.Float(0.0f, 0.0f, 10.0f, 10.0f);

if (line1.equals(line2))
```

```
System.out.println("The lines are equal!");
System.out.println("The lines are not equal!");
...
```

Drawing Rectangles in 2D

Many real-world objects commonly contain rectangular plane surfaces. A square is a specific form of rectangle in which all the sides are of equal size. Java 2D supports classes to directly create rectangles with different accuracies. The abstract class RectangularShape in java.awt.geom is the parent class for all types of rectangles, including those with rounded corners. (Later in this chapter, the section "Drawing Rectangles with Rounded Corners" discusses rectangles with rounded corners.)

An abstract class called Rectangle2D represents the regular rectangles (with sharp corners). This class is a subclass of RectangularShape, and is available in the package java.awt.geom (see Figure 3.3). Note that the class RectangularShape implements the interface Shape.

```
java.lang.Object
  └─ java.awt.geom.RectangularShape
       └─ java.awt.geom.Rectangle2D
```

Figure 3.3
Class hierarchy of the parent class Rectangle2D.

The static inner classes of Rectangle2D (such as Rectangle2D.Float and Rectangle2D.Double) provide the concrete implementations for the float and double type data of rectangles. The concrete subclass Rectangle furnishes an implementation of rectangles with integer data. This class is mainly meant for backward compatibility with AWT graphics.

Creating Instances of Rectangles

To create rectangles of type Rectangle2D, you can use the float type or double type X and Y coordinates for the top-left corner, width, and height of the rectangle. You can change the X and Y coordinates to relocate a rectangle. The values of width and height are useful to control the size.

The classes Rectangle2D.Float and Rectangle2D.Double support constructors with and without arguments. Here are the constructors supported in the classes Rectangle2D.Float and Rectangle2D.Double:

```
public Rectangle2D.Float()
public Rectangle2D.Float(float x, float y, float w, float h)

public Rectangle2D.Double()
public Rectangle2D.Double(double x, double y, double w, double h)
```

The constructors without arguments create rectangles at (0, 0) with width and height (0, 0). This type of rectangle can be redefined later by assigning proper values for the top-left corner coordinates, width, and height. The remaining constructors with arguments take the location coordinates (x, y) for the top-left corner, and width w and height h for the ofsize of rectangle.

2D Rectangle Example

Listing 3.2 contains a sample program that creates five rectangles, as shown in Figure 3.4. The first rectangle does not contain any fill pattern or color. The remaining rectangles are filled with gradient and texture patterns and simple color styles. The rectangles overlap each other, and you can adjust the Color-Composite slider to alter the alpha value for compositing colors.

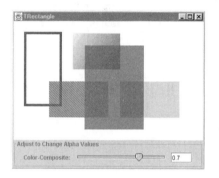

Figure 3.4

2D rectangles filled with different color patterns.

Listing 3.2   2D Rectangle Drawing Example (TRectangle.java)

```
// Demonstrates creating rectangles with different fill patterns

import javax.swing.*;
import javax.swing.event.*;
import javax.swing.border.*;
import java.awt.*;
import java.awt.event.*;
import java.awt.geom.*;
import java.awt.image.*;

class TRectangle extends JFrame {
    RectanglesCanvas canvas;
    JTextField textField;
    float alphaValue = 0.65f;

    public TRectangle() {
        super("TRectangle");
        Container container = getContentPane();
```

```
// 1. Add the canvas with rectangles
canvas = new RectanglesCanvas();
container.add(canvas);

// 2. Create the control panel with titled border
JPanel panel = new JPanel();
TitledBorder border = new TitledBorder
("Adjust to Change Alpha Values");
panel.setBorder(border);

// 3. Create a label, slider and text field
JLabel label = new JLabel("Color-Composite: ", JLabel.RIGHT);

JSlider slider = new JSlider(JSlider.HORIZONTAL, 0, 100, 65);
slider.addChangeListener(new SliderListener());

textField = new JTextField("0.65", 4);

// 4. Add the label, slider and text field to the panel
panel.add(label);
panel.add(slider);
panel.add(textField);

// 5. Add the panel to the frame
container.add(BorderLayout.SOUTH, panel);

// 6. Add a frame closing listener and display the frame
addWindowListener(new WindowEventHandler());
pack(); // Packs around the contents with suitable size
show(); // Display the frame
}

// 7. Slider listener to obtain and store the slider values.
// The slider values are converted to the alpha values, and
// displayed in the text field. Then call repaint() on canvas.
class SliderListener implements ChangeListener {
    public void stateChanged(ChangeEvent e) {
        JSlider tempSlider = (JSlider) e.getSource();
        alphaValue = (float)(tempSlider.getValue()/100.0);
        textField.setText(Float.toString(alphaValue));
        canvas.repaint();
    }
}

// 8. Code to handle closing of the frame
class WindowEventHandler extends WindowAdapter {
    public void windowClosing(WindowEvent e) {
```

continues

Listing 3.2   continued

```
            System.exit(0);
        }
    }


    // 9. The main method...
    public static void main(String arg[]) {
        new TRectangle();
    }


    // 10. Canvas to draw rectangles
    class RectanglesCanvas extends Canvas {
        Rectangle2D rec1, rec2, rec3, rec4, rec5;

        // 11. Constructor
        RectanglesCanvas() {
            // Create instances of 2D rectangles
            rec1 = new Rectangle2D.Float(25, 25, 75, 150);
            rec2 = new Rectangle2D.Float(125, 25, 100, 75);
            rec3 = new Rectangle2D.Float(75, 125, 125, 75);
            rec4 = new Rectangle2D.Float(225, 125, 125, 75);
            rec5 = new Rectangle2D.Float(150, 50, 125, 175);

            setBackground(Color.white);
            setSize(400, 225);  // canvas width=400 height=225
        }

    public void paint(Graphics g) {
        // 12. Set up the 2D graphics context
        Graphics2D g2D = (Graphics2D) g;

        // 13. Create an instance of alpha composite and assign
        // to the graphics context.
        AlphaComposite ac = AlphaComposite.getInstance(
                    AlphaComposite.SRC_OVER, alphaValue);
        g2D.setComposite(ac);

        // 14. Create a stroke object with the prescribed width
        // and assign it to the graphics context.
        g2D.setStroke(new BasicStroke(5.0f));

        // 15. Draw rectangle1.
        g2D.draw(rec1);

        // 16. Create a gradient paint object and assign it
        // to the graphics context. Next, call the fill() method
        // to draw the filled rectangle2.
        GradientPaint gp = new GradientPaint(125f, 25f,
                                    Color.yellow,
```

```
                                         225f, 100f,
                                         Color.blue);
        g2D.setPaint(gp);
        g2D.fill(rec2);


        // 17. Create a buffered image object, and create
        // the texture paint. Assign the texture paint to
        // the graphics context. Next, call the fill() method
        // to draw the filled rectangle.
        BufferedImage bi = new BufferedImage(5,5,
                            BufferedImage.TYPE_INT_RGB);
        Graphics2D big = bi.createGraphics();
        big.setColor(Color.magenta);
        big.fillRect(0,0,5,5);
        big.setColor(Color.black);
        big.drawLine(0,0,5,5);
        Rectangle r = new Rectangle(0,0,5,5);
        // Create the texture using the buffered image and rectangle.
        TexturePaint tp = new TexturePaint(bi, r);

        g2D.setPaint(tp);
        g2D.fill(rec3);


        // 18. Finally, assign different colors to the graphics
        // context and draw the filled rectangles rectangle4 and
        // rectangle5.
        g2D.setColor(Color.green);
        g2D.fill(rec4);
        g2D.setColor(Color.red);
        g2D.fill(rec5);
    }
  }
}
```

Code Analysis

The TRectangle.java program is an application that uses the Swing frame. The main class TRectangle extends JFrame and contains the other classes as inner classes. The canvas on which the rectangles are drawn, the text field that displays the alpha value of color compositing, and the float variable for alpha values are defined as fields of TRectangle.

Inside the constructor, the first statement simply assigns a title to the application frame. The second statement obtains a reference to the underlying container. Snippet-1 creates an instance of the canvas displaying rectangles, and adds it to the content pane.

Snippet-2 creates the control panel and decorates it with a titled border. Snippet-3 creates the instances of a label, slider, and text field. These components are positioned over the control panel as given in snippet-4. Snippet-5 adds the control panel to the bottom portion of the application frame. Snippet-6 shows the code to add a window listener to close the frame. You can also find the statements to pack the contents with suitable size and display the frame.

Snippet-7 defines the listener class for the slider created in snippet-3. The implementation method `stateChanged()` retrieves the slider value and assigns it to the parameter `alphaValue` that is defined as a field of the `TRectangle` class. The `alphaValue` is later passed as an argument to `AlphaComposite` while creating an instance. The program uses this instance to prepare the required graphics context. The method `stateChanged()` also contains a statement to display the `alphaValue` inside the text field defined in snippet-3. The last statement in the method invokes `repaint()` on the instance of drawing canvas.

Snippet-8 defines the class for handling the window events. The implementation method `windowClosing()` defines the statement to exit the application when you click the close button at the top corner of the window. Snippet-9 defines the `main` method that creates an instance of `TRectangle`.

Snippet-10 defines the canvas `RectanglesCanvas` to draw the 2D rectangles. Inside the constructor of this class, five rectangles are created using the constructors that take the location coordinates (x, y) and size (width, height). This code is shown in snippet-11.

Snippet-12 (inside the `paint()` method) creates the graphics context. Snippet-13 creates an instance of alpha composite for color composition and assigns it to the graphics context. Snippet-14 creates a new stroke object with line thickness equal to 5.0, and assigns this object to the graphics context. The code statement in snippet-15 draws the `rectangle1`.

Snippet-16 shows the code to create an object of gradient paint with yellow color at one end and blue color at the other end. Next, statements assign the gradient paint to the graphics context and draw the `rectangle2` that is filled with the gradient paint.

Snippet-17 shows the code to create a texture paint with black stripes. The last two statements in this snippet assign the texture paint to the graphics context and draw the `rectangle3` that is filled with the texture paint.

The last segment, snippet-18, assigns the green color to the graphics context and draws the filled `rectangle4`. Then the snippet assigns the red color to the graphics context and draws the filled `rectangle5`.

Working Further with Rectangles

This section discusses the operations that are performed on objects of rectangles. These operations are based on the methods encapsulated in the abstract classes `RectangularShape` and `Rectangle2D`, and the concrete classes `Rectangle2D.Float` and `Rectangle2D.Double`.

Redefining a Rectangle

After a rectangle is created, especially with the constructors that do not take any arguments, you can redefine the location (x, y) and size (w, h) of the rectangle using realistic or more accurate data. The following methods in `Rectangle2D.Float` help to achieve this:

```
public void setRect(float x, float y, float w, float h)
public void setRect(double x, double y, double w, double h)
public void setRect(Rectangle2D r)
```

The first method allows you to change the location (x, y) and the size (w, h) of the rectangle. The second method lets you redefine the rectangle using double precision values. The third method assigns the data of a specified rectangle to the data of the current rectangle. Note that the class `Rectangle2D.Double` also supports similar methods, except for the method `setRect()` with float precision.

Retrieving the Rectangle Parameters

In some programs, you might need to use the location (x, y) and size (w, h) of the rectangle. These data values can be retrieved in double precision by using the following get methods:

```
public double getX()
public double getY()
public double getWidth()
public double getHeight()
```

In addition to these methods, the abstract class `RectangularShape` supports the following methods to retrieve the X and Y coordinates of the top-left edge, bottom-right edge, and center of the rectangle:

```
// Retrieves the top-left corner x- and y- coordinates
public double getMinX()
public double getMinY()

// Retrieves the bottom-right corner x- and y- coordinates
public double getMaxX()
public double getMaxY()

// Retrieves the center (x, y) coordinates
public double getCenterX()
public double getCenterY()
```

Unions and Intersections of Rectangles

The classes `Rectangle2D.Float` and `Rectangle2D.Double` support methods to create rectangles from the unions or intersections of the specified rectangles. Here are these methods:

```
public Rectangle2D createUnion(Rectangle2D r)
public Rectangle2D createIntersection(Rectangle2D r)
```

The first method creates and returns a new rectangle of type `Rectangle2D`. The new rectangle is created using the union of the current rectangle with the specified rectangle. The second method creates and returns a rectangle that's an intersection of the current rectangle with the specified rectangle.

In addition to these methods, the abstract class `Rectangle2D` supports the following static methods that receive two source rectangles `src1` and `src2`, create the union or intersection rectangle, and assign the object reference `dest`:

```
public static void union(Rectangle2D src1, Rectangle2D src2,
                         Rectangle2D dest)

public static void intersect(Rectangle2D src1, Rectangle2D src2,
                             Rectangle2D dest)
```

You can also use the following method to test whether the current rectangle intersects a rectangle specified by its location (x, y) and size (w, h):

```
public boolean intersects(double x, double y, double w, double h)
```

Position of a Point Relative to a Rectangle

The following method determines the position of a point (x, y) with reference to the current rectangle:

```
public int outcode(double x, double y)
```

This method computes a binary `OR` of the appropriate mask values indicating the given point's location relative to the rectangle's outer sides. The bit-mask values are defined as data members of the abstract class `Rectangle2D`. The values `OUT_LEFT`, `OUT_TOP`, `OUT_RIGHT`, and `OUT_BOTTOM` indicate that the point is to the left, top, right, and bottom of the rectangle, respectively.

Adding a Point to a Rectangle

Sometimes you might be interested in creating a rectangle that contains the specified point and the current rectangle. Here are the methods you can use to perform this kind of operation:

```
public void add(double newx, double newy)
public void add(Point2D p)
```

This method adds the specified double precision point (x, y) or point object p to the current rectangle. The result is a modification of the current rectangle to encompass the point and the current rectangle.

In addition to these methods, the following method modifies the current rectangle so that it becomes the union of the current rectangle and specified rectangle:

```
public void add(Rectangle2D r)
```

Testing Whether a Point or Rectangle Is Inside

The abstract class `RectangularShape` supports the following two methods to test whether a specified point p of type `Point2D` or rectangle r of type `Rectangle2D` is inside the current rectangle:

```
public boolean contains(Point2D p)
public boolean contains(Rectangle2D r)
```

These methods return `true` if the current rectangle contains the specified object, and `false` otherwise. Note that these methods comply with the definition of "inside" as presented at the beginning of this chapter.

You can also test whether the current rectangle is empty by invoking the following method from the class `Rectangle2D.Float` or `Rectangle2D.Double`:

```
public boolean isEmpty()
```

Testing Equality of Rectangles

In a program, a given rectangle can be compared to the current rectangle to test whether it has the same location (x, y) and size (w, h). You can invoke the following method in `Rectangle2D` to test the equality of rectangles:

```
public boolean equals(java.lang.Object rectangle)
```

This method returns `true` if the object to be compared is an instance of `Rectangle2D` and has the same location and size values; the method returns `false` otherwise.

Retrieving Boundaries of a Rectangle

The abstract class `RectangularShape` provides a method to obtain a bounding box of type `Rectangle` around the current rectangle. The abstract class `Rectangle2D` supports another method that retrieves a high-precision bounding box around the current rectangle. Note that the low-precision box might not fit exactly around the current shape due to insufficient accuracy in data. The following are the low- and high-precision methods that retrieve the bounding boxes:

```
public Rectangle getBounds()
public Rectangle2D getBounds2D()
```

Testing Intersection with a Line

The abstract class `Rectangle2D` supports the following two methods to test whether a given line segment, specified either by (x1, y1) and (x2, y2) or as an object of `Line2D`, intersects the interior of the current rectangle:

```
public boolean intersectsLine(double x1, double y1,
                              double x2, double y2)
public boolean intersectsLine(Line2D l)
```

These methods return the boolean value `true` if the specified line intersects the rectangle interior; otherwise, they return `false`.

Retrieving the Outline Iterator

The outline iterator of a shape (a rectangle, in this case) contains the information of the shape boundary. The iterator object is of type `PathIterator`. The following methods from the parent class `Rectangle2D` retrieve the iteration object that defines the boundary of the current rectangle:

```
public PathIterator getPathIterator(AffineTransform at)
public PathIterator getPathIterator(AffineTransform at,
                              double flatness)
```

The second method retrieves an iteration object that defines the boundary of the flattened shape. The arguments are the affine transform object that is used to transform the points, and the error limit (in double precision) that is exercised while creating the flattened path.

Drawing Rectangles with Rounded Corners

In addition to the classes for regular rectangles with sharp corners, Java 2D also supports classes for low- and high-precision rectangles with rounded corners. These classes help to model objects containing rectangular planes with round corners.

The abstract class `RectangularShape` also serves as the parent for the classes representing the rectangles with rounded corners. The rectangles with rounded corners are of the abstract class type `RoundRectangle2D`. This class is a subclass of `RectangularShape`, and is stored in the package `java.awt.geom` (see Figure 3.5).

Figure 3.5

The class hierarchy of RoundRectangle2D.

The abstract class `RoundRectangle2D` represents a round rectangle (see Figure 3.6) that requires the location coordinates (x, y), the width and height of the rectangle (w, h), and the width and height of the arc to round the corners (arcw, arch). Note that the actual fields representing these parameters are contained by the concrete subclasses `RoundRectangle2D.Float` and `RoundRectangle2D.Double`. These classes are also defined as the inner classes of `RoundRectangle2D`.

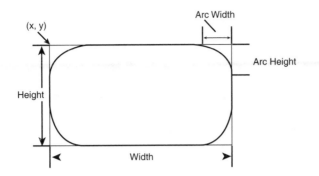

Figure 3.6
A round rectangle with its parameters.

Creating Rectangles with Rounded Corners

To create instances of rectangles with rounded corners, you can invoke constructors from RoundRectangle2D.Float or RoundRectangle2D.Double, depending on the required precision. The following are the lists of constructors from these classes:

```
public RoundRectangle2D.Float()
public RoundRectangle2D.Float(float x, float y,
                              float w, float h,
                              float arcw, float arch)


public RoundRectangle2D.Double()
public RoundRectangle2D.Double(double x, double y,
                               double w, double h,
                               double arcw, double arch)
```

The constructors without any arguments create round-corner rectangles that are initialized to the location (0.0, 0.0), with size (0.0, 0.0) and corner arcs of radius 0.0. These values can be reassigned at any later stage in the program.

The remaining constructors create rounded rectangles from the specified location coordinates (x, y), width and height (w, h), arc width (arcw), and arc height (arch).

Working Further with Rounded Rectangles

In this section, you will find the operations that are encapsulated as methods in the classes RoundRectangle2D, RoundRectangle2D.Float, and RoundRectangle2D.-Double. You can also invoke the methods from the abstract superclass RectangularShape. These operations have already been discussed in the previous section on rectangles with sharp corners.

Redefining a Round Rectangle

After creating a rounded rectangle, you can redefine the rectangle by changing its location or size or the dimensions of its rounded corners. You can also increase the precision to double type if it is currently in float form.

The methods for redefining are supported in the classes RoundRectangle2D.Float and RoundRectangle2D.Double. The methods also support assigning a new rectangle to the current rectangle. The following methods perform the necessary operations:

```
public void setRoundRect(float x, float y,
                         float w, float h,
                         float arcw, float arch)
public void setRoundRect(double x, double y,
                         double w, double h,
                         double arcw, double arch)
public void setRoundRect(RoundRectangle2D rr)
```

Retrieving the Geometric Parameters

In a program, you might need to use data values such as the location coordinates (x, y), size parameters (w, h), and arc parameters (arcw, arch) of the rectangles. To retrieve this data, the classes RoundRectangle2D.Float and RoundRectangle2D.Double support the following get methods. You can invoke these methods on the current rectangle:

```
public double getX()
public double getY()

public double getWidth();
public double getHeight()

public double getArcWidth()
public double getArcHeight()
```

Retrieving the Bounds

An object of the class Rectangle or Rectangle2D encapsulates the bounds of a rounded rectangle. The abstract class RectangularShape supports the following method that returns a low-precision bounding box of the rounded rectangle:

```
public Rectangle getBounds()
```

To obtain a high-precision bounding box that can accurately fit a rounded rectangle, you can invoke the following method from either RoundRectangle2D.Float or RoundRectangle2D.Double:

```
public Rectangle2D getBounds2D()
```

Testing Whether a Point or Rectangle Is Inside

The parent class RoundRectangle2D contains a method to determine whether a specified point (x, y) is inside the boundary of the current rectangle with rounded corners. Another method tests whether the current rounded rectangle completely contains the specified rectangle with location coordinates (x, y) and size (w, h). The following are those methods:

```
public boolean contains(double x, double y)
public boolean contains(double x, double y,
                        double w, double h)
```

Retrieving the Boundary Path Data

The abstract parent class RoundRectangle2D supports a method to retrieve the path iteration object. This iteration object contains the boundary information of a rounded rectangle. Here is the supported method:

```
public PathIterator getPathIterator(AffineTransform at)
```

For the path iteration object with the flatness parameter, you need to invoke the following method from the class RectangularShape:

```
public PathIterator getPathIterator(AffineTransform at, double flatness)
```

The flatness parameter controls the amount of subdivision of the curved segments.

Testing Intersection with a Rectangle

The class RoundRectangle2D supports the following method to test whether the current rectangle with rounded corners intersects the specified rectangle with location coordinates (x, y) and size (w, h):

```
public boolean intersects(double x, double y,
                          double w, double h)
```

Rounded Rectangle Drawing Example

Listing 3.3 shows a sample program that draws a collection of round-cornered rectangles over a canvas. This program provides code that lets the user interact with these rectangles using the mouse. The interactive operation fills the rectangles with different colors.

The user can click the mouse over any rectangle. The program recognizes the mouse clicks using the API methods supported for checking whether a rectangle contains a point. Then it uses the bounding box to draw small rectangular dots to indicate that the round-corner rectangle has received focus. Next, the user can select a color from the list of colors provided in a combo box. A Fill Color button supports the execution to fill the selected round-cornered rectangle with the specified color. The result of this program appears in Figure 3.7, with different colors selected for each round-cornered rectangle.

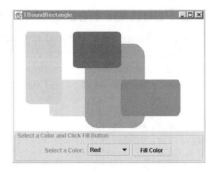

Figure 3.7

A program to interactively fill the round-cornered rectangles.

Listing 3.3   Round-Cornered Rectangle Drawing Example (TRoundRectangle.java)

```
// Demonstrates round-cornered rectangles, and provides code for
// interactively filling 2D shapes, in particular 2D round-cornered
// rectangles.

import javax.swing.*;
import javax.swing.event.*;
import javax.swing.border.*;
import java.awt.*;
import java.awt.event.*;
import java.awt.geom.*;
import java.util.Vector;

class TRoundRectangle extends JFrame {
    RectanglesCanvas canvas;
    String[] colorLabels = {"White", "Red", "Blue", "Green", "Yellow",
                            "Magenta", "Light Gray", "Black"};

    public TRoundRectangle() {
        // 1. Assign a title to the frame and get a handle on
        // the applet's content pane
        super("TRoundRectangle");
        Container container = getContentPane();

        // 2. Add the canvas with rectangles
        canvas = new RectanglesCanvas();
        container.add(canvas);

        // 3. Create a control panel with titled border
        JPanel panel = new JPanel();
        TitledBorder border = new TitledBorder(
```

```
                    "Select a Color and Click Fill Button");
         panel.setBorder(border);


         // 4. Create a label, combo box and button
         JLabel label = new JLabel("Select a Color: ", JLabel.RIGHT);

         JComboBox comboBox = new JComboBox(colorLabels);
         comboBox.addActionListener(new ComboBoxListener());

         JButton fillButton = new JButton("Fill Color");
         fillButton.addActionListener(new ButtonListener());

         // 5. Add the label, combo box, and button to the panel
         panel.add(label);
         panel.add(comboBox);
         panel.add(fillButton);

         // 6. Add the panel to the frame
         container.add(BorderLayout.SOUTH, panel);

         // 7. Add a frame closing listener and display the frame
         addWindowListener(new WindowEventHandler());
         pack(); // Packs around the contents with suitable size
         show(); // Display the frame
    }

    // 8. Code to handle closing of the frame
    class WindowEventHandler extends WindowAdapter {
        public void windowClosing(WindowEvent e) {
            System.exit(0);
        }
    }

    // 9. The main method...
    public static void main(String arg[]) {
        new TRoundRectangle();
    }

    // 10. Canvas to draw round-cornered rectangles
    class RectanglesCanvas extends Canvas {
        // Vectors to store rectangles and colors
        Vector recVector = new Vector();
        Vector filledRecs = new Vector();
        Vector filledColors = new Vector();

        // References for bounding and selected rectangles
        Rectangle2D boundingRec = null;
        RoundRectangle2D selectedRec = null;
```

continues

Listing 3.3   continued

```
// A reference and colors to fill the round-rectangles
Color fillColor = null;
Color[] colors = {Color.white, Color.red, Color.blue, Color.green,
                  Color.yellow, Color.magenta, Color.lightGray,
                  Color.black};

// Constructor
RectanglesCanvas() {
    // 11. Create instances of 2D rectangles
    recVector.addElement(
        new RoundRectangle2D.Float(25, 25, 75, 150, 20, 20));
    recVector.addElement(
        new RoundRectangle2D.Float(125, 25, 100, 75, 20, 10));
    recVector.addElement(
        new RoundRectangle2D.Float(75, 125, 125, 75, 20, 10));
    recVector.addElement(
        new RoundRectangle2D.Float(225, 125, 125, 75, 15, 20));
    recVector.addElement(
        new RoundRectangle2D.Float(150, 50, 125, 175, 50, 50));

    // 12. Add the mouse listener to receive a rectangle selection
    addMouseListener(new MyMouseListener());
    setBackground(Color.white);  // For canvas background color
    setSize(400, 225);  // Canvas width=400 height=225
}


public void paint(Graphics g) {
    // 13. Create the graphics context object
    Graphics2D g2D = (Graphics2D) g;

    // 14. Draw round rectangles defined in the constructor
    for (int i=0; i<recVector.size(); i++) {
        RoundRectangle2D r = (RoundRectangle2D) recVector.elementAt(i);
        g2D.draw(r);
    }

    // 15. This snippet draws all the selected rectangles with
    // specified colors while repainting.
    if (selectedRec != null) {
        for (int i=0; i<filledRecs.size(); i++) {
            Color currColor = (Color)filledColors.elementAt(i);
            g2D.setColor(currColor);
            RoundRectangle2D currRec =
(RoundRectangle2D)filledRecs.elementAt(i);
            g2D.fill(currRec);
```

```
            // Erase the black outline of selected rectangles; this is
            // one easy way!
            if (currColor == Color.white)
                g2D.setColor(Color.black);
            g2D.draw(currRec);
        }
    }
    // 16. Draw the dot-like rectangles whenever a rectangle is
    // selected
    if (boundingRec != null) {
        drawHighlightSquares(g2D, boundingRec);
    }
    // 17. Set the bounding rectangle back to null
    boundingRec = null;
}


public void drawHighlightSquares(Graphics2D g2D, Rectangle2D r) {
    double x = r.getX();
    double y = r.getY();
    double w = r.getWidth();
    double h = r.getHeight();
    g2D.setColor(Color.black);
    g2D.fill(new Rectangle.Double(x-3.0, y-3.0, 6.0, 6.0));
    g2D.fill(new Rectangle.Double(x+w*0.5-3.0, y-3.0, 6.0, 6.0));
    g2D.fill(new Rectangle.Double(x+w-3.0, y-3.0, 6.0, 6.0));
    g2D.fill(new Rectangle.Double(x-3.0, y+h*0.5-3.0, 6.0, 6.0));
    g2D.fill(new Rectangle.Double(x+w-3.0, y+h*0.5-3.0, 6.0, 6.0));
    g2D.fill(new Rectangle.Double(x-3.0, y+h-3.0, 6.0, 6.0));
    g2D.fill(new Rectangle.Double(x+w*0.5-3.0, y+h-3.0, 6.0, 6.0));
    g2D.fill(new Rectangle.Double(x+w-3.0, y+h-3.0, 6.0, 6.0));
    }
}

// 18. The mouse listener to handle hit detection of a rounded rectangle.
class MyMouseListener extends MouseAdapter {
    public void mouseClicked(MouseEvent e) {
        // Check if a rectangle contains the point of
        // mouse click
        for (int i=0; i<canvas.recVector.size(); i++) {
            RoundRectangle2D rec = (RoundRectangle2D)
                                canvas.recVector.elementAt(i);

            if (rec.contains(e.getX(), e.getY())) {
                canvas.selectedRec = rec;
                canvas.boundingRec = canvas.selectedRec.getBounds2D();
                canvas.repaint();
                return;
```

continues

Listing 3.3   continued

```
                    }
                }
            }
        }


    // 19. Combo box listener to handle color selections
    class ComboBoxListener implements ActionListener {
        public void actionPerformed(ActionEvent e) {
            JComboBox cBox = (JComboBox) e.getSource();
            String color = (String) cBox.getSelectedItem();
            for (int i=0; i<colorLabels.length; i++) {
                if(color.equals(colorLabels[i])) {
                    canvas.fillColor = canvas.colors[i];
                    return;
                }
            }
        }
    }


    // 20. Button listener to handle repainting of canvas by using
    // suitable colors for each of the selected rectangles.
    class ButtonListener implements ActionListener {
        public void actionPerformed(ActionEvent e) {
            if (canvas.selectedRec != null && canvas.fillColor != null) {
                canvas.filledRecs.addElement(canvas.selectedRec);
                canvas.filledColors.addElement(canvas.fillColor);
                canvas.repaint();
            }
        }
    }
}
```

Code Analysis

The TRoundRectangle.java program is a Swing application that uses the main class TRoundRectangle. This class declares an instance of a drawing canvas and a set of color labels as its fields. Inside the constructor, snippet-1 assigns a title to the application frame and obtains a reference to its content pane.

Snippet-2 creates and adds an instance of the canvas to display the collection of rectangles. Snippet-3 creates a panel and assigns a titled border. Snippet-4 creates a label, a combo box to select a color, and a button to execute the filling of a selected rectangle. Snippet-5 simply adds all these components to the panel, and snippet-6 adds the panel to the application frame. Snippet-7 is the code to register a window listener and display the frame. The window listener that implements the method to close the frame is given in snippet-8. Snippet-9 shows the main method.

Snippet-10 defines the class `RectanglesCanvas` in which the round-cornered rectangles are displayed. The vector type fields are meant for storing various rectangles and colors. You can also find the references for the bounding rectangle and selected rectangle.

Inside the constructor `RectanglesCanvas()`, snippet-11 creates five round-cornered rectangles and adds them to one of the vectors. Snippet-12 registers a mouse listener called `MyMouseListener` and assigns a background color and suitable size.

Inside the `paint()` method, snippet-13 creates the necessary graphics context object. Snippet-14 draws the round-cornered rectangles created in snippet-11. Snippet-15 is conditionally executed whenever a rectangle is selected using the mouse. The `for` loop draws all the previously selected rectangles with their respective colors. All the selected rectangles and colors are stored inside the vectors `filledRecs` and `filledColors`. The `if` statement in this snippet eliminates the black boundary with the color that is specified. Snippet-16 draws the dot-like rectangles to highlight the boundary of the selected round-cornered rectangle by using the `drawHighlightSquares()` method. The statement under snippet-17 resets the bounding rectangle to `null`.

Snippet-18 shows the mouse listener. The interface method `mouseClicked()` implements what should happen when the mouse is clicked. Basically, the method retrieves the X and Y coordinates of the point where the mouse click occurs, and then tests in a `for` loop whether any one of the rectangles contains the point. If the result is `true`, the bounding rectangle of the selected round-cornered rectangle is retrieved and drawn over the canvas. Notice that the code also registers the selected rectangle using the variable `selectedRec`.

Snippet-19 defines the combo box listener that implements the `ActionListener` interface. The method `actionPerformed()` implements the code to retrieve the selected color and stores it in a variable called `fillColor`. Snippet-20 is the button listener that implements code to specify what should happen when the user clicks the Fill Color button. Inside the `actionPerformed()` method, the selected rectangle and selected color are added to the respective arrays. Then the method calls `repaint()` on the canvas. The `paint()` method from the canvas draws all the rectangles that have been selected using the specified colors.

CHAPTER 4

Geometric Shapes: Curves, Arcs, and Ellipses

All objects in the world do not possess only linear and rectangular shapes. For modeling, objects commonly require primitives such as curves, arcs, circles, and ellipses. Similarly, these primitives play a significant role in a variety of graphics application areas. In presentation graphics, you require different curves and arcs that represent certain phenomena to plot the corresponding data as line graphs, bar charts, histograms, pie charts, and so on. Examples that use curves, arcs, circles, and ellipses include drawing the wing profile of an airplane, the top cover of a car, the face of a person, a plot of some mathematical function, or percentage sales of a product.

In the previous chapter, you were introduced to geometric shapes such as lines and rectangles. In this chapter, you will explore how to draw and operate on some more geometric shapes: quadratic and cubic curves; arcs of open type, chord type, and pie type; and circles and ellipses. The sample programs demonstrate the features of implementing methods from these shapes, applying specific attributes from a graphics context and interactive drawing.

Drawing Quadratic Curves

A quadratic curve or parabola is the simplest of all curves, and is represented by a second-degree polynomial $y(x) = A*x^2+B*x+C$. Quadratic curves are often useful to represent (or approximate) the shapes of objects with curvature in a single direction. If shapes have curvature in multiple directions, you need to represent them using cubic curves.

Using Java 2D, you can draw quadratic curves just as you do any other shapes. The abstract class QuadCurve2D represents the quadratic curves; it's stored in the package java.awt.geom. This class implements the Shape interface. The inner classes QuadCurve2D.Float and QuadCurve2D.Double of QuadCurve2D represent the float and double precision quadratic curves. The objects of these inner classes store the actual values of parameters that specify the quadratic curves.

Creating Quadratic Curves

A quadratic curve requires three points to completely specify the curve. The constructors of QuadCurve2D.Float and QuadCurve2D.Double that contain arguments require you to specify the starting point (x1, y1) and the ending point (x2, y2), along with a control point (ctrlx, ctrly).

The control point is any intermediate point that controls the degree of curvature of the curve. You can create a symmetric curve by choosing the coordinates of the control point exactly at the central location of the starting and ending points.

The other constructors that do not take any arguments initialize the respective quadratic curve objects using the value 0 for all the coordinates of the starting and ending points and the control point. The following are the sets of constructors from the float and double precision classes:

```
public QuadCurve2D.Float()
public QuadCurve2D.Float(float x1, float y1,
                         float ctrlx, float ctrly,
                         float x2, float y2)


public QuadCurve2D.Double()
public QuadCurve2D.Double(double x1, double y1,
                          double ctrlx, double ctrly,
                          double x2, double y2)
```

Working Further with Quadratic Curves

The abstract class QuadCurve2D and the concrete inner classes QuadCurve2D.Float and QuadCurve2D.Double support methods for a number of operations such as retrieving the curve parameters, flatness index, roots of the quadratic, and so on. The following sections will discuss these operations.

Redefining a Quadratic Curve

After a quadratic curve is created by using certain values or by using the constructor that does not take any arguments, you can redefine the parameters of the curve with certain new values for the starting point (x1, y1), control point (ctrlx, ctrly), and ending point (x2, y2). You do so using the following method:

```
public void setCurve(double x1, double y1,
                     double ctrlx, double ctrly,
                     double x2, double y2)
```

This method is supported in both the classes `QuadCurve2D.Float` and `QuadCurve2D.Double`. It assigns the starting point, ending point, and control point of the quadratic curve to the specified double precision coordinates. This method is also useful to update the parameters in floating precision to the double precision values by operating on a curve object of type `QuadCurve2D.Float`:

```
public void setCurve(float x1, float y1,
                     float ctrlx, float ctrly,
                     float x2, float y2)
```

This method is only supported in the class `QuadCurve2D.Float`. The method assigns new values for the starting point, ending point, and control point of the curve to the specified floating precision coordinates.

Retrieving Points or Coordinates of a Curve

Often you need to retrieve the coordinates of a curve in the middle of a program to use the curve for some other operation. The following access methods from both the classes `QuadCurve2D.Float` and `QuadCurve2D.Double` return various curve parameters:

```
public double getX1()
public double getY1()

public double getCtrlX()
public double getCtrlY()

public double getX2()
public double getY2()
```

These methods retrieve the starting, control, and ending point coordinates x1, y1, ctrlx, ctrly, x2, and y2 of the curve. Note that the methods return the respective values in double precision, even when they are operating on an object of type `QuadCurve2D.Float`.

The following methods retrieve the point objects of type `Point2D` that contain coordinates of the respective starting, control, and ending points:

```
public Point2D getP1()
public Point2D getCtrlPt()
public Point2D getP2()
```

Retrieving the Flatness Index of a Curve

The *flatness* of a curve is the maximum distance or offset of the control point from the line connecting the starting and ending points of the curve. The flatness is inversely proportional to the degree of curvature of a curve. The flatness is indicated by a double precision index number.

The parent class QuadCurve2D supports a set of methods to compute the flatness and square of flatness of a quadratic curve. The following methods return the flatness index and square of the flatness of a curve object in double precision:

```
public double getFlatness()
public double getFlatnessSq()
```

The following static methods also compute the flatness index or square of the flatness index when you supply the coordinate values such as the starting point (x1, y1), ending point (x2, y2), and control point (ctrlx, ctrly) of a curve:

```
public static double getFlatness(double x1, double y1,
                      double ctrlx, double ctrly,
                      double x2, double y2)

public static double getFlatnessSq(double x1, double y1,
                      double ctrlx, double ctrly,
                      double x2, double y2)
```

Here are two more static methods that enable you to compute the flatness index or square of the flatness index of a curve. You can supply any array of double precision numbers indicating exactly where the coordinate values (x1, y1, ctrlx, ctrly, x2, and y2) of the curve will begin in the array. You indicate the beginning of the coordinate values by using an offset to the first element x1 of the coordinate values:

```
public static double getFlatness(double[] coords, int offset)
public static double getFlatnessSq(double[] coords, int offset)
```

The following sample code statements will make the concept clearer:

```
double[] coords = {100, 0, 50, 25, 20, 30, 80, 160, 120, 20};
int offset = 0;
double flatness2 = QuadCurve2D.getFlatness(coords, 0);

int offset = 4;
double flatness2 = QuadCurve2D.getFlatness(coords, 0);

int offset = 6;
double flatness2 = QuadCurve2D.getFlatness(coords, 0);
```

The first statement defines an array of numbers. Now you set the offset to the numbers shown and examine what happens. The offset at value 0 begins the curve coordinates at the value 100 in the array. Thus, 100 and the next number (0) are taken as the values for the starting point (x1, y1); 50 and 25 are taken as the values for the control point (ctrlx, ctrly); and 25 and 20 are taken as the values for the ending point (x2, y2).

If you change the offset value to 4, the coordinate values are taken as (20, 30), (80, 160), and (120, 20) for the starting point, control point, and ending point, respectively. Finally, when you alter the offset to the value of 6, the coordinate values begin at the number 80. However, because you have an insufficient number of elements to define a quadratic curve, you will encounter an "array index out of bounds exception" when you execute these statements of code in a program.

Solving for the Roots of a Quadratic Curve

Sometimes you need to find the roots of a quadratic curve. You can use the following method from the class QuadCurve2D to solve for the roots of a quadratic equation whose coefficients A, B, and C in the equation of form $A*x^2+B*x+C = 0$ are available:

```
public static int solveQuadratic(double[] eqn)
```

This method is static and requires the specification of coefficients A, B, and C of the curve in the form of an array. If you know only the coordinate values of the starting point (x1, y1), control point (ctrlx, ctrly), and end point (x2, y2) of the curve, you can pose a linear mathematical problem by substituting the values of x and y from these points in the equation $y(x) = A*x^2 +B*x+C$. Then the resulting set of three linear equations can be solved to find out the coefficients A, B, and C of the curve. Note that the argument array must contain A, B, and C in reverse order, as given below:

```
double[] eqn = {C, B, A};
```

In case any real roots exist, the method returns the number of real roots, and stores the actual roots in the array that has been passed as its argument value. For example, if n1 and n2 are two real roots, the argument array eqn is filled with n1 and n2 as

```
eqn = {n1, n2, A}
```

If no real roots are available, the array remains the same and contains the coefficients of the curve equation.

Subdividing a Curve

The sub-curves of a quadratic curve are sometimes useful. You can retrieve a pair of sub-curves from a given quadratic by using the methods supported in the abstract class QuadCurve2D. These sub-curves are also of the type QuadCurve2D and can be subjected to further subdivision. Thus, you can retrieve any number of sub-curves from a given quadratic curve. The ending point of the first sub-curve will be the starting point of the second sub-curve. The following are the supported methods to create sub-curves:

```
public void subdivide(QuadCurve2D left, QuadCurve2D right)
public static void subdivide(QuadCurve2D src, QuadCurve2D left,
                             QuadCurve2D right)
public static void subdivide(double[] src, int srcoff,
                             double[] left, int leftoff,
                             double[] right, int rightoff)
```

The first method creates two sub-curves of the quadratic curve on which the method has been invoked. These sub-curves are then referenced by the argument curve references. You can create two references of type QuadCurve2D and pass them as argument values for this method.

The second method is a static method that receives a curve object called src and creates two sub-curves out of it. These curves are then assigned to the references left and right, which are passed as argument values of the method.

The third method is also a static method that creates sub-curves using arrays of data. The first argument src is an array that contains the coordinates of the quadratic curve to be subdivided. You need to specify the index or offset srcoff indicating exactly where the data of the curve (x1, y1, ctrlx, ctrly, x2, y2) starts. Notice that you need to count the offset in the array from 0.

The arguments left and right are any arrays that store the data of the resulting sub-curves of type QuadCurve2D. You can specify the respective offsets leftoff and rightoff to begin the storage of the resulting sub-curves.

Retrieving Boundaries and the Outline Iteration Object

The boundary of any geometric shape is often useful for hit detection, such as recognizing a mouse click in the vicinity of the shape. If the mouse click falls within the boundary of the shape, you can perform some further operation, such as resizing or dragging the shape.

The boundary of a shape is represented by a bounding rectangle of type Rectangle or Rectangle2D. The bounding rectangle of type Rectangle provides a low (integer) precision rectangle. The object of type Rectangle2D provides a high-precision rectangle.

Depending on the precision requirement, you can retrieve the bounding rectangle of a quadratic curve using either of the following methods supported in QuadCurve2D and its inner classes:

```
public Rectangle getBounds()
public Rectangle2D getBounds2D()
```

The path iteration object that contains the path information of a quadratic curve can be retrieved by invoking the following methods on the quadratic curve object:

```
public PathIterator getPathIterator(AffineTransform at)
public PathIterator getPathIterator(AffineTransform at, double flatness)
```

The first method retrieves an iteration object that contains the boundary of the quadratic curve. The second method retrieves an iteration object that defines the boundary of the flattened quadratic curve.

Testing the Containment or Intersection

Very often you need to test whether an event has occurred in the vicinity of a quadratic curve. For example, you might need to test whether a mouse click falls within the vicinity of the curve to interactively drag a quadratic curve in its container. You can implement such operations by invoking the following methods on a quadratic curve object:

```
public boolean contains(double x, double y)
public boolean contains(Point2D p)
public boolean contains(double x, double y, double w, double h)
public boolean contains(Rectangle2D r)
```

The first of these methods tests whether a quadratic curve contains the pair of coordinates (x, y). If the curve contains the coordinates, the method returns the boolean value true; otherwise, it returns false. The second method is a similar type, but takes an object of type Point2D as its argument value for testing. The point object contains the coordinate values of the point.

The third method tests whether the interior of the quadratic curve completely contains the rectangle specified by its location and size. The last method in the set is also similar to this method, but takes an object of type Rectangle2D as its argument value. You can expect the return value true if the curve entirely contains the rectangle, or false otherwise.

An Interactive Quadratic Curve Example

Listing 4.1 demonstrates how to draw quadratic curves and interactively select a curve by clicking the mouse. The quadratic curves are drawn using the constructors that take arguments. The arguments represent the starting, ending, and control points of the curves. Some of the curves are made symmetric by locating the control point on the line passing exactly in between the starting and ending points. The output of this program is shown in Figure 4.1.

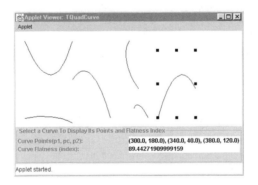

Figure 4.1

An applet displaying quadratic curves.

To select a curve, you can click the mouse in the vicinity of the curve. If the mouse click is inside the bounding box of the curve, the corners of the bounding box are displayed using small highlighting squares. The applet also displays the parameters of the selected curve that includes its flatness index.

Listing 4.1   Interactive Quadratic Curve Example (TQuadCurve.java)

```java
/*
 * <Applet code=TQuadCurve width=400 height=250>
 * </Applet>
 */

import javax.swing.*;
import javax.swing.border.*;
import javax.swing.event.*;
import java.awt.*;
import java.awt.event.*;
import java.awt.geom.*;
import java.util.Vector;

public class TQuadCurve extends JApplet {
    DrawingCanvas canvas;
    JLabel curveParamValues, curveFlatValue;

    public void init() {
        // 1. Get the content pane
        Container container = getContentPane();

        // 2. Create a display panel with titled border
        JPanel panel = new JPanel();
        panel.setLayout(new GridLayout(3, 2)); // 3rows&2columns
        TitledBorder border = new TitledBorder(
            "Select a Curve To Display Its Points and Flatness Index");
        panel.setBorder(border);

        // 3. Add the display labels to display curve points and
        // flatness index.
        JLabel curveParam = new JLabel("Curve Points(p1, pc, p2): ");
        panel.add(curveParam);
        curveParamValues = new JLabel("");
        curveParamValues.setOpaque(true);
        curveParamValues.setBackground(Color.white);
        curveParamValues.setForeground(Color.black);
        panel.add(curveParamValues);

        JLabel curveFlat = new JLabel("Curve Flatness (index): ");
        panel.add(curveFlat);
        curveFlatValue = new JLabel("");
        curveFlatValue.setOpaque(true);
        curveFlatValue.setBackground(Color.white);
        curveFlatValue.setForeground(Color.black);
        panel.add(curveFlatValue);

        // 4. Add the panel to the applet
        container.add(panel, BorderLayout.SOUTH);
```

```java
    // 5. Add the drawing canvas to the applet
    canvas = new DrawingCanvas();
    container.add(canvas);
}


// 6. Definition of 'DrawingCanvas' class
class DrawingCanvas extends Canvas {
    Vector quadCurves;
    QuadCurve2D selectedCurve = null;
    Rectangle2D boundingRec = null;

    // 7. Constructor
    public DrawingCanvas() {
        setBackground(Color.white);
        setSize(400,200);  // width and height of canvas
        addMouseListener(new MyMouseListener());

        // 8. Store the quadratic curves in a vector. Parameters
        // of the constructors are in the order P1(x1, y1),
        // P2(x2, y2) and P3(x3, y3).
        quadCurves = new Vector();
        quadCurves.addElement(
            new QuadCurve2D.Float(20,20, 80,160, 120,20));
            // x1, y1, ctrlx, ctrly, x2, y2 (see the constructors)
        quadCurves.addElement(
            new QuadCurve2D.Float(120,100, 160,40, 200,180));
        quadCurves.addElement(
            new QuadCurve2D.Float(240,20, 220,60, 260,120));
        quadCurves.addElement(
            new QuadCurve2D.Float(250,160, 260,140, 280,180));
        quadCurves.addElement(
            new QuadCurve2D.Float(300,180, 340,40, 380,120));
        quadCurves.addElement(
            new QuadCurve2D.Float(20,180, 80,170, 120,190));
    }


    // 9. The Overriding paint method
    public void paint(Graphics g) {
        Graphics2D g2D = (Graphics2D) g;

        // 10. Display quadratic curves from the vector
        for (int i=0; i<quadCurves.size(); i++) {
            g2D.draw((QuadCurve2D) quadCurves.elementAt(i));
        }

        // 11. Conditionally display the bounding rectangle of
        // the selected curve.
```

continues

Listing 4.1   continued

```
        if (boundingRec != null) {
            drawHighlightSquares(g2D, boundingRec);
        }
    }


// 12. Method to draw small highlight squares with fill style
public void drawHighlightSquares(Graphics2D g2D, Rectangle2D r) {
    double x = r.getX();
    double y = r.getY();
    double w = r.getWidth();
    double h = r.getHeight();
    g2D.setColor(Color.black);

    g2D.fill(new Rectangle.Double(x-3.0, y-3.0, 6.0, 6.0));
    g2D.fill(new Rectangle.Double(x+w*0.5-3.0, y-3.0, 6.0, 6.0));
    g2D.fill(new Rectangle.Double(x+w-3.0, y-3.0, 6.0, 6.0));
    g2D.fill(new Rectangle.Double(x-3.0, y+h*0.5-3.0, 6.0, 6.0));
    g2D.fill(new Rectangle.Double(x+w-3.0, y+h*0.5-3.0, 6.0, 6.0));
    g2D.fill(new Rectangle.Double(x-3.0, y+h-3.0, 6.0, 6.0));
    g2D.fill(new Rectangle.Double(x+w*0.5-3.0, y+h-3.0, 6.0, 6.0));
    g2D.fill(new Rectangle.Double(x+w-3.0, y+h-3.0, 6.0, 6.0));
}


// 13. The mouse listener class
class MyMouseListener extends MouseAdapter {
    public void mouseClicked(MouseEvent e) {
        // Check if a quadratic curve receives mouse focus
        for (int i=0; i<quadCurves.size(); i++) {
            QuadCurve2D curve = (QuadCurve2D) quadCurves.elementAt(i);

            if (curve.contains(e.getX(), e.getY())) {
                // Store a reference to the selected curve and
                // its bounding rectangle.
                selectedCurve = curve;
                boundingRec = curve.getBounds2D();

                // To display the curve points on the applet
                double x1,y1, ctrlX,ctrlY, x2,y2;
                x1 = selectedCurve.getX1();
                y1 = selectedCurve.getY1();
                ctrlX = selectedCurve.getCtrlX();
                ctrlY = selectedCurve.getCtrlY();
                x2 = selectedCurve.getX2();
                y2 = selectedCurve.getY2();

                String string = "(" + Double.toString(x1)
                        + ", "+ Double.toString(y1) + "),"
                        + " (" + Double.toString(ctrlX)
```

```
                                    + ", "+ Double.toString(ctrlY) + "),"
                                    + " (" + Double.toString(x2)
                                    + ", " + Double.toString(y2) + ")";
                    curveParamValues.setText(string);

                    // To display the flatness index of a curve
                    double flatness = selectedCurve.getFlatness();
                    curveFlatValue.setText(Double.toString(flatness));

                    // Finally call repaint() and return when a
                    // curve has been selected.
                    canvas.repaint();
                    return;
                }
            }
          }
        }
      }
    }
```

Code Analysis

This program is a Swing applet called TQuadCurve; it extends JApplet. The applet is attached to a drawing canvas and some labels to display the parameters of a quadratic curve. The objects of the classes DrawingCanvas and JLabel are declared as the fields of the applet.

Inside the init() method, snippet-1 gets a handle to the applet's content pane. Snippet-2 creates a display panel with a titled border. Snippet-3 adds the necessary labels to this panel. Snippet-4 adds the display panel to the content pane of the applet.

Snippet-5 creates an instance of DrawingCanvas and adds it at the center of the applet. The class DrawingClass is defined in snippet-6. This class extends java.awt.Canvas and contains a vector of quadratic curves and a reference to the selected curve and bounding rectangle as its fields.

Snippet-7 is the constructor of the drawing canvas class. The constructor initially assigns a suitable background color and size, and then registers a mouse listener with the canvas. Snippet-8 creates the vector of quadratic curves and then adds six quadratic curves with different parameters.

Snippet-9 shows the overridden paint method. Inside this method, snippet-10 displays the quadratic curves that are created in snippet-8. Snippet-11 displays the bounding rectangle of a curve when it is selected. The snippet calls the drawHighlightSquares() method that is defined in snippet-12.

Snippet-13 defines the mouse listener class. This class implements the mouseClicked() method. Inside this method, the real action takes place when the user clicks the mouse on a quadratic curve. Initially, it checks whether any quadratic curve (displayed on the canvas) receives focus. For this purpose, an if statement tests whether a quadratic curve contains a mouse click by invoking the method `contains()` with the mouse coordinates as its argument values.

If a quadratic curve contains the coordinates of the mouse when the user clicks it, that curve is registered as the selected curve by storing a reference to it in the variable `selectedCurve`. The bounding rectangle of the selected curve is also retrieved by invoking the method `getBounds2D()` on the selected curve object. Then the parameters of the curve are obtained to display them on the applet. Next, the flatness index is retrieved by invoking the method `getFlatness()` on the selected curve; the index is displayed on the applet.

The last set of statements in snippet-13 invoke the `repaint()` method of the canvas to update its display. The `return` statement makes sure that the initial `for` loop is no longer executed for this mouse click because a particular quadratic curve has already received the focus.

Drawing Cubic Curves

Cubic curves (or third-degree curves) of the form $y(x) = A*x^3 + B*x^2 + Cx + D$ are well recognized for their ability to meet a wide range of requirements when you're drawing curved shapes. A cubic curve is the smallest degree curve that has the smoothness properties for describing a curved shape with a fair amount of accuracy. The curves can also represent shapes that have curvature facing in multiple directions. The other good feature is that cubic curves closely resemble the way a drafter uses a mechanical spline. In Java 2D, the cubic curves are of the abstract class type `CubicCurve2D`. This class contains the inner classes `CubicCurve2D.Float` and `CubicCurve2D.Double` to represent the curves with float and double precision parameters. These classes contain the actual values of the objects that represent the cubic curves.

Creating Cubic Curves

Just as for quadratic curves, you need to specify a starting point (x1, y1) and ending point (x2, y2). But for a cubic curve, two control points (ctrlx1, ctrly1) and (ctrlx2, ctrly2) need to be specified to completely define the required curve. These control points will impose the constraints to create the expected shape of the curve. The classes `CubicCurve2D.Float` and `CubicCurve2D.Double` define the following sets of constructors:

```
public CubicCurve2D.Float()
public CubicCurve2D.Float(float x1, float y1,
                          float ctrlx1, float ctrly1,
                          float ctrlx2, float ctrly2,
                          float x2, float y2)


public CubicCurve2D.Double()
public CubicCurve2D.Double(double x1, double y1,
                           double ctrlx1, double ctrly1,
                           double ctrlx2, double ctrly2,
                           double x2, double y2)
```

The constructors without any arguments create objects by initializing all coordinates of the starting and ending points and control points to the value 0. You can redefine the values of the curve parameters to take new values at a later stage in a program.

Working with Cubic Curve Operations

The cubic curve classes CubicCurve2D, CubicCurve2D.Float, and CubicCurve2D.- Double support a number of useful methods to perform various operations. The operations are similar, as you saw in the case of quadratic curves. Following is a concise discussion of these operations to show the different methods available in these classes.

Redefining a Cubic Curve

To assign new values of float precision or more accurate values of double precision for the starting point, control point 1, control point 2, and ending point of a cubic curve, the class CubicCurve2D.Float supports the following two methods:

```
public void setCurve(float x1, float y1,
                     float ctrlx1, float ctrly1,
                     float ctrlx2, float ctrly2,
                     float x2, float y2)


public void setCurve(double x1, double y1,
                     double ctrlx1, double ctrly1,
                     double ctrlx2, double ctrly2,
                     double x2, double y2)
```

The second method, which takes double precision values for the curve parameters, is also available in CubicCurve2D.Double.

Retrieving the Coordinates

The following methods from classes CubicCurve2D.Float and CubicCurve2D.Double retrieve the double precision coordinate values of the starting point, control point 1, control point 2, and ending point of a curve:

```
public double getX1()
public double getY1()
public double getCtrlX1()
public double getCtrlY1()
public double getCtrlX2()
public double getCtrlY2()
public double getX2()
public double getY2()
```

In addition to these methods, the classes support the following methods to retrieve the point objects for the starting point P1, control point 1 CtrlP1, control point 2 CtrlP2, and ending point P2.

```
public Point2D getP1()
public Point2D getCtrlP1()
public Point2D getCtrlP2()
public Point2D getP2()
```

Testing Containment and Intersections

The class `CubicCurve2D` supports the following methods to test whether a cubic curve object completely contains a point (by using its coordinate values or the point object) or a rectangle:

```
public boolean contains(double x, double y)
public boolean contains(Point2D p)

public boolean contains(double x, double y,
                        double w, double h)

public boolean contains(Rectangle2D r)
```

Similarly, you can invoke the following methods to test whether a cubic curve object intersects the interior of a specified rectangle by using the rectangle's location and size, or the rectangle object itself:

```
public boolean intersects(double x,
                          double y,
                          double w,
                          double h)

public boolean intersects(Rectangle2D r)
```

Retrieving the Flatness Index

The parent class `CubicCurve2D` supports the following methods to compute the flatness or square of the flatness of a cubic curve:

```
public double getFlatness()
public double getFlatnessSq()
```

The following static methods in the `CubicCurve2D` class are useful to find out the flatness and square of the flatness of any cubic curve object that is specified through the values of its starting point, control point 1, control point 2, and ending point:

```
public static double getFlatness(double x1, double y1,
                        double ctrlx1, double ctrly1,
                        double ctrlx2, double ctrly2,
                        double x2, double y2)
public static double getFlatnessSq(double x1, double y1,
                        double ctrlx1, double ctrly1,
                        double ctrlx2, double ctrly2,
                        double x2, double y2)
```

Other methods enable you to compute the flatness or its square by specifying the coordinates in an array. The array can be of any length, but the coordinates of the cubic curve must be in this order: starting point (x1, y1), control point 1 (ctrlX1, ctrlY1), control point 2 (ctrlX2, ctrlY2), and ending point (x2, y2). You can specify an index called offset to point out the first coordinate x1 of the curve in the array. Here are the methods that take the array and the offset as their arguments:

```
public static double getFlatness(double[] coords, int offset)
public static double getFlatnessSq(double[] coords, int offset)
```

Solving for Roots of a Cubic Curve

Cubic curves are represented by a third-degree polynomial as $A*x^3 + B*x^2 + C*x + D = 0$. You can find out the real roots of this equation by passing an array of coefficients prepared as $eqn = \{D, C, B, A\}$ to the following method:

```
public static int solveCubic(double[] eqn)
```

This method places the real roots back in the array eqn that is passed as its argument. The method also returns the number of roots of the cubic curve.

Subdividing a Cubic Curve

The class CubicCurve2D supports methods to obtain sub-curves of a given cubic curve. You can invoke the following method to obtain two sub-curves left and right from a curve on which the method is invoked:

```
public void subdivide(CubicCurve2D left, CubicCurve2D right)
```

The class also supports the following static methods to create sub-curves out of any cubic curve objects:

```
public static void subdivide(CubicCurve2D src,
                        CubicCurve2D left, CubicCurve2D right)
public static void subdivide(double[] src, int srcoff,
                        double[] left, int leftoff,
                        double[] right, int rightoff)
```

The first method requires a cubic curve src that needs to be divided to generate sub-curves left and right. The second static method takes an array of data src that contains the cubic curve coordinates. The cubic curve coordinates are indicated by the offset srcoff. The array arguments left and right store the sub-curve coordinates at the specified offsets leftoff and rightoff in the respective arrays.

Retrieving Boundaries of a Cubic Curve

CubicCurve2D and its inner classes support the following methods to obtain the low- and high-precision bounding rectangle of a cubic curve. The low-precision method that returns a rectangle of type Rectangle is supported in CubicCurve2D:

```
public Rectangle getBounds()
public Rectangle2D getBounds2D()
```

Cubic Curve Drawing Example

Listing 4.2 demonstrates how to interactively draw cubic curves. The application frame contains a canvas and a panel that displays the current location of the mouse pointer. To draw a cubic curve, you can press the mouse button at a location (x1, y1) and drag to draw a straight line, and release the mouse button at the ending point (x2, y2) of the straight line.

You can press the mouse button again at an intermediate control point, and drag to draw a quadratic curve that possesses the starting and ending points of the straight line as its starting and ending coordinates. The quadratic curve settles at the final location of the mouse pointer after dragging, and takes the present location of the mouse pointer as its control point (ctrlX1, ctrlY1).

Finally, you can press the mouse button a third time at any point and drag it to draw a cubic curve. The cubic curve considers the points (x1, y1), (x2, y2), and (ctrlX1, ctrlY1) as its starting point, ending point, and control point 1. The curve considers the final location of the mouse pointer as its control point 2 (ctrlX2, ctrlY2). The program also erases the previously drawn straight line and quadratic curve that are used for guide lines. Figure 4.2 displays an application frame with a number of cubic curves that are drawn interactively.

NOTE

For the sake of brevity, this program does not store and repaint the cubic curve objects. So, the program cannot support painting during iconifying and de-iconifying, hiding and showing, resizing, moving, or activating the application window. To compensate for this limitation, you need to store the cubic curve objects—for example, in a vector—and paint them (in the `paint()` method) by calling from the implementation methods in the window and component listener classes (see the interfaces `ComponentListener` and `WindowListener`).

Figure 4.2

An application window displaying cubic curves.

Listing 4.2   Cubic Curve Drawing Example (TCubicCurve.java)

```java
import javax.swing.*;
import javax.swing.event.*;
import java.awt.*;
import java.awt.event.*;
import java.awt.geom.*;
import java.util.Vector;

public class TCubicCurve extends JFrame {
    DrawingCanvas canvas;
    JLabel label, coords;

    public TCubicCurve() {
        // 1. Assign a name and get the content pane
        super("TCubicCurve");
        Container container = getContentPane();

        // 2. Create a display panel
        JPanel panel = new JPanel();
        panel.setLayout(new GridLayout(1,2)); //1 row&2 cols

        // 3. Add the display labels
        label = new JLabel("Mouse Location (x, y):  ", JLabel.RIGHT);
        panel.add(label);
        panel.add(label);

        coords = new JLabel("");
        panel.add(coords);

        // 4. Add the panel to the container
        container.add(panel, BorderLayout.SOUTH);

        // 5. Add the drawing canvas
        canvas = new DrawingCanvas();
        container.add(canvas);

        // 6. Add the window closing listener and display the
        // frame with proper size
        addWindowListener(new WindowEventHandler());
        pack();
        show();
    }

    // 7. Definition of window listener class
    class WindowEventHandler extends WindowAdapter {
        public void windowClosing(WindowEvent e) {
            System.exit(0);
```

continues

Listing 4.2   continued

```
      }
  }


// 8. The main method...
public static void main(String arg[]) {
    new TCubicCurve();
}


// 9. Definition of Drawing Canvas
class DrawingCanvas extends Canvas {
    // Coordinates to draw a straight line, quadratic curve,
    // and a cubic curve
    float x1,y1,
          xc1cur,yc1cur, xc1new, yc1new,
          xc2cur,yc2cur, xc2new, yc2new,
          x4cur,y4cur, x4new, y4new;

    // Some useful flags
    int pressNo = 0;
    int dragFlag1 = -1;
    int dragFlag2 = -1;
    boolean clearFlag = false;

    // For creating a dashed stroke
    float dashes[] = {5f, 5f}; //stroke and gap
    BasicStroke stroke;

    // 10. Constructor
    public DrawingCanvas() {
        setBackground(Color.white);
        addMouseListener(new MyMouseListener());
        addMouseMotionListener(new MyMouseMotionListener());
        setSize(400, 400);
        stroke = new BasicStroke(1f, BasicStroke.CAP_BUTT,
                        BasicStroke.JOIN_BEVEL,
                        10f, dashes, 0f);
    }

    // 11. The overriding update() method
    public void update(Graphics g) {
        paint(g);
    }

    // 12. The overriding paint method
    public void paint(Graphics g) {
        // Set up the graphics context
        Graphics2D g2D = (Graphics2D) g;
```

```
// 13. Interactively draw a straight line
if (pressNo == 1) {
    g2D.setXORMode(getBackground());
    g2D.setColor(Color.black);
    g2D.setStroke(stroke);

    // Erase the currently existing line
    g2D.draw(new Line2D.Float(x1, y1, x4cur, y4cur));
    // Draw the new line
    g2D.draw(new Line2D.Float(x1, y1, x4new, y4new));

    // Update the currently existing coordinate values
    x4cur = x4new;
    y4cur = y4new;
}

// 14. Interactively draw a quadratic curve
else if (pressNo == 2) {
    g2D.setXORMode(getBackground());
    g2D.setColor(Color.black);
    g2D.setStroke(stroke);

    if (dragFlag1 != -1) {
    // Erase the previously existing quadratic curve
    g2D.draw(
        new QuadCurve2D.Float(x1,y1, xc1cur,yc1cur, x4new,y4new));
    }
    dragFlag1++;  // Reset the drag-flag

    // Draw the new quadratic curve
    g2D.draw(
        new QuadCurve2D.Float(x1,y1, xc1new,yc1new, x4new,y4new));

    // Update the coordinate values
    xc1cur = xc1new;
    yc1cur = yc1new;
}

// 15. Interactively draw a cubic curve
else if (pressNo == 3) {
    g2D.setXORMode(getBackground());
    g2D.setColor(Color.black);

    if (dragFlag2 != -1) {
    // Erase the currently existing curve
    g2D.draw(
        new CubicCurve2D.Float(
            x1,y1, xc1new,yc1new, xc2cur,yc2cur, x4new,y4new));
```

continues

Listing 4.2   continued

```
        }
        dragFlag2++;    // Reset the drag flag

        // Draw the new curve
        g2D.draw(
            new CubicCurve2D.Float(
                x1,y1, xc1new,yc1new, xc2new,yc2new, x4new,y4new));

        // Update the current coordinate values
        xc2cur = xc2new;
        yc2cur = yc2new;
    }

    // 16. Clear the guiding straight line and quadratic curve.
    if (clearFlag) {
        g2D.setXORMode(getBackground());
        g2D.setColor(Color.black);
        g2D.setStroke(stroke);

        g2D.draw(new Line2D.Float(x1, y1, x4new, y4new));
        g2D.draw(
            new QuadCurve2D.Float(x1,y1, xc1new,yc1new, x4new,y4new));

        // Reset the flag
        clearFlag = false;
    }
}

// 17. Definition of the mouse listener
class MyMouseListener extends MouseAdapter {
    // 18. When a mouse button is pressed...
    public void mousePressed(MouseEvent e) {
        if (pressNo == 0) { // Note: This is the first press
            pressNo++;

            // Update the starting and current coordinates
            x1 = x4cur = e.getX();
            y1 = y4cur = e.getY();
        }
        else if (pressNo == 1) { // Note: This is the second press
            pressNo++;

            // Update the current control coordinates-1
            xc1cur = e.getX();
            yc1cur = e.getY();
        }
        else if (pressNo == 2) { // Note: This is the third press
            pressNo++;
```

```java
        // Update the current control coordinates-2
        xc2cur = e.getX();
        yc2cur = e.getY();
    }
}


// 19. When the mouse is released...
public void mouseReleased(MouseEvent e) {
    if (pressNo == 1) {
        x4new = e.getX();
        y4new = e.getY();
        canvas.repaint();
    }
    else if (pressNo == 2) {
        xc1new = e.getX();
        yc1new = e.getY();
        canvas.repaint();
    }
    else if (pressNo == 3) {
        xc2new = e.getX();
        yc2new = e.getY();
        canvas.repaint();

        // Reset the flags after the drawing a curve
        pressNo = 0;
        dragFlag1 = -1;
        dragFlag2 = -1;
        clearFlag = true;
    }
  }
}


// 20. Definition of mouse motion listener
class MyMouseMotionListener extends MouseMotionAdapter {
    // 21. When the mouse is dragged...
    public void mouseDragged(MouseEvent e) {
        if (pressNo == 1) {
            // Update for the new values of coordinates of the
            // ending point of a straight line.
            x4new = e.getX();
            y4new = e.getY();

            // Display the location coordinates of the mouse
            String string = "(" + Integer.toString(e.getX())
                            + ", " + Integer.toString(e.getY())
                            + ")";
            coords.setText(string);
```

continues

Listing 4.2 continued

```
                    // Call the repaint() on canvas
                    canvas.repaint();
                }
                else if (pressNo == 2) {
                    // Update for the control point-1 of the quadratic
                    // curve. This curve uses the starting and ending
                    // points as those of the straight line.
                    xc1new = e.getX();
                    yc1new = e.getY();

                    // Display the location coordinates of the mouse
                    String string = "(" + Integer.toString(e.getX())
                                    + ", " + Integer.toString(e.getY())
                                    + ")";
                    coords.setText(string);

                    // Call the repaint() on canvas
                    canvas.repaint();
                }
                else if (pressNo == 3) {
                    // Update for the control point-2 of the cubic curve;
                    // The starting and ending points, and the control
                    // point-2 are the same as that of the quadratic curve.
                    xc2new = e.getX();
                    yc2new = e.getY();

                    // Display the location coordinates of the mouse
                    String string = "(" + Integer.toString(e.getX())
                                    + ", " + Integer.toString(e.getY())
                                    + ")";
                    coords.setText(string);

                    // Call the repaint() on canvas
                    canvas.repaint();
                }
            }

            // 22. When the mouse is moved...
            public void mouseMoved(MouseEvent e) {
                // Display the coordinates of the mouse pointer
                String string = "(" + Integer.toString(e.getX())
                                + ", " + Integer.toString(e.getY())
                                + ")";
                coords.setText(string);
            }
        }
    }
}
```

Code Analysis

The class TCubicCurve represents an application frame by extending the Swing class JFrame. This class declares a canvas object and two label objects to display the coordinates of the mouse pointer as it moves over the canvas. Inside the constructor of TCubicCurve, snippet-1 assigns a title to the frame, and then obtains a reference to its content pane.

Snippets-2, 3, and 4 create a panel with display labels for the coordinates of the mouse pointer, and add the panel to the frame. Snippet-5 creates the drawing canvas and adds it to the frame. Snippet-6 provides the widow event handler that implements the method to exit the application on closing the frame. Snippet-7 defines the window listener class. The snippet also contains statements to display the frame with a packing size around the canvas and display panel. Snippet-8 is the main method that creates an instance of the main frame.

Snippet-9 defines the drawing canvas. This class declares the parameters to draw a straight line, quadratic curve, and cubic curve. Certain useful flags and parameters for the dashed style of the stroke are also declared. Snippet-10 shows the constructor of this class, in which you will find code to assign the background color of the canvas, register mouse and mouse-motion listeners, assign the size of canvas, and define a stroke object to draw geometric shapes.

Snippet-11 is the update() method that calls the paint() method of the canvas given in snippet-12. The paint() method initially creates a graphics context object and then conditionally executes different snippets of code shown in snippets-13, 14, 15, and 16. The if and else if clauses test the count of the mouse press for drawing different shapes. For example, in snippet-13, if the press count is equal to 1, the program draws a straight line that guides further drawing. For interactive drawing and to avoid clearing the entire canvas, the graphics context is set to the XOR mode. The code statements also assign appropriate stroke objects (such as dashed stroke) to the graphics context. Finally, snippet-13 updates the current drawing coordinates to the new coordinates. You will find similar functionality in snippets-14 and 15. But in those snippets you will draw quadratic and cubic curves interactively.

Snippet-16 shows the code to clear the straight line and quadratic curve. These curves remain onscreen to serve as guide lines until you finish drawing the cubic curves.

Snippet-17 defines the mouse listener class that contains methods to perform operations when the mouse button is pressed or released. Snippet-18 defines what should happen when the mouse buttons is pressed in the beginning (pressNo == 0) to draw a straight line, and subsequently pressed to draw quadratic and cubic curves (pressNo == 1 and pressNo == 2). These three conditions are tested in the snippet. Then the snippet retrieves the respective location coordinates of the mouse to initialize the corresponding starting and control points.

In a similar manner, snippet-19 implements the code to perform operations when the mouse button is released after drawing a straight line, and quadratic and cubic curves. Here, the ending point of the straight line and the final control points after dragging the mouse are initialized with the mouse values. To display the resulting effect, the repaint() method is invoked on the canvas object. This snippet also contains the statements to reset various flags after drawing a cubic curve.

Snippet-20 defines the mouse motion listener class. Snippet-21 is the method that is activated when the mouse is dragged over the canvas. Also inside this method, the parameters of the straight line and quadratic and cubic curves are updated as the mouse is dragged. Other code displays the location coordinates of the mouse pointer as the mouse is being dragged. Finally, snippet-22 displays the method that is activated when the mouse pointer is moved over the canvas. This is the place where you provide the code to display the coordinates of the mouse location.

Drawing Ellipses and Circles

An *ellipse* is an elongated circle. Geometrically, an ellipse is defined as the set of points such that the sum of the distances from two fixed positions (called *foci* of the ellipse) is constant for all points. That is, if d1 and d2 are the distances from the foci to any point P(x,y) on the ellipse, the equation of the ellipse becomes

```
d1 + d2 = constant
```

By expressing the distances d1 and d2 in terms of the coordinates of the foci F1(x1, y1) and F2(x2, y2), and by framing an equation in terms of x and y, you will obtain the following ellipse equation in terms of the coefficients *A*, *B*, *C*, *D*, *E*, and *F*:

```
A*x2+B*y2+C*x*y+D*x+E*y+F = 0
```

Using Java 2D, fortunately you need not compute the coefficients to specify the dimensions of an ellipse. Instead, a bounding rectangle serves as the mechanism to specify an ellipse. An ellipse contains a major axis and a minor axis whose sizes specify the size of the ellipse. The major axis passes through the foci of the ellipse from one end of the ellipse to the other. The minor axis is perpendicular to the major axis, bisecting it at its center. The width of the bounding rectangle is equal to the length of the major axis and the height is equal to the length of the minor axis. Thus, you can use the dimensions of the rectangle to specify the size of an ellipse (see Figure 4.3).

An ellipse in Java 2D is represented by the abstract class Ellipse2D. This class is stored in the package java.awt.geom and extends the superclass RectangularShape. The inner classes Ellipse2D.Float and Ellipse2D.Double support the floating point and double precision shapes, respectively. Note that these classes extend Ellipse2D, and the respective instances hold the actual data of the ellipses.

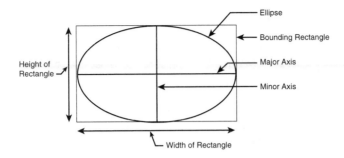

Figure 4.3

An ellipse and its bounding rectangle.

Circles

A circle in Java 2D is simply an ellipse in which the major and minor axes are of equal lengths. Thus, circles are specific cases of ellipses when the bounding rectangle's width and height are equal. In a circle, the foci meet at the center of the ellipse and form the center of the circle. You can create circles by assigning the same value for both the width and height of the bounding rectangle of the ellipse.

Creating Ellipses

The concrete classes Ellipse2D.Float and Ellipse2D.Double support constructors to create instances of ellipses at the specified location and size. You can also create ellipses that are located at the origin (0,0), but without any size. These ellipses can be redefined at a later stage using the values for a new location and size. The constructors that contain arguments require you to specify the location coordinates (x, y) and the width and height of the bounding rectangle (w, h). The following are the supported constructors from the floating point and double precision classes Ellipse2D.Float and Ellipse2D.Double:

```
public Ellipse2D.Float()
public Ellipse2D.Float(float x, float y, float w, float h)

public Ellipse2D.Double()
public Ellipse2D.Double(double x, double y, double w, double h)
```

Working with Ellipse Operations

The abstract classes RectangularShape and Ellipse2D and the concrete classes Ellipse2D.Float and Ellipse2D.Double support a number of operations that you can perform on an ellipse object. The following sections discuss these features.

Redefining an Ellipse

After an ellipse is created in float precision, you can redefine the ellipse by using new values for its location coordinates and size. The following method in `Ellipse2D.Float` supports this functionality:

```
public void setFrame(float x, float y, float w, float h)
```

Similarly, an ellipse can be redefined by using double precision values for the coordinates. The classes `Ellipse2D.Float` and `Ellipse2D.Double` support the governing method:

```
public void setFrame(double x, double y, double w, double h)
```

Retrieving the Coordinates of an Ellipse

As you have already seen, an ellipse is created by using a pair of coordinates for its location (x, y) along with its width and height (w, h). The following methods retrieve the values of these parameters in double precision:

```
public double getX()
public double getY()
public double getWidth()
public double getHeight()
```

Testing Containment and Intersections

The classes `RectangularShape` and `Ellipse2D` support the following methods to test whether an ellipse object completely contains the specified point or rectangle. A point can be specified by using its coordinates or the point object. Similarly, a rectangle can be specified by using its location coordinates and size, or the rectangle object itself:

```
public boolean contains(double x, double y)
public boolean contains(Point2D p)
```

```
public boolean contains(double x, double y, double w, double h)
public boolean contains(Rectangle2D r)
```

You can also test whether the bounding box of an ellipse is completely empty by invoking the following method:

```
public boolean isEmpty()
```

The classes `RectangularShape` and `Ellipse2D` also support the following methods to test whether the interior of an ellipse intersects the interior of the specified rectangle:

```
public boolean intersects(double x, double y, double w, double h)
public boolean intersects(Rectangle2D r)
```

Retrieving the Bounding Rectangle of an Ellipse

The classes `RectangularShape`, `Ellipse2D.Float`, and `Ellipse2D.Double` support the methods to retrieve the low-precision and high-precision bounding rectangles of an ellipse. The following are these methods:

```
public Rectangle getBounds()
public Rectangle2D getBounds2D()
```

Retrieving the Outline Information

The classes `RectangularShape` and `Ellipse2D` support the following methods to retrieve the path iteration object that contains the outline information of the shape:

```
public PathIterator getPathIterator(AffineTransform at)
public PathIterator getPathIterator(AffineTransform at,
                                    double flatness)
```

Retrieving the Center of the Bounding Rectangle

The class `RectangularShape` supports the following methods to retrieve the center coordinates (xc, yc) of the bounding rectangle of the ellipse in double precision:

```
public double getCenterX()
public double getCenterY()
```

Interactive Ellipse Example

Listing 4.3 creates an interactive program that displays an ellipse in an application frame. You can click the mouse in the bounding box of the ellipse to get the focus to the ellipse. You can also drag the ellipse to move it around the frame. The applet displays the coordinates of the mouse pointer as it is being dragged. Notice that the mouse pointer changes to a pointing hand as the mouse enters the bounding box of the ellipse. The output of this program is shown in Figure 4.4.

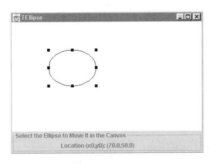

Figure 4.4

An application window displaying a movable ellipse.

Listing 4.3   Interactive Ellipse Example (TEllipse.java)

```java
import javax.swing.*;
import javax.swing.event.*;
import javax.swing.border.*;
import java.awt.*;
import java.awt.event.*;
import java.awt.geom.*;

public class TEllipse extends JFrame {
    DrawingCanvas canvas;
    JLabel location;

    public TEllipse() {
        // 1. Assign a title and get a reference to the content
        // pane of the swing frame
        super("TEllipse");
        Container container = getContentPane();

        // 2. Add the drawing canvas
        canvas = new DrawingCanvas();
        container.add(canvas);

        // 3. Create a display panel with titled border
        JPanel panel = new JPanel();
        panel.setLayout(new GridLayout(1,2));
        panel.add(new JLabel("Location (x0,y0): ", JLabel.RIGHT));
        location = new JLabel("");
        panel.add(location);
        TitledBorder border = new TitledBorder(
            "Select the Ellipse to Move It in the Canvas");
        panel.setBorder(border);

        // 4. Add the panel to the container
        container.add(panel, BorderLayout.SOUTH);

        // 5. Add a window listener to close the frame and display it
        // with a suitable packing size for the contents.
        addWindowListener(new WindowEventHandler());
        pack();
        show();
    }

    // 6. Definition of the window listener
    class WindowEventHandler extends WindowAdapter {
        public void windowClosing(WindowEvent e) {
            System.exit(0);
        }
    }
}
```

```
// 7. The main method...
public static void main(String arg[]) {
    new TEllipse();
}


// 8. Definition of the drawing canvas class
class DrawingCanvas extends Canvas {
    double x,y, w,h;  // parameters of ellipse
    int x1,y1, x2,y2;
    Ellipse2D ellipse;
    Ellipse2D selectedShape;
    Rectangle2D boundingRec;
    Cursor curCursor;

    // 9. Constructor
    public DrawingCanvas() {
        // Values for the ellipse parameters
        x = 20; y = 20; w = 100; h = 75;
        setBackground(Color.white);
        addMouseListener(new MyMouseListener());
        addMouseMotionListener(new MyMouseMotionListener());
        setSize(400, 300); // canvas width and height
    }

    // 10. The overriding paint method
    public void paint(Graphics g) {
        Graphics2D g2D = (Graphics2D) g;

        // Draw the ellipse
        ellipse = new Ellipse2D.Double(x,y, w,h);
        g2D.draw(ellipse);

        // When the ellipse is selected using mouse, highlight it.
        if (boundingRec != null) {
            drawHighlightSquares(g2D, boundingRec);
        }

        // Change the mouse cursor if necessary
        if (curCursor != null)
            setCursor(curCursor);
    }

    // 11. Method to draw highlight squares
    public void drawHighlightSquares(Graphics2D g2D, Rectangle2D r) {
        double x = r.getX();
        double y = r.getY();
        double w = r.getWidth();
        double h = r.getHeight();
```

continues

Listing 4.3   continued

```
        g2D.setColor(Color.black);

        g2D.fill(new Rectangle.Double(x-3.0, y-3.0, 6.0, 6.0));
        g2D.fill(new Rectangle.Double(x+w*0.5-3.0, y-3.0, 6.0, 6.0));
        g2D.fill(new Rectangle.Double(x+w-3.0, y-3.0, 6.0, 6.0));
        g2D.fill(new Rectangle.Double(x-3.0, y+h*0.5-3.0, 6.0, 6.0));
        g2D.fill(new Rectangle.Double(x+w-3.0, y+h*0.5-3.0, 6.0, 6.0));
        g2D.fill(new Rectangle.Double(x-3.0, y+h-3.0, 6.0, 6.0));
        g2D.fill(new Rectangle.Double(x+w*0.5-3.0, y+h-3.0, 6.0, 6.0));
        g2D.fill(new Rectangle.Double(x+w-3.0, y+h-3.0, 6.0, 6.0));
    }

    // 12. Definition of the mouse listener class
    class MyMouseListener extends MouseAdapter {
        // When the mouse button is pressed
        public void mousePressed(MouseEvent e) {
            // Check if the mouse pointer is inside the ellipse
            if (ellipse.contains(e.getX(), e.getY())) {

                //Initialize the selection status and bounding rectangle
                selectedShape = ellipse;
                if (boundingRec != null)
                    boundingRec = ellipse.getBounds2D();

                // To display the location and size of ellipse
                displayParameters(selectedShape);
            }
            else { // If the mouse pointer is not over the ellipse
                boundingRec = null;
                location.setText("");
            }
            // Update the canvas
            canvas.repaint();

            // Store the mouse coordinates
            x1 = e.getX(); y1 = e.getY();
        }

        // When the mouse button is released
        public void mouseReleased(MouseEvent e) {
            // Test if the mouse pointer is inside the ellipse
            if (ellipse.contains(e.getX(), e.getY())) {
                boundingRec = ellipse.getBounds2D();
                selectedShape = ellipse;

                // To display the location and size of ellipse
                displayParameters(selectedShape);
            }
```

```
        // Update the canvas
        canvas.repaint();
    }


    // When the mouse button is clicked
    public void mouseClicked(MouseEvent e) {
        // Test if the mouse pointer is inside the ellipse
        if (ellipse.contains(e.getX(), e.getY())) {
            selectedShape = ellipse;
            // Need to draw the bounding box when the mouse
            // button is clicked
            boundingRec = ellipse.getBounds2D();

            // To display the location and size of ellipse
            displayParameters(selectedShape);
        }
        else {
            if (boundingRec != null)
                boundingRec = null;
            location.setText("");
        }

        // Update the canvas
        canvas.repaint();
    }
}


// 13. The mouse motion listener
class MyMouseMotionListener extends MouseMotionAdapter {
    public void mouseDragged(MouseEvent e) {
        // Test if the mouse pointer is inside the ellipse
        if (ellipse.contains(e.getX(),e.getY())) {
            boundingRec = null;
            selectedShape = ellipse;

            // Retrieve the mouse coordinates
            x2 = e.getX(); y2 = e.getY();

            // Update the values for the location of the
            // ellipse by adding/subtracting the difference
            // in the mouse movement.
            x = x + x2 - x1;
            y = y + y2 - y1;

            // Store the latest mouse location as (x1, y1).
            x1 = x2;
            y1 = y2;
```

continues

Listing 4.3   continued

```
        }
        if (selectedShape != null)
            displayParameters(selectedShape);

        // Update the canvas
        canvas.repaint();
    }

    // When the mouse is moved, this method controls the
    // type of mouse cursor.
    public void mouseMoved(MouseEvent e) {
        if (ellipse != null) { // Averts a null pointer in
                               // event dispatch thread
            if (ellipse.contains(e.getX(),e.getY())) {
                // Set the cursor to the hand type.
                curCursor = Cursor.getPredefinedCursor(
                            Cursor.HAND_CURSOR);
            }
            else {
                // Set the cursor to the default one.
                curCursor = Cursor.getDefaultCursor();
            }
        }
        canvas.repaint();
    }
}

// 14. To display the instantaneous location coordinates while
// dragging the ellipse.
public void displayParameters(Shape shape) {
    double x = selectedShape.getX();
    double y = selectedShape.getY();
    double w = selectedShape.getWidth();
    double h = selectedShape.getHeight();
    String locString = "(" + Double.toString(x)
                    + "," + Double.toString(y) + ")";
    String sizeString = "(" + Double.toString(w)
                    + "," + Double.toString(h) + ")";
    location.setText(locString);
}
    }
}
```

Code Analysis

This program is a Swing application. The application frame `TEllipse` extends `JFrame`. The application class declares the objects `DrawingCanvas` and `JLabel` as its fields.

Inside the constructor of TEllipse, snippet-1 assigns a title to the frame and obtains a reference to the content pane of the underlying frame. Snippet-2 creates an instance of the drawing canvas and attaches it to the main frame. Snippet-3 creates a display panel, and snippet-4 adds the frame. Snippet-5 adds a window event listener to properly close the application frame. You will also find the statements to pack and display the frame.

Snippet-6 defines the window listener in which the windowClosing() method provides the code to exit the application on closing the frame. Snippet-7 is the main method that creates an instance of TEllipse.

Snippet-8 provides the definition of the class DrawingCanvas. This class declares the parameters of the ellipse, an ellipse object and its bounding rectangle, and the mouse pointer as its fields. Snippet-9 is the constructor of the class where the initial location (x, y) and size (w, h) of the ellipse are defined. The remaining statements in the constructor assign a background color to the canvas, register mouse and mouse-motion listeners with the canvas, and assign a suitable size to the canvas.

Snippet-10 shows the overriding paint() method. The first statement in this method prepares the graphics context. The next couple of statements create an ellipse and draw it over the canvas. The remaining code statements draw the highlighting squares and change the mouse pointer if necessary. Snippet-11 is the method to draw highlighting squares.

Snippet-12 defines the mouse listener class. This class provides the code for the methods mousePressed(), mouseReleased(), and mouseClicked(). Inside the mousePressed() method, the first code statement tests whether the ellipse contains the mouse pointer. If this happens to be true, the bounding rectangle is retrieved and initialized to the variable boundingRec.

If the condition is false, the bounding rectangle is reset to null. The location coordinates are also displayed. Then the canvas is updated by using the repaint() method. Next, the mouse coordinates are stored. The mouseReleased() and mouseClicked() methods also implement similar functionality.

Snippet-13 implements the mouse-motion listener class. This class implements the mouseDragged() and mouseMoved() methods. Inside this snippet, you will find the code to compute the location coordinates of the ellipse as the ellipse is being dragged. Then the location of the ellipse is updated on the canvas. The mouseMoved() method implements the code to change the mouse pointer as it enters or leaves the ellipse. Finally, snippet-14 shows the method that supports code to display the coordinates of the mouse pointer's location.

Drawing Open Arcs, Chords, and Pies

An *arc* is a portion of an ellipse. Thus, an arc has a certain radius, a starting angle, and an angular extent. Arcs in Java 2D are specified by means of the location and dimensions of the bounding rectangle of the ellipse from which an arc is created. Thus, you will need the location and size of bounding rectangle of the ellipse, a starting angle, and an angular extent to specify an arc (see Figure 4.5).

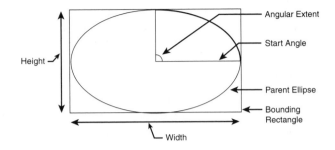

Figure 4.5

Parameters of an arc to specify its dimensions.

There are three types of arcs: open arcs, chords of a circle or ellipse, and pies of a circle or ellipse. Open arcs represent the outlines of arch-type structures or objects. Chords are formed when both ends of an open arc are joined by means of a straight line (see Figure 4.6). A semicircle is a chord when the angular extent of the governing arc is π radians.

A pie is a type of arc that has an important role in presentation graphics. A pie is created when the starting point and ending point of an arc are connected to the center of the arc by means of straight lines (see Figure 4.6). The center of the arc is the center of the ellipse in which the arc is a portion.

Figure 4.6

Arc types: an open arc, a chord, and a pie.

An arc is represented by the abstract class Arc2D. This class extends the super class RectangularShape. Because RectangularShape implements the Shape interface, the arcs are also shapes described in Java2D. You can call the methods draw() and fill() from the graphics context to paint the arcs.

This abstract class Arc2D contains a number of useful fields and methods you can use to operate on arcs. More importantly, this class contains the inner classes Arc2D.Float and Arc2D.Double. These concrete subclasses of Arc2D support the floating point and double precision shapes.

Creating Open, Chord, and Pie Type Arcs

The classes `Arc2D.Float` and `Arc2D.Double` support constructors to create arcs at the specified location with the specified size, starting angle, angular extent, and arc type. Some constructors take no arguments, and others take argument values for various arc parameters.

You can also specify the arc type by using the constructors with arguments. The constructors without any arguments create open-type arcs. In a suitable constructor, an arc type can be specified by using suitable field from the `Arc2D` class. The following encapsulated fields specify the open type, chord type, and pie type arcs, respectively:

```
public static final int OPEN
public static final int CHORD
public static final int PIE
```

Next, the following constructors are supported in the `Arc2D.Float` and `Arc2D.Double` classes:

```
public Arc2D.Float()
public Arc2D.Float(int type)
public Arc2D.Float(float x, float y, float w, float h,
                   float start, float extent, int type)
public Arc2D.Float(Rectangle2D ellipseBounds,
                   float start, float extent, int type)

public Arc2D.Double()
public Arc2D.Double(int type)
public Arc2D.Double(double x, double y, double w, double h,
                    double start, double extent, int type)
public Arc2D.Double(Rectangle2D ellipseBounds,
                    double start, double extent, int type)
```

The first methods in the preceding two sets of constructors create an open arc at the origin without any size, and with a starting angle and angular extents of zero degrees. Such arcs can be redefined to certain realistic values at a later time in a program. The second methods are similar to the first methods, but you can specify the type of the arc such as `Arc2D.OPEN`, `Arc2D.CHORD`, and `Arc2D.PIE`.

The third methods create new arcs that are initialized to the specified location, size, starting angle, angular extent, and arc type. The last methods in the sets create new arcs that are initialized to the specified location, size, angular extents, and arc type. Notice that in these constructors, you need to specify the objects of type `Rectangle2D` to specify the location and size. This rectangle object specifies the boundary of the ellipse of which the arc is a portion.

Interactive Arc Example

Listing 4.4 demonstrates the open, chord, and pie type arcs. The program creates an applet with six control sliders in its top portion, and a couple of combo boxes at the bottom. The sliders provide control over parameters of the arc, such as location, size, starting angle, and angular extent. From the combo boxes, you can select the arc type and fill color. At the center of the applet is the drawing canvas that displays an arc. The output of this program is shown in Figures 4.7, 4.8, and 4.9 when different arc types are selected.

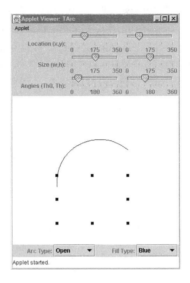

Figure 4.7

An applet demonstrating the open type arcs.

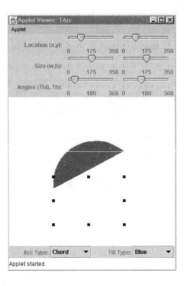

Figure 4.8

An applet demonstrating the chord type arcs.

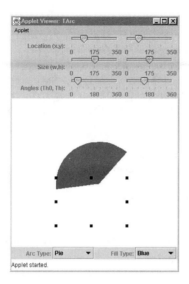

Figure 4.9

An applet demonstrating the pie type arcs.

Listing 4.4   Interactive Arc Example (TArc.java)

```
/*
 * <Applet code=TArc width=350 height=400>
 * </Applet>
 */

import javax.swing.*;
import javax.swing.event.*;
import java.awt.*;
import java.awt.event.*;
import java.awt.geom.*;

public class TArc extends JApplet {
    // Canvas for drawing an arc
    DrawingCanvas canvas;

    // Combo boxes for arc type and fill color selections
    JComboBox arcBox, fillBox;

    // Sliders to control arc parameters
    JSlider slider,
            sliderX, sliderY,
            sliderW, sliderH,
            sliderT0, sliderT;
```

continues

Listing 4.4   continued

```
// Arrays to be used for the arc and color selection comboboxes
String[] arcLabels = {"Open", "Chord", "Pie"};
int[] arcTypes = {Arc2D.OPEN, Arc2D.CHORD, Arc2D.PIE};
String[] colorLabels = {"Black", "White", "Red", "Green", "Blue"};
Color[] colors = {Color.black, Color.white, Color.red,
                  Color.green, Color.blue};


public void init() {
    // 1. Get the content pane
    Container container = getContentPane();

    // 2. Create the drawing canvas
    canvas = new DrawingCanvas();

    // 3. Create sliders to control arc parameters by using the method
    // defined in snippet-9
    setSlider(0, canvas.getWidth(), canvas.getWidth()/4,
            canvas.getWidth()/2, canvas.getWidth()/4);
    sliderX = slider;
    setSlider(0, canvas.getHeight(), canvas.getHeight()/4,
            canvas.getHeight()/2, canvas.getHeight()/4);
    sliderY = slider;
    setSlider(0, canvas.getWidth(), canvas.getWidth()/2,
            canvas.getWidth()/2, canvas.getWidth()/4);
    sliderW = slider;
    setSlider(0, canvas.getHeight(), canvas.getHeight()/2,
            canvas.getHeight()/2, canvas.getHeight()/4);
    sliderH = slider;
    setSlider(0, 360, 45, 180, 45); //See the setSlider() arguments.
    sliderT0 = slider;
    setSlider(0, 360, 135, 180, 45);
    sliderT = slider;

    // 4. Add the labels and sliders to a panel
    JPanel panel1 = new JPanel();
    panel1.setLayout(new GridLayout(3,3));
    panel1.add(new JLabel("Location (x,y): ", JLabel.RIGHT));
    panel1.add(sliderX); panel1.add(sliderY);
    panel1.add(new JLabel("Size (w,h): ", JLabel.RIGHT));
    panel1.add(sliderW); panel1.add(sliderH);
    panel1.add(new JLabel("Angles (Th0, Th): ", JLabel.RIGHT));
    panel1.add(sliderT0); panel1.add(sliderT);

    container.add(panel1, BorderLayout.NORTH);

    // 5 Create combo boxes for selecting arc type and fill color
    arcBox = new JComboBox(arcLabels);
```

```
arcBox.setSelectedIndex(0);
arcBox.setAlignmentX(Component.LEFT_ALIGNMENT);
arcBox.addActionListener(new ComboBoxListener());

fillBox = new JComboBox(colorLabels);
fillBox.setSelectedIndex(0);
fillBox.setAlignmentX(Component.LEFT_ALIGNMENT);
fillBox.addActionListener(new ComboBoxListener());

// 6. Add the comboboxes to another panel
JPanel panel2 = new JPanel();
panel2.setLayout(new GridLayout(1, 4));
panel2.add(new JLabel("Arc Type: ", JLabel.RIGHT));
panel2.add(arcBox);
panel2.add(new JLabel("Fill Type: ", JLabel.RIGHT));
panel2.add(fillBox);

// 7. Add panel-2 to the container
container.add(panel2, BorderLayout.SOUTH);

// 8. Add the drawing canvas
container.add(canvas);
}

// 9. Method to create sliders with necessary configuration
public void setSlider(int min, int max, int init,
                      int mjrTkSp, int mnrTkSp) {
    slider = new JSlider(JSlider.HORIZONTAL, min, max, init);
    slider.setPaintTicks(true);
    slider.setMajorTickSpacing(mjrTkSp);
    slider.setMinorTickSpacing(mnrTkSp);
    slider.setPaintLabels(true);
    slider.addChangeListener(new SliderListener());
}

// 10. Definition of the drawing canvas
class DrawingCanvas extends Canvas {
    Arc2D arc;
    double x,y, w,h, T0,T; // location, size, start angle, extent
    Color fillColor;
    int arcType;
    Rectangle2D boundingRec = null;

    // 11. Constructor
    public DrawingCanvas() {
        // Assign a size to the canvas
        setSize(350,350); // canvas width and height
```

continues

Listing 4.4   continued

```
        // Initialize the arc parameters for display when
        // the applet first showed up.
        x = getWidth()/4; y = getHeight()/4;
        w = getWidth()/2; h = getHeight()/2;
        T0 = 0; T = 135; // Start angle and extent
        arcType = Arc2D.OPEN;
        fillColor = Color.black;

        // Assign white color to the canvas
        setBackground(Color.white);
    }

    // 12. The overriding paint method
    public void paint(Graphics g) {
        Graphics2D g2D = (Graphics2D) g;

        // 13. Create an arc using the parameters for location (x, y),
        // size (w, h), start angle and angular extent (T0, T), and
        // arc type such as open, pie, or chord.
        arc = new Arc2D.Double(x,y, w,h, T0,T, arcType);
        if (fillColor == Color.white || arcType == Arc2D.OPEN) {
            g2D.setColor(Color.black);
            g2D.draw(arc);
        }
        else {
            g2D.setColor(fillColor);
            g2D.fill(arc);
        }

        // 14. Display the bounding rectangle using highlight squares
        boundingRec = arc.getBounds2D();
        drawHighlightSquares(g2D, boundingRec);
    }

    // 15. Method to draw highlight squares
    public void drawHighlightSquares(Graphics2D g2D, Rectangle2D r) {
        double x = r.getX();
        double y = r.getY();
        double w = r.getWidth();
        double h = r.getHeight();
        g2D.setColor(Color.black);

        g2D.fill(new Rectangle.Double(x-3.0, y-3.0, 6.0, 6.0));
        g2D.fill(new Rectangle.Double(x+w*0.5-3.0, y-3.0, 6.0, 6.0));
        g2D.fill(new Rectangle.Double(x+w-3.0, y-3.0, 6.0, 6.0));
        g2D.fill(new Rectangle.Double(x-3.0, y+h*0.5-3.0, 6.0, 6.0));
```

```
        g2D.fill(new Rectangle.Double(x+w-3.0, y+h*0.5-3.0, 6.0, 6.0));
        g2D.fill(new Rectangle.Double(x-3.0, y+h-3.0, 6.0, 6.0));
        g2D.fill(new Rectangle.Double(x+w*0.5-3.0, y+h-3.0, 6.0, 6.0));
        g2D.fill(new Rectangle.Double(x+w-3.0, y+h-3.0, 6.0, 6.0));
    }
}


// 16. Define the combo box listener to draw the selected arc type or
// to fill the selected color.
class ComboBoxListener implements ActionListener {
    public void actionPerformed(ActionEvent e) {
        JComboBox cb = (JComboBox) e.getSource();
        if(cb == arcBox) {
            canvas.arcType = arcTypes[cb.getSelectedIndex()];
        }
        else if (cb == fillBox) {
            canvas.fillColor = colors[cb.getSelectedIndex()];
        }

        // Update the canvas with the new settings
        canvas.repaint();
    }
}


// 17. Define the slider listener to alter different parameters
// of the arc
class SliderListener implements ChangeListener {
    public void stateChanged(ChangeEvent e) {
        JSlider slider = (JSlider) e.getSource();
        if (slider == sliderX)
            canvas.x = slider.getValue();
        else if (slider == sliderY)
            canvas.y = slider.getValue();
        else if (slider == sliderW)
            canvas.w = slider.getValue();
        else if (slider == sliderH)
            canvas.h = slider.getValue();
        else if (slider == sliderT0)
            canvas.T0 = slider.getValue();
        else if (slider == sliderT)
            canvas.T = slider.getValue();

        // Update the drawing with new values of arc parameters
        canvas.repaint();
    }
}
}
```

Code Analysis

The applet TArc declares a drawing canvas, combo boxes, and sliders as fields of the class. You can also find the declaration of arrays, arcLabels, arcTypes, colorLabels, and colors that are used with the combo boxes as fields.

Inside the init() method, snippet-1 gets a handle on the applet's content pane. Snippet-2 creates a drawing canvas, and snippet-3 creates the control sliders using the method defined in snippet-9. Snippet-4 adds the sliders to the applet with suitable description labels.

Snippet-5 creates the combo box panel on which you select the arc type and color of the fill. Snippet-6 adds these combo boxes to the bottom portion of the applet. Snippet-7 adds the combo box panel to the applet. Finally, snippet-8 adds the drawing canvas to the applet.

Snippet-9 defines the method to create sliders with the necessary configuration. Snippet-10 defines the DrawingCanvas class. This class declares an arc, along with its parameters, fill color, arc type, and bounding rectangle as its fields.

Snippet-11 is the constructor of the drawing canvas. The constructor assigns a suitable size to the canvas, and provides the arc parameters with initial values. You will also find a statement to assign the background color of the canvas.

Snippet-12 shows the paint() method that overrides that of its parent. This method sets up the graphics context for 2D drawing. Snippet-13 conditionally draws the arc when its fill color is white, or if it is the open type. If the arc is of the chord or pie type or the fill color is not white, the else clause draws an arc with the specified fill color.

NOTE

If the fill color is specified for an open type arc, according to the Java 2D API, the color will fill in the entire open arc. However, this program implements the open arc in a different way, so that it does not receive any fill color.

Snippet-14 shows the code statements to display the bounding rectangle of the arc. The corresponding method drawHighlightSquares() is given in snippet-15. Snippet-16 defines the combo box listener that implements the code to recognize the combo box in operation by using an if-else statement. Inside the clauses, the selected items of the respective combo boxes are registered by using the variables arcType and fillColor. Then the canvas is updated with the new values of arc type and fill color by calling repaint().

Snippet-17 defines the listener class for sliders. The implementation method contains the code to recognize the slider in operation, and then to obtain the corresponding value of the slider by invoking the getValue() method on the slider object. The method then updates the canvas to display the arc by using the new value of the parameter.

Working with Arc Operations

The abstract parent classes `RectangularShape` and `Arc2D` and the concrete classes `Arc2D.Float` and `Arc2D.Double` support various methods to perform operations such as redefining the arc parameters, retrieving the parameters, retrieving the bounding box, testing containment, and so on. Here is the concise discussion of these methods.

Redefining an Arc

After an arc is created, especially with the constructor that does not take any arguments, you can redefined the values of the parameters by invoking the following methods on the arc object:

```
public void setArc(double x, double y,
                   double w, double h,
                   double angSt, double angExt,
                   int arcType)
```

The following method is similar to the preceding method, but requires the arc location `loc` as a point object and the arc `size` as an object of type `Dimension2D`:

```
public void setArc(Point2D loc, Dimension2D size,
                   double angSt, double angExt,
                   int arcType)
```

The next method is the same as the previous methods, but you need to specify the location and size of the arc by using an object `rect` of type `Rectangle2D` that encompasses the arc:

```
public void setArc(Rectangle2D rect,
                   double angSt, double angExt,
                   int arcType)
```

The following method is useful when the current arc needs to be initiated to another existing arc:

```
public void setArc(Arc2D arc)
```

These coordinates of the center can define the location of an arc, and the radius can define the size of the arc. Here is another important method that is useful to redefine an arc object by using the coordinates of the center, radius, starting angle, angular extent, and arc type:

```
public void setArcByCenter(double x, double y,
                           double radius,
                           double angSt,
                           double angExt,
                           int arcType)
```

In addition to the previous methods, the following methods are useful to assign the respective parameters of an arc:

```
public void setArcType(int type)
public void setAngleStart(double angSt)
public void setAngleExtent(double angExt)
```

You can also use the coordinates or point objects to define arc parameters, such as the starting angle, angular extent, and size. A line passing through a point (represented by its object p) can subtend an angle at the center of the arc with the prescribed reference line where the initial angle is zero. The following method supports this functionality:

```
public void setAngleStart(Point2D p)
```

In a similar way, the next two methods define the starting angle and angular extent by using the coordinate values (x1, y1) and (x2, y2), or the point objects p1 and p2:

```
public void setAngles(double x1, double y1, double x2, double y2)
public void setAngles(Point2D p1, Point2D p2)
```

The next method redefines the size of an arc by specifying the location and size of the bounding rectangle of the arc:

```
public void setFrame(double x, double y, double w, double h)
```

Retrieving the Parameters of the Arc

The classes Arc2D.Float and Arc2D.Double support the following methods to retrieve different parameters of the arc such as its location coordinates, size parameters, starting angle, angular extent, arc type, starting point, and ending point:

```
public double getX()
public double getY()

public double getWidth()
public double getHeight()

public double getAngleStart()
public double getAngleExtent()

public int getArcType()

public Point2D getStartPoint()
public Point2D getEndPoint()
```

Testing the Containment and Intersection

The classes RectangularShape and Arc2D support the following methods to test whether the arc object completely contains a point, rectangle, or angle:

```
public boolean contains(double x, double y)
public boolean contains(Point2D point)
```

```
public boolean contains(double x, double y, double w, double h)
public boolean contains(Rectangle2D r)

public boolean containsAngle(double angle)
```

In these methods, for points and rectangles you can use either the coordinate values or the respective objects.

The classes RectangularShape and Arc2D support the following methods to test whether the arc object intersects the specified rectangle:

```
public boolean intersects(double x, double y, double w, double h)
public boolean intersects(Rectangle2D r)
```

Retrieving the Bounding Box of an Arc

The classes RectangularShape and Arc2D support the following methods to retrieve the low-precision and high-precision bounding rectangles of an ellipse:

```
public Rectangle getBounds()
public Rectangle2D getBounds2D()
```

CHAPTER 5

General Paths and Composite Shapes

The previous two chapters have discussed various graphics primitives such as lines, rectangles, round-cornered rectangles, quadratic and cubic curves, ellipses, and arcs. This chapter will take you beyond creating those basic shapes by discussing how to create shapes with complex outlines. Java 2D supports a class for creating arbitrary shapes that are made up of lines, quadratic curves, and cubic curves. The outlines of these shapes are referred as *general paths*.

This chapter also discusses how to create shapes that are made up of two or more available geometric shapes by using constructive area geometry (CAG). The CAG creates custom shapes by performing add, subtract, intersect, or exclusive-OR operations. You can prepare areas of different shapes and then subject them to these operations to create composite shapes.

Drawing General Paths

General paths are shapes that are created by using lines and/or quadratic curves and/or cubic curves. You need to specify the coordinates of the starting, ending, and control points of these primitives that form the subpaths of a general path. Thus, the general paths can represent complex shapes that are composed of straight and curved edges.

In Java 2D, a general path object is represented by the class GeneralPath. This class implements the Shape interface and is a direct subclass of Object. The package java.awt.geom contains GeneralPath.

By using the class GeneralPath, you can create shapes of considerable complexity. The shapes can also have overlapped regions. The overlapped regions must be identified to be interior or exterior for the purpose of filling them. The algorithms based on winding rules decide whether an overlapped region is interior or exterior to the shape.

Winding Rules

For geometric shapes whose edges meet only at the vertices, the identification of interior regions is straightforward. However, the identification becomes complex for general paths that contain intersecting edges (see Figure 5.1).

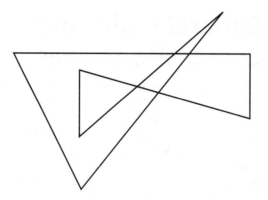

Figure 5.1

A simple general path with intersecting edges.

As in the case of many graphics packages, Java 2D supports the usage of either the *odd-even rule* (also called the *odd-parity rule*) or the *non-zero winding number rule* to identify the interior of a shape. The algorithms for these rules are summarized here.

Odd-Even Rule

To use the odd-even rule, follow these steps:

1. Conceptually draw a line from any point P of a shape to a distant point outside its coordinate extents. Make sure that the line must never pass through any of the vertices.
2. Count the number of edge crossings along the line.
3. If the number of polygon edges crossed by the line is odd, P is interior to the shape; otherwise, P is an exterior point.

Figure 5.2 demonstrates the odd-even rule by using the geometric shape shown in Figure 5.1.

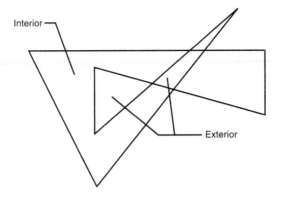

Figure 5.2

Demonstration of the odd-even rule.

Non-zero Winding Number Rule

To use the non-zero winding rule, follow these steps:

1. Count the number of times the edges of a shape wind around a particular point P in the counter-clockwise direction. This count is called the *winding number*.
2. The winding number is non-zero for the interior points of a 2D shape.
3. For polygons, initialize the winding number to zero and imagine a line drawn from any point P to a remote point existing beyond the coordinate limits of the shape. Make sure that the line does not pass through any of the vertices on the way.
4. As the line moves from the point P to the remote point, count the number of times the line crosses edges in each direction.
5. Add one to the winding number every time the line intersects an edge that crosses from left to right.
6. The position of point P is determined by obtaining the final value of the winding number after all the edges are crossed.
7. If the winding number is non-zero, the point P is in the interior of the shape; otherwise, it lies outside the shape.

Figure 5.3 demonstrates the non-zero winding rule using the shape shown in Figure 5.1. Note that the odd-even method and the non-zero winding rule yield the same results for standard polygons and other simple shapes. But for more complex shapes, the two methods might give different interior and exterior regions.

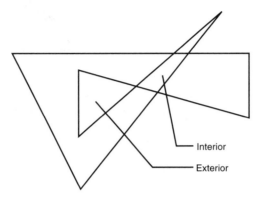

Figure 5.3

Demonstration of the non-zero winding rule.

Specifying a Rule

To specify the general path object to use the even-odd rule or the non-zero winding rule, you can use the following fields from the class GeneralPath:

```
public static final int WIND_EVEN_ODD
```

```
public static final int WIND_NON_ZERO
```

To assign one of these fields, you can pass it as an argument value in the relevant constructor of the class GeneralPath. If an object of GeneralPath is readily available, you can invoke the following method to assign a field:

```
public void setWindingRule(int rule)
```

This method throws an illegal argument exception if the assigned rule is anything other than the two rules we've discussed. The class also supports the following method to retrieve the current winding rule at any point in a program:

```
public int getWindingRule()
```

Constructing a General Path

The class GeneralPath defines four different constructors to create instances. The following are those constructors:

```
public GeneralPath()
public GeneralPath(int windingRule)
public GeneralPath(int windingRule, int initialCapacity)
public GeneralPath(Shape shape)
```

The constructor without any arguments creates a general path object using the non-zero winding rule by default. The second constructor requires the specification of one of the winding rules defined in the class.

The third constructor is similar to the second one, but it requires the specification of the initial capacity `initialCapacity` to store the coordinates of the sub-paths. The capacity is automatically expandable at any stage to store more coordinates as more sub-paths are added to the general path object. Therefore, you can initially assume some reasonable value for this parameter.

Because a general path can represent any specific geometric shape, you can create a general path object out of that shape. The fourth constructor requires the specification of an object of type `Shape`. The shape of this object will be used to create the general path.

Retrieving Boundaries of a General Path

As you have seen with the classes for standard primitives, the class `GeneralPath` also supports the methods to retrieve its bounding box. The bounding box can be a low-precision rectangle of type `Rectangle`, or a high-precision rectangle of type `Rectangle2D`. The following methods support the retrieval operations:

```
public Rectangle getBounds()
public Rectangle2D getBounds2D()
```

Testing Containment and Intersection

The class `GeneralPath` supports two methods to test whether its object contains any specified point. The overloaded methods require the specification of the point as a pair of coordinates (x, y) or as an object of type `Point2D`. The following are these methods:

```
public boolean contains(double x, double y)
public boolean contains(Point2D p)
```

Similarly, you can test whether a general path object completely contains a rectangle. You must specify the rectangle by using either its location coordinates (x, y) and size (w, h), or by using the object itself. Here are the supported methods:

```
public boolean contains(double x, double y, double w, double h)
public boolean contains(Rectangle2D r)
```

If the general path object does not contain a rectangle, you can test whether it intersects or overlaps a portion of the rectangle by using the following two methods:

```
public boolean intersects(double x, double y, double w, double h)
public boolean intersects(Rectangle2D r)
```

General Path Example

Listing 5.1 shows the code for a Swing applet that displays eight general path objects. These objects range from very simple to complex shapes. As you can see in Figure 5.4, the applet displays a control panel that contains radio buttons to select a winding rule and push buttons to control the filling of shapes.

Clicking the No Fill button simply repaints the outline of the objects. If you click the Fill button when none of the shapes have been filled, all the shapes are filled with the selected winding rule. At any time, you can also select a single general path object by clicking the mouse in the interior of the shape.

Selecting the winding rule and clicking the Fill button will fill that shape according to the selected winding rule. The output shown in Figure 5.4 renders the general paths using the non-zero winding rule. Figure 5.5 shows the general path objects when they are filled using the odd-even rule.

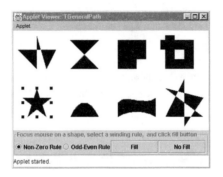

Figure 5.4

General path objects filled using the non-zero rule.

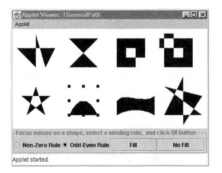

Figure 5.5

General path objects filled using the odd-even rule.

Listing 5.1   General Path Example (TGeneralPath.java)

```
/*
 * <Applet code=TGeneralPath width=400 height=275>
 * </Applet>
 */
```

```
import javax.swing.*;
import javax.swing.border.*;
import java.awt.*;
import java.awt.event.*;
import java.awt.geom.*;
import java.util.Vector;

public class TGeneralPath extends JApplet {
    DrawingCanvas canvas;
    JRadioButton oddEvenBox, nonZeroBox;
    JButton fillButton, noFillButton;

    public void init() {
        // 1. Get the content pane of the applet
        Container container = getContentPane();

        // 2. Create a control panel with titled border
        JPanel panel = new JPanel();
        panel.setLayout(new GridLayout(1, 3));
        TitledBorder border = new TitledBorder(
            "Focus mouse on a shape, select a winding rule, "
            + " and click fill button");
        panel.setBorder(border);

        // 3. Create and add radio buttons and fill buttons to the panel
        nonZeroBox = new JRadioButton("Non-Zero Rule", true);
        oddEvenBox = new JRadioButton("Odd-Even Rule");
        ButtonGroup group = new ButtonGroup();
        group.add(nonZeroBox); group.add(oddEvenBox);

        nonZeroBox.addActionListener(new ActionEventHandler1());
        oddEvenBox.addActionListener(new ActionEventHandler1());

        fillButton = new JButton("Fill");
        noFillButton = new JButton("No Fill");
        noFillButton.addActionListener(new ActionEventHandler2());
        fillButton.addActionListener(new ActionEventHandler2());

        panel.add(nonZeroBox);
        panel.add(oddEvenBox);
        panel.add(fillButton);
        panel.add(noFillButton);

        // 4. Add the panel to the applet
        container.add(panel, BorderLayout.SOUTH);

        // 5. Add the drawing canvas to the applet
        canvas = new DrawingCanvas();
```

continues

Listing 5.1   continued

```
        container.add(canvas);
    }


// 6. Definition of the 'DrawingCanvas' class
class DrawingCanvas extends Canvas {
    Vector generalPaths;
    GeneralPath selectedGPath = null;
    Rectangle2D boundingRec = null;
    int selectedRule = GeneralPath.WIND_NON_ZERO;
    boolean drawNoFill = false;


// 7. Constructor
public DrawingCanvas() {
    setBackground(Color.white);
    setSize(400,200);   // width and height of canvas
    addMouseListener(new MouseEventHandler());

    // Initialize the vector that stores general paths
    generalPaths = new Vector();

    // General Path references
    GeneralPath gp1, gp2, gp3, gp4,
                gp5, gp6, gp7, gp8;

    // Create different general paths and add them to the vector.
    // See the program output for the shapes.
    gp1 = new GeneralPath();
    gp1.moveTo(50, 10);
    gp1.lineTo(70, 80); gp1.lineTo(90, 40);
    gp1.lineTo(10, 40); gp1.lineTo(50, 80);
    gp1.closePath();
    generalPaths.addElement(gp1);

    gp2 = new GeneralPath();
    gp2.moveTo(120, 20);
    gp2.lineTo(180, 20); gp2.lineTo(120, 80);
    gp2.lineTo(180, 80);
    gp2.closePath();
    generalPaths.addElement(gp2);

    gp3 = new GeneralPath();
    gp3.moveTo(220, 20);
    gp3.lineTo(280, 20); gp3.lineTo(280, 60);
    gp3.lineTo(240, 60); gp3.lineTo(240, 40);
    gp3.lineTo(260, 40); gp3.lineTo(260, 80);
    gp3.lineTo(220, 80);
    gp3.closePath();
    generalPaths.addElement(gp3);
```

```
gp4 = new GeneralPath();
gp4.moveTo(310, 20);
gp4.lineTo(380, 20); gp4.lineTo(380, 80);
gp4.lineTo(320, 80); gp4.lineTo(320, 10);
gp4.lineTo(340, 10); gp4.lineTo(340, 60);
gp4.lineTo(360, 60); gp4.lineTo(360, 40);
gp4.lineTo(310, 40);
gp4.closePath();
generalPaths.addElement(gp4);

gp5 = new GeneralPath();
gp5.moveTo(50, 120);
gp5.lineTo(70, 180); gp5.lineTo(20, 140);
gp5.lineTo(80, 140); gp5.lineTo(30, 180);
gp5.closePath();
generalPaths.addElement(gp5);

gp6 = new GeneralPath();
gp6.moveTo(120, 180);
gp6.quadTo(150, 120, 180, 180);
gp6.closePath();
generalPaths.addElement(gp6);

gp7 = new GeneralPath();
gp7.moveTo(220, 150);
gp7.curveTo(240, 130, 280, 160, 300, 140);
gp7.lineTo(300, 180);
gp7.quadTo(260, 160, 220, 180);
gp7.closePath();
generalPaths.addElement(gp7);

gp8 = new GeneralPath();
gp8.moveTo(360, 100);
gp8.lineTo(360, 200); gp8.lineTo(400, 140);
gp8.lineTo(320, 120); gp8.lineTo(400, 180);
gp8.lineTo(320, 180);
gp8.closePath();
generalPaths.addElement(gp8);
}

// 8. The Overriding paint method
public void paint(Graphics g) {
    Graphics2D g2D = (Graphics2D) g;

    // 9. Display the general paths from the vector
    for (int i=0; i<generalPaths.size(); i++) {
        if (drawNoFill) { // Render non-filled shapes
```

continues

Listing 5.1   continued

```
                g2D.draw((GeneralPath) generalPaths.elementAt(i));
        }
        else { // Render filled shapes
            g2D.fill((GeneralPath) generalPaths.elementAt(i));
        }
    }

    // 10. Conditionally display the bounding rectangle of
    // the selected shape.
    if (boundingRec != null) {
        drawHighlightSquares(g2D, boundingRec);
    }
}

// 11. Method to draw small highlight squares with fill style
public void drawHighlightSquares(Graphics2D g2D, Rectangle2D r) {
    double x = r.getX();
    double y = r.getY();
    double w = r.getWidth();
    double h = r.getHeight();
    g2D.setColor(Color.black);

    g2D.fill(new Rectangle.Double(x-3.0, y-3.0, 6.0, 6.0));
    g2D.fill(new Rectangle.Double(x+w*0.5-3.0, y-3.0, 6.0, 6.0));
    g2D.fill(new Rectangle.Double(x+w-3.0, y-3.0, 6.0, 6.0));
    g2D.fill(new Rectangle.Double(x-3.0, y+h*0.5-3.0, 6.0, 6.0));
    g2D.fill(new Rectangle.Double(x+w-3.0, y+h*0.5-3.0, 6.0, 6.0));
    g2D.fill(new Rectangle.Double(x-3.0, y+h-3.0, 6.0, 6.0));
    g2D.fill(new Rectangle.Double(x+w*0.5-3.0, y+h-3.0, 6.0, 6.0));
    g2D.fill(new Rectangle.Double(x+w-3.0, y+h-3.0, 6.0, 6.0));
}

// 12. The mouse listener class
class MouseEventHandler extends MouseAdapter {
    public void mouseClicked(MouseEvent e) {
        // Check if a general path received mouse focus
        for (int i=0; i<generalPaths.size(); i++) {
            GeneralPath gPath = (GeneralPath) generalPaths.elementAt(i);

            // If the mouse click is inside the shape...
            if (gPath.contains(e.getX(), e.getY())) {
                // Store a reference to the selected path and
                // its bounding rectangle.
                selectedGPath = gPath;
                boundingRec = gPath.getBounds2D();

                // Finally, call repaint() and return when a
                // general path has been selected.
```

```
                    canvas.repaint();
                    return;
                 }
              }
           }
        }
     }

// 13. Event handler for events from radio buttons: Implements the
// functionality to register the selected winding rule.
class ActionEventHandler1 implements ActionListener {
    public void actionPerformed(ActionEvent e) {
        JRadioButton temp = (JRadioButton) e.getSource();

        if (temp.equals(oddEvenBox)) {
            canvas.selectedRule = GeneralPath.WIND_EVEN_ODD;
        }
        else if (temp.equals(nonZeroBox)) {
            canvas.selectedRule = GeneralPath.WIND_NON_ZERO;
        }
    }
}

// 14. Event handler for events from buttons: Implements the functionality
// to repaint canvas with the modified values of winding rule, fill style.
class ActionEventHandler2 implements ActionListener {
    public void actionPerformed(ActionEvent e) {
        JButton temp = (JButton) e.getSource();

        if (temp.equals(fillButton)) {
            if (canvas.selectedGPath != null) {
                canvas.selectedGPath.setWindingRule(canvas.selectedRule);
                canvas.drawNoFill = false;
                canvas.repaint();
            }
        }
        else if (temp.equals(noFillButton)) {
            canvas.drawNoFill = true;
            canvas.repaint();
        }
    }
}
}
```

Code Analysis

The applet TGeneralPath declares the references to a drawing canvas, radio buttons, and push buttons as its fields. Inside the init() method, snippet-1 retrieves a reference to the content pane of the applet. Snippet-2 creates a control panel with a titled border. Snippet-3 creates a set of radio buttons and push buttons and adds them to a panel.

Snippet-4 adds the panel at the bottom portion of the applet. Snippet-5 creates an instance of the drawing canvas and adds it at the center of the applet.

Snippet-6 shows the definition of the `DrawingCanvas` class. This class declares a vector, a general path object, and some flags as its fields. Snippet-7 is the constructor of the class where the background color and a suitable dimension are assigned to the canvas. A mouse listener object is also registered with the canvas. The remaining portion of the code creates a number of general path objects and adds them to the vector object `generalPaths`.

Snippet-8 shows the overriding `paint()` method. This method begins by creating the graphics context object. Snippet-9 conditionally renders the general path objects stored in the vector with or without the fill style. Snippet-10 shows the code to display the bounding rectangle to highlight the selected shape. This snippet makes use of the method shown in snippet-11.

Snippet-12 provides the definition of the mouse listener. The class `MouseEventHandler` implements the `mouseClicked()` method. Inside this method, the code checks whether a mouse click occurs in the interior region of a shape. If a mouse click occurs in a shape, the snippet stores a reference to that object. The bounding rectangle is also retrieved to highlight the shape. Then the `repaint()` method is invoked on the canvas object. Because the mouse-click operation is successful on a shape object, the control returns from this method.

Snippet-13 is the class `ActionEventHandler1`, which implements the code to register the selected winding rule (even-odd or non-zero). The winding rules are selected by operating the mutually exclusive radio buttons.

Finally, snippet-14 shows the code for the class `ActionEventHandler2`. This class simply implements the code to call the `repaint()` method on the canvas object after a suitable winding rule is selected. This action is performed when you click the Fill button. The implementation method also provides the code to reset the applet to its normal condition. This is executed when you click the No Fill button.

Composite Shapes

In addition to the general path objects, Java 2D also supports creating composite shapes made up of the areas of two or more existing shapes. The binary operations such as add, subtract, intersect, and exclusive-OR are performed to create new shapes.

To handle these binary operations, the package `java.awt.geom` supports a class called `Area`. This class implements the `Shape` interface and represents the closed area of a specified shape. The `Area` class uses the winding rule information of the shape to determine its interior and exterior regions.

You can create the area object of a geometric shape and then perform the required operations to create a composite shape. Because the `Area` class implements the `Shape` interface, you can invoke graphics context methods such as `draw()` and `fill()` to render the area.

Creating the Instances of the Area Class

The class Area supports two constructors to create its instances:

```
public Area()
public Area(Shape shape)
```

The constructor without any arguments creates an object that possesses any area. The constructor that takes an argument value of type Shape creates an enclosed area for the specified shape.

Applying Constructive Area Geometry

Constructive area geometry (CAG) is a standard technique in 2D modeling to combine areas of multiple shapes using certain binary operations. This technique creates new area objects by applying add (union), subtract, intersect, and exclusive-OR operations on existing area objects.

Figure 5.6 shows an object that is made up of three separate objects: a rectangle, an arc, and a triangle (general shape). To create this object, initially the arc and rectangle are combined by applying the union operation. Then the resulting shape is combined with the triangle (again, using the union operation) to create the pointer at the end of the shape.

Figure 5.6
A composite object made up of three separate objects.

Next, let's discuss the operations—add (union), subtract, intersect, and exclusive-OR—that can be performed on area objects.

Addition (Union) Operation

By using the addition operation, you can add the specified area to the currently existing geometric area. The class Area supports the following method to perform this operation on the current area by applying the specified area as its argument value:

```
public void add(Area specifiedArea)
```

Subtraction Operation

The subtraction operation subtracts the overlapped or common region of the specified area on the current area object. The class Area supports the following method to perform this operation on the current area object from which the overlapped portion of the specified area is removed.

```
public void subtract(Area specifiedArea)
```

Intersecting Operation

The intersection operation retains only the region that is common to the current and specified area objects. The remaining areas of the shapes are discarded. The following method supports this operation:

```
public void intersect(Area anotherArea)
```

Exclusive-OR Operation

The exclusive-OR operation retains only the region that is not common to the current and specified area objects. Thus, the overlapped region is discarded from the total area. The following method supports this operation:

```
public void exclusiveOr(Area specifiedArea)
```

Testing for the Type of Shape

You can test an area object to find out whether it is made up of a single geometric primitive. To do so, you invoke the following method:

```
public boolean isSingular()
```

You can also test whether the geometric shape of the area object is a rectangle or polygon by invoking the following boolean methods:

```
public boolean isRectangular()
public boolean isPolygonal()
```

Testing Containment and Intersection

You can test an area object composed of multiple shapes to find out whether the boundary of the shape contains a set of coordinates (x, y) of a point. You can also specify the point object of type `Point2D` for the purpose of testing. The following are the supported methods in the `Area` class:

```
public boolean contains(double x, double y)
public boolean contains(Point2D p)
```

Similarly, the following two methods can test whether the bounding box of the area object completely contains the specified rectangle with location (x, y) and size (w, h) (you can also specify the object `rectangle` of type `Rectangle2D`):

```
public boolean contains(double x, double y, double w, double h)
public boolean contains(Rectangle2D rectangle)
```

Next, you can test whether the interior of the area object intersects the interior of a specified rectangle with location (x, y) and size (w, h) (you can also specify the object rectangle of type `Rectangle2D`) by using the following methods:

```
public boolean intersects(double x, double y, double w, double h)
public boolean intersects(Rectangle2D r)
```

You can also test whether the area object is empty—that is, doesn't contain any geometric shape—by calling the following method:

```
public boolean isEmpty()
```

Note that all these boolean methods return the value `true` if the respective operation is satisfied; otherwise, the methods return the value `false`.

Retrieving Boundaries

You can retrieve the low-precision or high-precision bounding box of an area object composed of multiple shapes by invoking the following methods:

```
public Rectangle getBounds()
public Rectangle2D getBounds2D()
```

Retrieving the Path Iterator of a Shape

After you've operated on an area object to arrive at a composite shape, you can invoke the following methods to retrieve the iteration object that provides the path information:

```
public PathIterator getPathIterator(AffineTransform trans)
public PathIterator getPathIterator(AffineTransform trans, double flatness)
```

In these methods, the argument `trans` is the affine transform object that can be applied. In case you do not want to exercise any transformation on this shape, you can apply `null` for this value. The `flatness` argument is the maximum allowable flatness of the curve for flattened sub-paths. Note that the flatness factor is inversely related to the degree of curvature of the curve.

Composite Shapes Example

Listing 5.2 creates the demonstration applet shown in Figure 5.7. Initially, the applet displays two overlapped shapes: a general path as a diamond shape and an ellipse. At the top of the applet is the control panel in which you can select a specific CAG operation by using one of the radio buttons. At the bottom of the applet is the Reset button that returns the canvas to its initial state.

You can choose a CAG operation—add, subtract, intersect, or exclusive-OR—to study its effect. Note that when you perform an operation, the corresponding method is invoked on the general path area object. The elliptical area is passed as an argument to the operation method. Figures 5.8 through 5.11 show the area objects from Figure 5.7 when a CAG operation is selected.

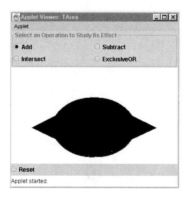

Figure 5.7

An applet used to demonstrate CAG operations.

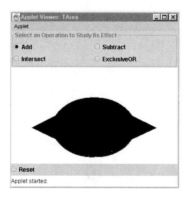

Figure 5.8

Applet demonstrating the add operation.

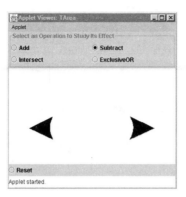

Figure 5.9

Applet demonstrating the subtract operation.

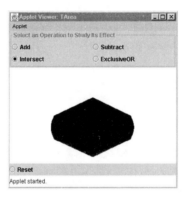

Figure 5.10

Applet demonstrating the intersect operation.

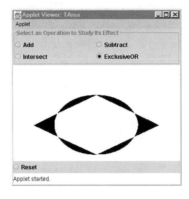

Figure 5.11

Applet demonstrating the exclusive-OR operation.

Listing 5.2   Composite Shapes Example (TArea.java)

```
/*
 * <Applet code=TArea width=350 height=300>
 * </Applet>
 */

import javax.swing.*;
import javax.swing.border.*;
import java.awt.*;
import java.awt.event.*;
import java.awt.geom.*;

public class TArea extends JApplet {
    DrawingCanvas canvas;
    JRadioButton addButton, subtractButton, intersectButton,
                exclusiveORButton, resetButton;

    public void init() {
        // 1. Get the content pane
        Container container = getContentPane();

        // 2. Create a control panel with titled border
        JPanel panel = new JPanel();
        panel.setLayout(new GridLayout(2, 2)); // 2 rows & 2 cols
        TitledBorder border = new TitledBorder(
            "Select an Operation to Study Its Effect");
        panel.setBorder(border);

        // 3. Create radio buttons
        resetButton = new JRadioButton("Reset", true);
```

```java
addButton = new JRadioButton("Add");
subtractButton = new JRadioButton("Subtract");
intersectButton = new JRadioButton("Intersect");
exclusiveORButton = new JRadioButton("ExclusiveOR");

// Group the radio buttons for mutual exclusion
ButtonGroup group = new ButtonGroup();
group.add(resetButton);
group.add(addButton); group.add(subtractButton);
group.add(intersectButton); group.add(exclusiveORButton);
group.add(resetButton);

// Register action listeners to the radio buttons
resetButton.addActionListener(new ActionEventHandler());
addButton.addActionListener(new ActionEventHandler());
subtractButton.addActionListener(new ActionEventHandler());
intersectButton.addActionListener(new ActionEventHandler());
exclusiveORButton.addActionListener(new ActionEventHandler());

// Add the CAG operation buttons to the control panel
panel.add(addButton);
panel.add(subtractButton);
panel.add(intersectButton);
panel.add(exclusiveORButton);

// 4. Add the panel to the applet and reset button separately
// to the applet.
container.add(panel, BorderLayout.NORTH);
container.add(resetButton, BorderLayout.SOUTH);

// 5. Add the drawing canvas to the applet
canvas = new DrawingCanvas();
container.add(canvas);
}

// 6. Definition of the 'DrawingCanvas' class
class DrawingCanvas extends Canvas {
    GeneralPath gp;
    Ellipse2D ellipse;
    Area area1, area2;
    boolean drawFlag = true;
    boolean fillFlag = false;

    // 7. Constructor
    public DrawingCanvas() {
        setBackground(Color.white);
        setSize(350,250); // width and height of canvas
        int w = getWidth(); int h = getHeight();
```

continues

Listing 5.2   continued

```
            // Create area objects from the general path
            // and ellipse objects
            gp = new GeneralPath();
            gp.moveTo(w/8, h/2);
            gp.lineTo(w/2, h/4); gp.lineTo(7*w/8, h/2);
            gp.lineTo(w/2, 3*h/4);
            gp.closePath();
            area1 = new Area(gp);    // General path area object

            ellipse = new Ellipse2D.Double(w/4, h/4, w/2, h/2);
            area2 = new Area(ellipse); // Ellipse area object
        }

    // 8. The Overriding paint method
    public void paint(Graphics g) {
        // Create the graphics context object
        Graphics2D g2D = (Graphics2D) g;
        // Assign a slightly wider stroke
        g2D.setStroke(new BasicStroke(2.0f));

        // This is executed when the paint() method is called
        // initially, or when the reset button is selected.

        if (drawFlag) {
            g2D.draw(area1);
            g2D.draw(area2);
        }

        // The manipulated area object is redrawn in fill style.
        if (fillFlag)
            g2D.fill(area1);
        }
    }

    // 9. Event handler for events from radio buttons
    class ActionEventHandler implements ActionListener {
        public void actionPerformed(ActionEvent e) {
            JRadioButton temp = (JRadioButton) e.getSource();

            // For the add button
            if (temp.equals(addButton)) {
                canvas.area1 = new Area(canvas.gp);
                canvas.area1.add(canvas.area2);
                canvas.drawFlag = false;
                canvas.fillFlag = true;
                canvas.repaint();
            }
```

```
        // For the subtract button
        else if (temp.equals(subtractButton)) {
            canvas.area1 = new Area(canvas.gp);
            canvas.area1.subtract(canvas.area2);
            canvas.drawFlag = false;
            canvas.fillFlag = true;
            canvas.repaint();
        }
        // For the intersect button
        else if (temp.equals(intersectButton)) {
            canvas.area1 = new Area(canvas.gp);
            canvas.area1.intersect(canvas.area2);
            canvas.drawFlag = false;
            canvas.fillFlag = true;
            canvas.repaint();
        }
        // For the exclusiveOR button
        else if (temp.equals(exclusiveORButton)) {
            canvas.area1 = new Area(canvas.gp);
            canvas.area1.exclusiveOr(canvas.area2);
            canvas.drawFlag = false;
            canvas.fillFlag = true;
            canvas.repaint();
        }
        // For the Reset button
        else if (temp.equals(resetButton)) {
            if (canvas.drawFlag == false) {
                canvas.area1 = new Area(canvas.gp);
                canvas.drawFlag = true;
                canvas.fillFlag = false;
                canvas.repaint();
            }
        }
    }
  }
 }
}
```

Code Analysis

The Swing applet TArea declares a reference to the drawing canvas and five JRadioButton references as its fields. Inside the init() method, snippet-1 gets a handle to the applet's content pane. Snippet-2 creates a control panel with titled border. Snippet-3 creates radio button objects for the reset, add, subtract, intersect, and exclusive-OR operations. These controls are added to the button group to form a mutually exclusive set. Next, the controls are registered with suitable action listener objects and added to the panel. Snippet-4 adds the panel and Reset radio button separately to the applet. Snippet-5 creates the drawing canvas and adds it to the applet.

Snippet-6 provides the definition of the drawing canvas. The class `DrawingCanvas` declares the references for a general path object, an ellipse object, two area objects, and certain boolean flags as its fields. Snippet-7 shows the constructor of the class. The constructor initially assigns the background color and a suitable size for the canvas. Next, the snippet creates a general path object and the corresponding area object. Similarly, the ellipse object and its area object are created.

Snippet-8 shows the overriding `paint()` method. Inside this method, the graphics context object is prepared with a suitable stroke width. Next, the area objects are rendered over the canvas. The `if` statement that takes the `drawFlag` renders the areas of both the general path and ellipse when the condition is satisfied. The other `if` statement conditionally renders the filled area. This area is the manipulated area used to create the composite area.

Snippet-9 is the event handler for the events fired by the radio buttons. The implementation method provides the code to execute a specific operation when the corresponding radio button is selected. Inside this method, you will find the conditional statements that manipulate the area object. The manipulations are the `add()`, `subtract()`, `intersect()`, and `exclusiveOr()` operations. After performing a suitable operation, the canvas is repainted with the updated rendering flags. The `if` statement for the Reset button simply resets the flags to draw the areas as they appeared when the applet started.

CHAPTER 6

Platform Fonts and Text Layout

The Java 2D API extends the Java font and text handling features significantly. The developments include enhancements to the Font class existing in the previous releases of JDK, and the introduction of a new text layout mechanism. For example, the Font class now includes functionality to draw various scripts—such as Chinese, Japanese, Roman, and Devanagari—with the appropriate base lines.

The text layout mechanism helps to display text that can receive user inputs. The text layout also supports highlighting text, using cursors, and building custom text components.

For example, you can build text boxes, callout boxes, and format callout boxes for a sophisticated word processor program. A text box allows the user to embed a text string in a drawing. A callout box is used to describe a component in a drawing by using text. The format callout box is used to format the selected text in a callout box.

NOTE

The Swing library already provides a set of lightweight user interface components, such as a text field, password field, text area, text pane, and editor pane. These components are discussed in the book *Pure JFC: Swing* from Sams. You can determine whether any of these components suit your requirements.

The text layout mechanism enables you to apply suitable affine transformations on a specified font to create newly derived fonts. Basically, the text layout mechanism applies the affine transform to the character shapes (also called glyphs) to generate the transformed shapes.

The first part of this chapter focuses on the enhanced font support to harness the fonts from the given platform. The next section discusses the text layout mechanism. That section contains topics such as hit testing, highlighting, and positioning and moving the caret or cursor. The remaining sections will focus on how to make use of various text and graphic attributes, and create paragraphs of text.

Working with Fonts

The Java 2D enhances the existing font support to create and retrieve various attributes that help to display characters and text with more sophisticated features. The enhanced Font class encapsulates certain new properties and operations that are added to the already existing features in the class. For example, the base line property is useful when laying out text in scripts such as Chinese, Japanese, Korean, Devanagari, and Roman.

The Font class is available in the package java.awt. The instances of the Font class can represent the fonts existing on a platform. Thus, you can retrieve the fonts on a platform and store them in an array of type Font.

Font Terminology

Before you know how to retrieve the fonts on a platform, you must understand the font terminology. When creating font objects, you'll encounter three types of names: the *font name* or *font face name*, the *family name*, and the *logical name*. These names are defined as follows:

- Font name and font face name—These two names mean the same thing. They refer to the name of a font based on its appearance. Various fonts or font faces are available on a given platform. Sample font face names are Arial, Arial Black, Arial Rounded Black, and Arial Narrow. (The output of the sample program in Listing 6.1 shows various font faces available on the Windows 95 operating system.)

NOTE

You can use the font face name while creating a font object. The font face name is commonly used to refer to a font, rather than using its other names.

- Family name—The family name refers to the family of a collection of font faces on a platform. Thus, the font families are specific to a platform. For example, Arial, Book Antique, and Courier New are family names. A font family contains different font faces that are based on different typographic styles. For example, Arial and Arial Narrow are two different font faces in the Arial font family. These fonts have different font faces (plain and narrow), although the general look of the Arial family is preserved.

- Logical name—This name refers to a particular font available in a system like the Abstract Windowing Toolkit (AWT). For example, *dialog* is a logical font name. The logical name is independent of the platform. The logical font names are mapped onto the font names available on a platform. This is the name used to specify a font in the previous releases of JDK. In Java 2D, you must use the font face names to refer to fonts, rather than using the logical names.

Fonts have sizes that are expressed in points. The point sizes are specified by using positive integers. The default point size used by a Font object is 12.

Fonts also use styles such as plain, italic, bold, bold italic, and so on. The font styles can be specified directly by using integer bit masks such as PLAIN, ITALIC, and BOLD, which are available as fields of the Font class. You can also specify the new style by using the bitwise operation; for example, you can indicate both BOLD and ITALIC by using BOLD¦ITALIC.

In addition to these styles, the Java 2D allows you to create more styles of fonts by applying the affine transforms on font objects (see the sample program given in Listing 6.1). You can also derive new fonts by specifying the size, style, affine transform, and other font attributes. (See "Deriving New Fonts from the Given Font," later in this chapter.)

Text strings made up of characters are laid out in rows to create a message of statements. To lay out text in multiple rows, a measurement system must address the dimensions of a character and properly position characters in rows. Figure 6.1 illustrates the measurements or metrics of a font to exactly position text strings.

Figure 6.1

Illustration of font measurements.

The following terms define the font measurements given in Figure 6.1:

- Base Line—An imaginary horizontal line that passes at the base of various characters as shown in Figure 6.1. For example, the letters *F*, *l*, and *a* rest their bases on this line. Characters such as *g* also sit on the base line, but their bottom portions descend below the base line.
- Ascent—The vertical distance between the top of the font and the base line.
- Descent—The vertical distance from the base line to the bottom of the font.

- Leading—The distance from the line at the descent of a character (such as *g*) to the top of the next row of characters. If you set the leading to zero, adjacent rows will touch each other.

Creating Fonts

The Font class supports two constructors to create font objects. The first constructor requires the font face name (or the logical name, as in JDK 1.1), font style, and font size. The second constructor uses the font attributes that are of type Map. The following are these constructors:

```
public Font(String name, int style, int size)
public Font(Map attributes)
```

Retrieving Various Font Names

The font family name, font face name, and logical name were defined previously. You can invoke the following methods to retrieve the respective names:

```
public String getFamily()
```
retrieves the font family name of the current font. Sample font family names include Arial, Book Antiqua, Courier New, and Helvetica.

```
public String getFontName()
```
retrieves the font face name of the current font. Sample font faces are Arial Bold, Helvetica Bold, Arial Italic, and so on.

```
public String getName()
```
retrieves the logical name of the current font as dialog, serif, sans serif, and so on.

Retrieving Platform Fonts

Most often, you might prefer to use the fonts provided on a platform. The java.awt.GraphicsEnvironment class helps to retrieve the fonts available to a Java application when it is running on a platform. You can obtain an instance of the graphics environment available on a platform by calling the following static method:

```
public static GraphicsEnvironment
getLocalGraphicsEnvironment()
```

The font resources need not be available on the local machine; instead, they can reside on a remote machine connected through a network. The following methods help to retrieve the fonts on a platform:

```
public abstract Font[] getAllFonts()
```
retrieves an array containing instances of all fonts available in the platform. The font size is one point. The application developer can change the sizes of fonts to realistic sizes.

```
public abstract String[] getAvailableFontFamilyNames()
```
returns a `String` array that contains the names of all font families available on a platform.

```
public abstract String[] getAvailableFontFamilyNames(Locale locale)
```
retrieves a `String` array that contains the localized names of all font families available on a platform. This method requires the `locale` object as its argument.

NOTE

The typical implementation approach with the available font family names on a platform is to first retrieve all font family names. Then, apply a certain font style and size to a font family to derive the font face you're interested in.

Deriving New Fonts from the Given Font

A Java application can alter the size of a font and assign various other font attributes by invoking one of the `deriveFont()` methods on the font object. The following are the overloaded `deriveFont()` methods available in the `Font` class.

```
public Font deriveFont(float size)
```
creates a new font object by creating a copy of the current font object and applying the specified size to the font. The replicated font is then returned. Note that you must often apply this method to the platform fonts because their size is only one point when they are retrieved.

```
public Font deriveFont(int style)
```
creates a new font by creating a copy of the current font object, and then applying a new style to it. The replicated font is then returned.

```
public Font deriveFont(int style, float size)
```
creates a font object by creating a copy of the current font object and applying the specified font style and font size. The replicated object is returned by the method.

```
public Font deriveFont(AffineTransform trans)
```
creates a font object by creating a copy of the current font object and applying an affine transform to it. The affine transform geometrically transforms the current font to create a new font.

```
public Font deriveFont(int style, AffineTransform trans)
```
creates a new font object by copying the current font object and applying the specified style and transform. The affine transform geometrically transforms the current font to create new shapes by shearing, rotating, and scaling.

```
public Font deriveFont(Map attributes)
```
creates a font object by copying the current font object and applying a set of font attributes represented by the Map interface.

Platform Fonts Example

Listing 6.1 shows a sample program that retrieves various platform fonts. These fonts are displayed in the pull-down list of a combo box to allow selection of a font. The combo box is attached to a control panel. The control panel also displays two more combo boxes in which the user can select a font style and size. Whenever the user selects a new parameter, the program creates a new font face using these parameters. The new font face is applied to the text that is displayed in the display panel. Figure 6.2 shows the output of the program.

Figure 6.2

An application using platform fonts.

Listing 6.1   Retrieving and Modifying Platform Fonts (TFont.java)

```java
import javax.swing.*;
import javax.swing.event.*;
import javax.swing.border.*;
import java.awt.*;
import java.awt.event.*;
import java.awt.geom.*;

class TFont extends JFrame {
    DisplayPanel displayPanel;
    JComboBox fontsBox, fontStylesBox, fontSizesBox;

    String[] fontStyleLabels = {"Plain", "Bold", "Italic", "Bold&Italic"};
    int BOLDITALIC = Font.BOLD¦Font.ITALIC;
    int[] fontStyles = {Font.PLAIN, Font.BOLD, Font.ITALIC, BOLDITALIC};
    String[] fontSizeLabels = {"8", "9", "10", "11", "12",
                               "14", "18", "25", "36", "72"};

    public TFont() {
        // 1. Assign a title to the frame and get a handle on
        // the frame's content pane
```

```
super("TFont");
Container container = getContentPane();

// 2. Create a display panel and add it to the frame
displayPanel = new DisplayPanel();
container.add(displayPanel);

// 3. Create a control panel with titled border
JPanel controlPanel = new JPanel();
controlPanel.setLayout(new GridLayout(1,3));
TitledBorder border = new TitledBorder(
    "Select a Font, Font Style, and Font Size...");
controlPanel.setBorder(border);

// 4. Create combo boxes for font names, styles, and sizes
fontsBox = new JComboBox(displayPanel.fontFamilyNames);
fontsBox.setSelectedItem("Arial"); // default selection
fontsBox.addActionListener(new ComboBoxListener());

fontStylesBox = new JComboBox(fontStyleLabels);
fontStylesBox.addActionListener(new ComboBoxListener());

fontSizesBox = new JComboBox(fontSizeLabels);
fontSizesBox.setSelectedItem("36");
fontSizesBox.addActionListener(new ComboBoxListener());

// 5. Add the combo boxes to the control panel and add the
// panel to the main frame.
controlPanel.add(fontsBox);
controlPanel.add(fontStylesBox);
controlPanel.add(fontSizesBox);
container.add(BorderLayout.SOUTH, controlPanel);

// 6. Add a frame closing listener and display the frame
addWindowListener(new WindowEventHandler());
pack();
setSize(400, 250);
show(); // Display the frame
}

// 7. The main method...
public static void main(String arg[]) {
    new TFont();
}

// 8. Class to handle closing of the frame
class WindowEventHandler extends WindowAdapter {
```

continues

Listing 6.1   continued

```
    public void windowClosing(WindowEvent e) {
        System.exit(0);
    }
}


// 9. Combo box listener to handle font name, style and size
// selections in the respective combo boxes.
class ComboBoxListener implements ActionListener {
    public void actionPerformed(ActionEvent e) {
        JComboBox tempBox = (JComboBox) e.getSource();

        if (tempBox.equals(fontsBox)) {
            displayPanel.fontFamilyName =
                        (String) tempBox.getSelectedItem();
            displayPanel.repaint();
        }
        else if (tempBox.equals(fontStylesBox)) {
            displayPanel.fontStyle =
                        fontStyles[tempBox.getSelectedIndex()];
            displayPanel.repaint();
        }
        else if (tempBox.equals(fontSizesBox)) {
            displayPanel.fontSize =
                        Integer.parseInt((String)
tempBox.getSelectedItem());
            displayPanel.repaint();
        }
    }
}


// 10. Definition of display panel
class DisplayPanel extends JPanel {
    String displayText;
    Font currentFont;
    String fontFamilyName;
    int fontStyle;
    int fontSize;

    GraphicsEnvironment ge;
    String[] fontFamilyNames;

    // 11. Constructor
    public DisplayPanel() {
        // Logo to be displayed on the panel
        displayText = "Java 2D Fonts";
        fontFamilyName = "Arial";
        fontStyle = Font.PLAIN;
```

```
        fontSize = 36;

        // Retrieve all the font family names from the platform
        System.out.println("Loading Fonts... Please Wait...");
        ge = GraphicsEnvironment.getLocalGraphicsEnvironment();
        fontFamilyNames = ge.getAvailableFontFamilyNames();

        setBackground(Color.white);  // For canvas background color
        setSize(400, 225);  // Canvas width and height
    }

    // 12. The update method...
    public void update(Graphics g) {
        g.clearRect(0, 0, getWidth(), getHeight());
        paintComponent(g);
    }

    // 13. The painting method...
    public void paintComponent(Graphics g) {
        super.paintComponent(g);

        // 14. Create the graphics context object
        Graphics2D g2D = (Graphics2D) g;

        // 15. Prepare the current font and apply it to
        // the display text.
        currentFont = new Font(fontFamilyName,
                               fontStyle,
                               fontSize);
        g2D.setFont(currentFont);
        g2D.drawString(displayText, 25, 100);
    }
  }
}
```

Code Analysis

The class TFont extends JFrame and serves as the main frame. This class declares a display panel and three combo boxes. The display panel shows a text string with the selected font. The combo boxes allow the user to select three font attributes: the font name, font style, and font size.

Inside the constructor of the TFont class, snippet-1 assigns a title to the frame and then obtains a handle to the frame's content pane. Snippet-2 creates a display panel and adds it to the frame. Snippet-3 creates a control panel with a titled border. Three combo boxes are created as shown in snippet-4. Snippet-5 adds the combo boxes to the control panel. Snippet-6 registers a frame closing listener with the frame and then displays the frame at a suitable size. Snippet-7 is the main method. Snippet-8 defines the window closing listener.

Snippet-9 shows the combo box listener to handle the selections of font name, style, and size. Inside the `actionPerformed()` method, the code finds out which combo box has fired the action event and then stores the selection in a suitable data member of the display panel. Next, the `repaint()` method is called.

Snippet-10 defines the `DisplayPanel` class. This class declares the font name, font style, and font size as data members. You will also find the graphics environment and array of font family names. Inside the constructor shown in snippet-11, the text to be displayed is initialized along with the associated font parameters. Then the font family names are retrieved from the platform by using the `getAvailableFontFamilyNames()` method from the `GraphicsEnvironment` class.

Snippet-12 is the `update()` method that clears the background of the display panel and then calls `paintComponent()` method. Snippet-13 shows the `paintComponent()` method. Snippet-14 creates the 2D graphics context. Snippet-15 creates the font object that is assigned to the graphics context. Finally, the string is displayed with the selected font.

Laying Out Text

A text layout is a graphics layout mechanism meant for displaying or printing styled text. The class `TextLayout` represents a text layout object that encapsulates a number of text handling features and management capabilities. This class is stored in the package `java.awt.font`.

Using the text layout mechanism, you can handle bidirectional text, hit testing, caret positioning and moving, and highlighting text. Bidirectional text can display the characters running from left-to-right as well as right-to-left. For example, in Arabic, the numbers run from left-to-right and the letters run from right-to-left.

The text layout also allows developers to retrieve the baselines provided for different scripts. For example, scripts such as Roman, Devanagari, Chinese, Korean, and Japanese use different baselines. The Devanagari script uses a hanging baseline, whereas the Chinese, Korean, and Japanese scripts use a center baseline.

You can also use the text layout for retrieving the font metrics, such as ascent, descent, and advance. The following sections will discuss how to create text layout objects and work with various methods from the `TextLayout` class.

Shaping, Ordering, and Positioning Text

The text layout mechanism creates and positions the shapes for a text string based on the specified font and font rendering context. The font rendering context allows you to apply an affine transformation to the text shape to create as sophisticated (derived) shapes as the user wants (see the program given in Listing 6.2). After the shape of text is created, it is displayed or printed with the proper positioning order.

The shapes that are created, positioned, and displayed for each character of a text are called *glyphs*. Each character might require more than one glyph for its shape, as in the case of **a'**, where **a** and **'** are two separate glyphs constituting a single character. A single glyph can also be made from one or more characters, as in **fi**. Here **f** and **i** are joined to form a single shape. Glyphs of this sort are called *ligatures*. Various font faces are basically collections of glyphs and ligatures. The shape, size, and positioning of a glyph depends on the font and font rendering context.

For languages other than English, glyphs and ligatures are created before the text is displayed. In languages such as Arabic, a single character can take shapes depending on its connection with the adjacent characters. A character can have different glyphs when it is not connected in the text, or connected to the character on its left side or right side, or connected to characters on both sides.

Creating TextLayout Instances

The `TextLayout` class supports three constructors to create objects. The constructor

```
public TextLayout(String text, Font font, FontRenderContext frc)
```

creates a layout object using the `text` string to be displayed, a suitable `font`, and the font rendering context `frc`. The text string must be a single paragraph of text. The bidirectional algorithm used for laying out requires the entire paragraph.

The font rendering context measures the text metrics correctly. The font rendering context is represented by the class `FontRenderContext`, which is stored in the package `java.awt.font`. You can create an object of this class using its only `public` constructor:

```
public FontRenderContext(AffineTransform tx,
                         boolean isAntiAliased,
                         boolean usesFractionalMetrics)
```

This constructor requires an optional `AffineTransform` object as its first argument. The other two arguments are boolean values that determine whether the newly constructed object has anti-aliasing and uses fractional metrics.

The second constructor of the `TextLayout` requires the argument values `text`, font `attributes`, and font rendering context `frc`, as in

```
public TextLayout(String text, Map attributes,
FontRenderContext frc)
```

The constructor uses the attributes map to style the specified text. The font rendering context supplies the metrics of the text.

The third constructor uses the attributed character iterator and the font rendering context. The `AttributedCharacterIterator` class (stored in the `java.text` package) allows iteration through both text and related attribute information. The constructor is

```
public TextLayout(AttributedCharacterIterator text, FontRenderContext frc)
```

Rendering Text

After you create a text layout object specifying the text, font for styling, and font render context for the text metrics, you can render the text at the specified location on a graphics context. The following method supports this operation:

```
public void draw(Graphics2D g2, float x, float y)
```

Text Layout Example

Listing 6.2 shows a sample application that demonstrates how to apply geometric (affine) transformations on text using the text layout support in Java 2D. The application frame displays a text string and a set of sliders to translate, rotate, scale, and shear the text string. You can observe how a transformed (derived) font is created by applying various affine transforms. Figure 6.3 shows the output of this program.

NOTE

When a new affine transform is applied to text, it results in a new derived font. Thus, each transformed text shape that results in this program from adjusting the control sliders represents a derived font.

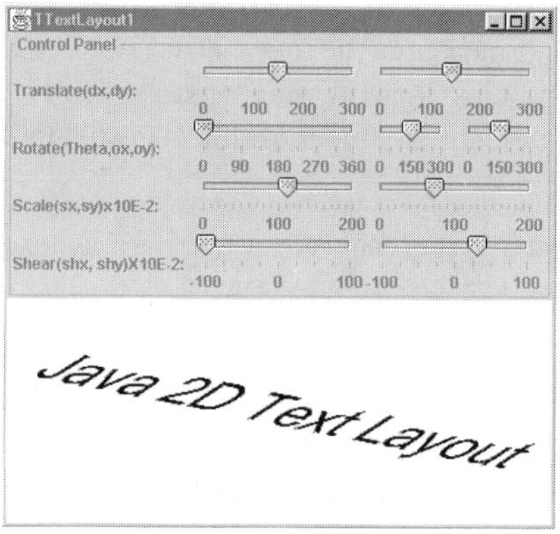

Figure 6.3

An application using text layout to create transformed fonts.

Listing 6.2   Applying Affine Transforms to Text (TTextLayout1.java)
```java
import javax.swing.*;
import javax.swing.event.*;
import javax.swing.border.*;
import java.awt.*;
import java.awt.event.*;
import java.awt.font.*;
import java.awt.geom.*;
```

```java
public class TTextLayout1 extends JFrame {
    DisplayPanel displayPanel;
    JSlider slider, slider1, slider2, slider3,
            slider4, slider5, slider6, slider7,
            slider8, slider9;

    // Translation distances in x- and y- directions
    double transX = 0.0, transY = 0.0;

    // Rotation parameters: Theta and center of rotation.
    double rotateTheta = 0.0, rotateX = 150.0, rotateY = 150.0;

    // Scale factors in the x- and y- directions
    double scaleX = 1.0, scaleY = 1.0;

    // Shear factors in the x- and y- directions
    double shearX = 0.0, shearY = 0.0 ;

    public TTextLayout1() {
        // 1. Assign a title and get the content pane
        super("TTextLayout1");
        Container container = getContentPane();

        // 2. Add a control panel with titled border
        JPanel controlPanel = new JPanel();
        controlPanel.setLayout(new GridLayout(4, 3));
        container.add(controlPanel, BorderLayout.NORTH);
        TitledBorder border = new TitledBorder("Control Panel");
        controlPanel.setBorder(border);

        // 3. Add various controls to the panel to adjust translation,
        // rotation, scaling and shearing.
        JLabel label1 = new JLabel("Translate(dx,dy): ");
        JLabel label2 = new JLabel("Rotate(Theta,ox,oy): ");
        JLabel label3 = new JLabel("Scale(sx,sy)x10E-2:");
        JLabel label4 = new JLabel("Shear(shx, shy)X10E-2: ");

        // To control translation
        controlPanel.add(label1);
        setSlider(controlPanel, JSlider.HORIZONTAL,
                0, 300, 150, 100, 50);
        slider1 = slider;
        setSlider(controlPanel, JSlider.HORIZONTAL,
                0, 300, 150, 100, 50);
        slider2 = slider;

        // To control rotation
        controlPanel.add(label2);
```

continues

Listing 6.2   continued

```
        setSlider(controlPanel, JSlider.HORIZONTAL,
                0, 360, 0, 90, 45);
        slider3 = slider;

        JPanel subPanel = new JPanel();
        subPanel.setLayout(new GridLayout(1, 2));

        setSlider(subPanel, JSlider.HORIZONTAL,
                0, 300, 150, 150, 50);
        slider4 = slider;
        setSlider(subPanel, JSlider.HORIZONTAL,
                0, 300, 150, 150, 50);
        slider5 = slider;
        controlPanel.add(subPanel);

        // To control scaling
        controlPanel.add(label3);
        setSlider(controlPanel, JSlider.HORIZONTAL,
                0, 200, 100, 100, 10);
        slider6 = slider;
        setSlider(controlPanel, JSlider.HORIZONTAL,
                0, 200, 100, 100, 10);
        slider7 = slider;

        // To control shearing
        controlPanel.add(label4);
        setSlider(controlPanel, JSlider.HORIZONTAL,
                -100, 100, 0, 100, 25);
        slider8 = slider;
        setSlider(controlPanel, JSlider.HORIZONTAL,
                -100, 100, 0, 100, 25);
        slider9 = slider;

        // 4. Add the display panel to the frame.
        displayPanel = new DisplayPanel();
        container.add(displayPanel);

        // 5. Add a frame closing listener and display the frame
        addWindowListener(new WindowEventHandler());
        setSize(400, 400);
        show(); // Display the frame
    }

    // 6. The main method...
    public static void main(String arg[]) {
        new TTextLayout1();
    }
```

```
// 7. Code to handle closing of the frame
class WindowEventHandler extends WindowAdapter {
    public void windowClosing(WindowEvent e) {
        System.exit(0);
    }
}


// 8. Creates a slider object with the required tick marks
public void setSlider(JPanel panel, int orientation,
                      int minimumValue, int maximumValue,
                      int initValue,
                      int majorTickSpacing,
                      int minorTickSpacing) {
    slider = new JSlider(orientation,
                         minimumValue, maximumValue,
                         initValue);
    slider.setPaintTicks(true);
    slider.setMajorTickSpacing(majorTickSpacing);
    slider.setMinorTickSpacing(minorTickSpacing);
    slider.setPaintLabels(true);
    slider.addChangeListener(new SliderListener());
    panel.add(slider);
}


// 9. Slider listener class; Methods retrieve the values from
// the sliders and assign them to the respective parameters.
// These parameters are used to apply to the font rendering context.
// Next call the repaint() method on canvas.
class SliderListener implements ChangeListener {
    public void stateChanged(ChangeEvent e) {
        JSlider tempSlider = (JSlider) e.getSource();

        if (tempSlider.equals(slider1)) {
            transX = slider1.getValue()-150.0;
            displayPanel.repaint();
        }
        else if (tempSlider.equals(slider2)) {
            transY = slider2.getValue()-150.0;
            displayPanel.repaint();
        }
        else if (tempSlider.equals(slider3)) {
            rotateTheta = slider3.getValue()*Math.PI/180;
            displayPanel.repaint();
        }
        else if (tempSlider.equals(slider4)) {
            rotateX = slider4.getValue();
            displayPanel.repaint();
        }
```

continues

Listing 6.2   continued

```
        else if (tempSlider.equals(slider5)) {
            rotateY = slider5.getValue();
            displayPanel.repaint();
        }
        else if (tempSlider.equals(slider6)) {
            if (slider6.getValue() != 0.0) {
                scaleX = slider6.getValue()/100.0;
                displayPanel.repaint();
            }
        }
        else if (tempSlider.equals(slider7)) {
            if (slider7.getValue() != 0.0) {
                scaleY = slider7.getValue()/100.0;
                displayPanel.repaint();
            }
        }
        else if (tempSlider.equals(slider8)) {
            shearX = slider8.getValue()/100.0;
            displayPanel.repaint();
        }
        else if (tempSlider.equals(slider9)) {
            shearY = slider9.getValue()/100.0;
            displayPanel.repaint();
        }
    }
}

// 10. Definition of the display panel
class DisplayPanel extends JPanel {
    // Constructor
    public DisplayPanel() {
        setBackground(Color.white);
        setSize(400, 200);
    }

    // The update method...
    public void update(Graphics g) {
        g.clearRect(0, 0, getWidth(), getHeight());
        paintComponent(g);
    }

    // The painting method...
    public void paintComponent(Graphics g) {
        super.paintComponent(g);
        Graphics2D g2D = (Graphics2D) g;

        // Assign the translation, rotation, scaling and shearing
        // to the affine transform.
```

```
            AffineTransform af = new AffineTransform();
            af.translate(transX, transY);
            af.rotate(rotateTheta, rotateX, rotateY);
            af.scale(scaleX, scaleY);
            af.shear(shearX, shearY);
            // Apply the affine transform to a fort rendering context.
            FontRenderContext frc =  new FontRenderContext(
                                    af, false, false);
            Font font = new Font("Dialog", Font.PLAIN, 36);
            // Assign the font and font rendering context to a text layout
            TextLayout layout = new TextLayout(
                                    "Java 2D Text Layout", font, frc);
            layout.draw(g2D, 25, 75); // draw the layout string
        }
    }
}
```

Code Analysis

The class TTextLayout1 creates the main frame by extending the JFrame class. This class declares a display panel and a set of control sliders as its fields. The class also declares initial parameters for translation, rotation, scaling, and shearing as its fields. These parameters are initialized with the default values when the main frame appears.

Inside the constructor, snippet-1 assigns a title to the frame and retrieves its content pane. Snippet-2 creates a control panel and adds it to the main frame. Snippet-3 creates the control sliders for translation, rotation, scaling, and shearing, and adds them to the control panel. Snippet-4 adds the display panel to the main frame. Snippet-5 registers a window closing listener to the frame and displays it at a suitable size. Snippet-6 is the main method that creates an instance of the main frame. Snippet-7 defines the window listener for closing the frame. Snippet-8 shows the method to create a slider and add it to the control panel.

Snippet-9 defines the slider listener class. The implementation method stateChanged() finds out which slider has been operated, and then assigns the slider value to the corresponding parameter declared in the display panel. Then it calls the repaint() method to display the effect of the change in slider value. The stateChanged() method implements this logic for the control sliders used for translation, rotation, scaling, and shearing.

Snippet-10 defines the display panel class. This class encapsulates the update() method to clear the panel background and then calls the paintComponent() method. The paintComponent() method initially sets up the 2D graphics context. Then it assigns the new parameters values obtained from the slider controls to the affine transform. Next, the affine transform is used to create the font rendering context object. Then the method creates a text layout object using the text string, font rendering context, and font. Finally, the text string is displayed by invoking the draw() method on the text layout object.

Detecting User Inputs over Text

Detecting user inputs, such as mouse clicks over text, is a common requirement in a variety of programs. For example, editors locate the insertion cursor (or caret) at the position of the mouse click in text. Similarly, a user can drag the mouse over a certain length of text to highlight that portion. In order to implement features of that sort in a program, the first step is to detect the inputs over text.

The classes `TextLayout` and `TextHitInfo` encapsulate the necessary operations for detecting user inputs or hits over the specified text. The following methods from the `TextLayout` class retrieve the `TextHitInfo` objects:

```
public TextHitInfo hitTestChar(float x, float y)
public TextHitInfo hitTestChar(float x, float y, Rectangle2D bounds)
```

These methods require the point coordinates (x, y) to retrieve the corresponding `TextHitInfo` objects. The bounds object is the bounding rectangle of the text layout. A point outside the bounds of the text layout maps to hits on the leading edge of the first logical character, or the trailing edge of the last logical character. Typically, the (x, y) coordinates represent the point where a mouse click occurs.

Using the `TextHitInfo` object that has been retrieved, you can retrieve the insertion index by invoking the following method on the `TextHitInfo` object (see Listing 6.3):

```
public int getInsertionIndex()
```

The return integer represents the character index if the leading edge of the character has been hit, or one greater than the character index if the trailing edge has been hit. If you want to retrieve the character index, the following method may be invoked:

```
public int getCharIndex()
```

Here is some typical hit-testing code that uses the location of the mouse click to initialize the insertion index:

```
public void mouseClicked(MouseEvent e) {
    // Create the hit info object corresponding to the mouse click
    hitInfo = layout.hitTestChar(e.getX(), e.getY(), bounds);

    // Retrieve the insertion index.
    hit = hitInfo.getInsertionIndex();
}
```

Displaying and Moving Carets

A caret (or insertion point marker) is often displayed in a text editor to indicate the position at which characters of text will be typed or where a piece of text will be inserted. Carets have features such as shape, position, and angle. The `TextLayout` class manages the information for these features. This class allows you to easily display carets in simple text in one direction as well as in complex text layouts, such as those using bidirectional text. The text layout also controls the angle of a caret, to suitably display it for font styles that are angled (as in the case of italic text). The following methods retrieve the caret shapes, attributes, and other information:

`public Shape getCaretShape(TextHitInfo hit)`
retrieves a `Shape` object representing the caret generated at the specified hit inside the natural bounds of this layout.

`public Shape[] getCaretShapes(int offset)`
retrieves two carets in the `Shape` array; the fist element in the array is a strong caret and the second element is a weak caret. This method uses the default caret policy and the natural bounds of the text layout. The default caret policy is used when the developer does not specify any caret policy. The argument `offset` is an offset to the text layout.

`public Shape getCaretShape(TextHitInfo hit, Rectangle2D bounds)`
retrieves a `Shape` object that represents the caret generated at the specified `hit` inside the specified `bounds`.

`public Shape[] getCaretShapes(int offset, Rectangle2D bounds,`
                      `TextLayout.CaretPolicy policy)`
retrieves two types of carets: strong and weak. The first element in the array is the strong caret, and the second element is the weak caret. The argument `offset` is the offset to the text layout. `bounds` represents the rectangular bounds to which the caret can extend, and `policy` represents the caret policy.

`public Shape[] getCaretShapes(int offset, Rectangle2D bounds)`
returns the caret paths corresponding to the strong and weak carets. The method uses the default caret policy.

`public float[] getCaretInfo(TextHitInfo hit, Rectangle2D bounds)`
retrieves the caret information about its `hit` when a hit is performed on a caret in the text layout. The first element of the array is the intersection of the caret with the baseline. The second element of the array is the slope (run/rise) of the caret.

`public float[] getCaretInfo(TextHitInfo hit)`
also retrieves the information about the caret `hit`. This method makes use of the natural bounds of the current text layout.

Retrieving Measurement Information

For the text layout that has been prepared for a text paragraph, you can retrieve various measurements as follows.

`public float getAdvance()`
retrieves the distance from the origin to the specific character position in the line direction. This distance is referred as the *advance*.

```
public float getVisibleAdvance()
```
retrieves the visual advance, which is the advance of the text layout minus trailing whitespace.

```
public float getAscent()
```
retrieves the ascent of the text layout. The *ascent* is the distance from the top of the text layout to the baseline. Its value is either positive or zero.

```
public float getDescent()
```
retrieves the descent of the text layout. The *descent* is the distance from the baseline to the bottom of the text layout. Its value is also either positive or zero.

```
public float getLeading()
```
retrieves the leading of the text layout. The *leading* is the spacing between two consecutive lines in the layout.

Finding the Direction of the Text Layout

The following methods indicate the direction of a text layout.

```
public boolean isLeftToRight()
```
returns the boolean value `true` if the text layout has a left-to-right base direction. If the text layout has a right-to-left base direction, the method returns `false`.

```
public boolean isVertical()
```
returns the boolean value `true` if the text layout is vertical; otherwise, the method returns `false`.

Retrieving the Bounds of the Text Layout

You can retrieve the bounds of a text layout by using the method

```
public Rectangle2D getBounds()
```

This method returns the bounding rectangle of type `Rectangle2D`.

Retrieving Character Information

The `TextLayout` class provides two methods to retrieve the number of characters in the text layout and the character level or position at a specified index. The following are the respective methods to perform these operations:

```
public int getCharacterCount()
public byte getCharacterLevel(int index)
```

Selecting Text by Highlighting

Highlighting is the process of making certain segments of text stand out, to attract the attention of the user. Highlighting normally involves changing the background of a text segment by using a prominent color. In many editors, selected text is highlighted by using a black background color and reversing the text foreground color to white. (This is basically a reversal of video for the highlighted text.)

Depending on the context, highlighting in bidirectional text can be either of two types, as follows:

- Logical highlighting—The selected text is contiguous and the highlighted area can be discontiguous.
- Visual highlighting—Multiple text segments are selected; however, the highlighted region is always contiguous.

Following are the methods for highlighting text from the `TextLayout` class.

```
public Shape getLogicalHighlightShape(int firstEndpoint,
                                      int secondEndpoint,
                                      Rectangle2D bounds)
```

retrieves a `Shape` object that encloses the logical selection in the specified range, extended to the specified `bounds`. The `firstEndpoint` is an endpoint in the range of selection. The `secondEndpoint` is the other endpoint of the selection. Note that the `secondEndpoint` can be less then the `firstEndpoint`. The `firstEndpoint` and `secondEndpoint` are usually retrieved through hit detection over text while highlighting (see Listing 6.3). The argument `bounds` is the bounding rectangle of the selection extent.

```
public Shape getLogicalHighlightShape(int firstEndpoint,
                                      int secondEndpoint)
```

also retrieves the `Shape` of the logical selection for highlighting. This method uses the original bounds of the text layout.

You can retrieve the shape that encloses the visual selection by using the following methods.

```
public Shape getVisualHighlightShape(TextHitInfo firstEndpoint,
                                     TextHitInfo secondEndpoint,
                                     Rectangle2D bounds)
```

requires the `TextHitInfo` objects and a bounds object of type `Rectangle2D` as arguments. An overloaded form of this method that uses the original bounds of the text layout is

```
public Shape getVisualHighlightShape(TextHitInfo firstEndpoint,
                                     TextHitInfo secondEndpoint)
```

The following code snippets illustrate how to implement highlighting of text:

```
// Create the highlighted shape using the hits over text
Shape hilight = layout.getLogicalHighlightShape(hit1, hit2);

// Apply translation transformation to shift the origin, if necessary.
hilight = at.createTransformedShape(hilight);

// Assign the highlight color and draw the filled-in shape of highlight.
g2.setColor(Color.lightGray);
g2.fill(hilight);
```

Hit Testing, Carets, and Highlighting Example

Listing 6.3 shows a program that demonstrates various operations such as hit testing over a text string, inserting carets, and highlighting selected text. The user can click the mouse over a character in the text to bring the caret to the location of the character. Basically, the mouse clicks are detected using hit testing methods provided in the TextLayout and HitTestInfo classes. The application also shows the code to create carets and move them over the text. Next, by dragging the mouse over a text segment, the user can select text by highlighting. Figure 6.4 shows the output of the program when a text segment is selected.

NOTE

If you change the font of the displayed text in this program to the italic style, the text layout will angle the caret to make it suitable to the font style.

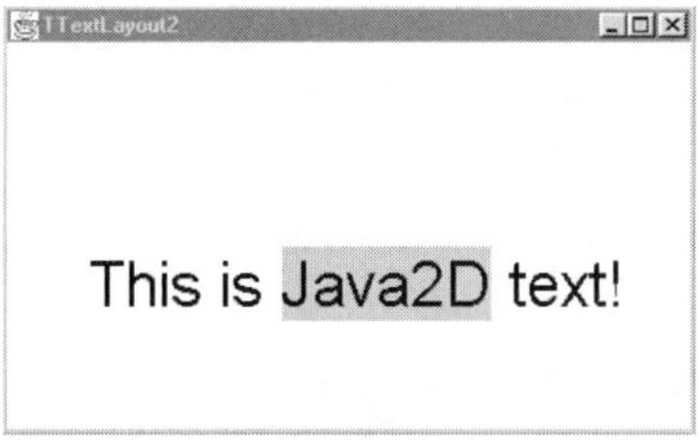

Figure 6.4

Demonstration of hit testing, carets, and highlighting.

Listing 6.3   Hit Testing, Inserting Carets, and Highlighting Selected Text (TTextLayout2.java)

```
import java.awt.*;
import java.awt.event.*;
import javax.swing.*;
import java.awt.font.*;
```

```
import java.awt.geom.*;

public class TTextLayout2 extends JFrame
    // 1. Constructor
    public TTextLayout2(String title) {
        super(title);
        setBackground(Color.white);
    }

    // 2. The main method...
    public static void main(String arg[]) {
        // Create a TextLayout2 object which is a frame
        TTextLayout2 frame = new TTextLayout2("TTextLayout2");

        // Add a listener to close the frame
        frame.addWindowListener(new WindowAdapter() {
            public void windowClosing(WindowEvent e) {System.exit(0);}
        });

        // Add the display panel to the frame
        frame.getContentPane().add("Center", new DisplayPanel());

        // Show the frame with a suitable size
        frame.pack();
        frame.setSize(new Dimension(400,300));
        frame.show();
    }
}

// 3. Definition of the display panel
class DisplayPanel extends JPanel {
    TextLayout layout;
    FontRenderContext frc;
    Font font;
    Rectangle2D rect;
    float rx, ry, rw, rh;

    TextHitInfo hitInfo;
    Color caretColor;
    int hit1, hit2;
    int w, h;

    // 4. Constructor
    public DisplayPanel() {
        setBackground(Color.white);
        setForeground(Color.black);
```

continues

Listing 6.3   continued

```
    setSize(400, 200);
    addMouseListener(new MouseHandler());
    addMouseMotionListener(new MouseMotionHandler());
    w = getWidth(); h = getHeight();

    // 5. Text string to be displayed with the specified
    // font, and layout.
    String text = "This is Java2D text!";
    font = new Font("Arial", Font.PLAIN, 36);
    frc = new FontRenderContext(null, false, false);
    layout = new TextLayout(text, font, frc);

    // 6. Compute the coordinates and dimensions of the
    // bounding rectangle of text.
    rx = (float) (w/2-layout.getBounds().getWidth()/2);
    ry = (float) 3*h/4;
    rw = (float) (layout.getBounds().getWidth());
    rh = (float) (layout.getBounds().getHeight());
    rect = new Rectangle2D.Float(rx, ry, rw, rh);

    // Caret color to be manipulated later
    caretColor = getForeground();
}

// 7. The update method...
public void update(Graphics g) {
    g.clearRect(0, 0, getWidth(), getHeight());
    paintComponent(g);
}

// 8. The paint method...
public void paintComponent(Graphics g) {
    super.paintComponent(g);
    Graphics2D g2 = (Graphics2D) g;

    // Create an instance of translated affine transform
    AffineTransform at = AffineTransform.getTranslateInstance(rx, ry);

    // First draw the highlighted shape
    Shape hilight = layout.getLogicalHighlightShape(hit1, hit2);
    hilight = at.createTransformedShape(hilight);
    g2.setColor(Color.lightGray);
    g2.fill(hilight);

    // Draw text, centering it horizontally in the frame
    g2.setColor(Color.black);
    layout.draw(g2, rx, ry);
```

```java
    // Draw caret
    Shape[] caretShapes = layout.getCaretShapes(hit1);
    Shape caret = at.createTransformedShape(caretShapes[0]);
    g2.setColor(caretColor);
    g2.draw(caret);
}

// 9. Method to retrieve the hit location
public int getHitLocation(int mouseX, int mouseY) {
    hitInfo = layout.hitTestChar(mouseX, mouseY, rect);
    return hitInfo.getInsertionIndex();
}

// 10. Mouse listener
class MouseHandler extends MouseAdapter {
    public void mouseClicked(MouseEvent e) {
        caretColor = getForeground();
        hit1 = getHitLocation(e.getX(), e.getY());
        hit2 = hit1;
        repaint();
    }

    public void mousePressed(MouseEvent e) {
        caretColor = getForeground();
        hit1 = getHitLocation(e.getX(), e.getY());
        hit2 = hit1;
        repaint();
    }

    public void mouseReleased(MouseEvent e) {
        hit2 = getHitLocation(e.getX(), e.getY());
        repaint();
    }
}

// 11. Mouse motion listener
class MouseMotionHandler extends MouseMotionAdapter {
    public void mouseDragged(MouseEvent e) {
        // Hide the cursor only when a selection is made
        // (not merely when the mouse is dragged!)
        if (hit1 != hit2)
            caretColor = getBackground();
        // Get the hit location index
        hit2 = getHitLocation(e.getX(), e.getY());
        repaint();
    }
}
}
```

Code Analysis

The class TTextLayout2 is the main frame that extends JFrame. Snippet-1 is the constructor of this class. Snippet-2 is the main() method that creates an instance of the main frame and configures it.

Snippet-3 defines the display panel that extends JPanel. This class declares the text layout, font rendering context, and font as its fields. The class also declares a 2D rectangle object that serves as the bounding rectangle for the text layout, and the text hit information object, caret color, hit indexes, and panel dimensions as fields.

The constructor shown in snippet-4 initially configures the panel for the background and foreground colors and registers the mouse and mouse motion listeners. Snippet-5 initializes the objects for the text string, font, font rendering context, and text layout. Snippet-6 computes the coordinates and dimensions of the bounding rectangle of text. Then the constructor concludes by assigning the foreground color to the caret color.

Snippet-7 is the update() method that clears the display panel and invokes the paintComponent() method. Snippet-8 shows the paintComponent() method. This method prepares the 2D graphics context and then creates an object of the translated affine transform.

Then the code draws the highlighted shape using the bounds of the highlight rectangle. Note that you need to draw the highlight first and then draw the selected text over it. The final cluster of code inside the paintComponent() method draws the caret. The caret shapes are obtained by invoking the getCaretShapes() method, which takes the hit index as its argument.

Snippet-9 defines the method that implements the code to retrieve the hit location from the mouse operations. The method uses the hitTestChar() from the layout object to retrieve the hit information object. Next, it calls the getInsertionIndex() method on the hit information object. The hit information object is of type TextHitInfo class. Snippet-10 defines the mouse listener class. When the mouse button is clicked, pressed, or released, the method retrieves the hit location by using the method defined in snippet-9. Snippet-11 defines the mouse motion listener that implements the mouseDragged() method. This method retrieves the final index of the highlight and then repaints the panel to exercise the effect.

Working with Text and Graphic Attributes

The Abstract Windowing Toolkit (AWT) supports assigning text attributes to a text string. This includes setting background and foreground colors, and assigning various system fonts. Java 2D allows you to create styled text by assigning sophisticated text and graphic attributes to individual characters and words in a text string. The following sections present the details of these concepts.

Using Text Attributes

By using the text attributes supported in Java 2D, you can assign the following attributes to individual segments in a text string:

- Background and foreground colors
- Fonts and their sizes
- Transforms to obtain derived fonts
- Font weights such as bold, heavy, light, demi-bold, extra bold, and so on
- Character replacement
- Underlining text
- Swapping background and foreground paints
- Paragraph justification
- Highlight styles
- Posture of fonts
- Run direction for bidirectional text

The class `java.awt.font.TextAttribute` defines the attribute keys and attribute values for these features. You can apply these attributes to different characters and words in a text. The class `TextAttribute` extends the inner class `AttributedCharacter-Iterator.Attribute` from the `java.text` package. See Chapter 10, "Inheritance Hierarchies and API Quick Reference," for a quick reference on attribute fields provided in the `TextAttribute` class.

To assign an attribute to a certain segment of a text string, you need to create an object of attributed string of type `java.text.AttributedString` by using the specified text. Then you can invoke the following method on the attributed string object:

```
public void addAttribute(AttributedCharacterIterator.Attribute attribute,
                         Object value,
                         int startIndex,
                         int endIndex)
```

This method allows you to specify the `startIndex` and `endIndex` of the text segment to be styled. The `attribute` argument is the attribute key, and the `value` is the attribute value from the `TextAttribute` class. Next, you can retrieve the attribute character iterator from the attributed string, and pass it as an argument value to a suitable constructor in the `TextLayout` class.

Using Graphic Attributes

Graphic attributes are the graphic objects embedded in a text string. The graphic objects are different shapes described by the `Shape` interface, and images of type `Image` or `BufferedImage`. The abstract class `java.awt.font.GraphicAttribute` represents a graphic. This class is extended to created different graphic attribute implementations. The package `java.awt.font` readily supports the concrete classes `ShapeGraphic-Attribute` and `ImageGraphicAttribute` for the shape attributes and image attributes, respectively.

NOTE

The graphic attributes are embedded in text by using the `TextAttribute.CHAR_REPLACEMENT` attribute key. The attribute value will be an object of type `GraphicAttribute`.

The `ShapeGraphicAttribute` class contains the following constructor to create its object:

```
public ShapeGraphicAttribute(Shape shape, int alignment, boolean stroke)
```

This constructor creates an object by using the specified `shape`, `alignment`, and `stroke` parameter. The shape could be any geometric or font shape that is of type `Shape`. The `stroke` parameter is a boolean argument. If its value is true, the shape is of stroke type. If the argument value is false, the shape is of filled type. The `alignment` argument takes one of the fields supported in the `GraphicAttribute` class as its value. The class `GraphicAttribute` supports the following alignment fields:

```
public static final int TOP_ALIGNMENT
```
aligns the top of a graphic to the top of text.

```
public static final int BOTTOM_ALIGNMENT
```
aligns the bottom of a graphic to the bottom of text.

```
public static final int ROMAN_BASELINE
```
aligns the origin of a graphic to the roman baseline of text.

```
public static final int CENTER_BASELINE
```
aligns the origin of a graphic to the center baseline of text.

```
public static final int HANGING_BASELINE
```
aligns the origin of a graphic to the hanging baseline of text.

The `ImageGraphicAttribute` class supports the following constructors to create its objects.

```
public ImageGraphicAttribute(Image image, int alignment)
```
constructs an object from the specified `image` with the specified `alignment` from the `GraphicAttribute` class. The origin is at (0, 0).

```
public ImageGraphicAttribute(Image image, int alignment, float originX, float originY)
```
constructs an object from the specified `image` and `alignment`. The coordinates `originX` and `originY` are from the image that appears at the origin of the `ImageGraphicAttribute` within the text.

After you create an object of type ImageGraphicAttribute, you can add this to an attributed string by using the addAttribute() method shown previously. The attribute key must be TextAttribute.CHAR_REPLACEMENT.

Using Text and Graphic Attributes Example

Listing 6.4 shows a sample application that demonstrates how to create the text string that is styled by using various attributes. The text string also contains graphic attribute objects of type ShapeGraphicAttribute and ImageGraphicAttribute. Figure 6.5 shows the output of this program.

Figure 6.5

An application displaying the styled text.

Listing 6.4   Applying Text and Graphic Attributes to a Text String (TAttributes.java)

```
import java.awt.*;
import java.awt.event.*;
import javax.swing.*;
import java.awt.font.*;
import java.text.*;
import java.awt.geom.*;
import java.awt.image.*;

public class TAttributes extends JFrame {
    // 1. Constructor
    public TAttributes(String title) {
        super(title);
        setBackground(Color.white);
    }

    // 2. The main method...
    public static void main(String arg[]) {
        TAttributes frame = new TAttributes("TAttributes");
```

continues

Listing 6.4   continued

```
        frame.addWindowListener(new WindowAdapter() {
            public void windowClosing(WindowEvent e) {System.exit(0);}
        });
        frame.getContentPane().add("Center", new DisplayPanel());
        frame.pack();
        frame.setSize(new Dimension(500,200));
        frame.show();
    }
}


// 3. Definition of the display panel class
class DisplayPanel extends JPanel {
    String text = "  This is  Java 2D Text!!!";
    AttributedString attribString;
    AttributedCharacterIterator attribCharIterator;
    Image javaImage;

    public DisplayPanel() {
        // 4. Prepare the display panel with suitable size and background
        setBackground(Color.lightGray);
        setSize(500, 200);

        // 5. Create the attributed string object using the given text.
        attribString = new AttributedString(text);

        // 6. Add a star shaped graphic attribute in the beginning of the
        // given text.
        GeneralPath star = new GeneralPath();
        star.moveTo(0, 0); // x and y coordinates
        star.lineTo(10, 30); star.lineTo(-10, 10);
        star.lineTo(10, 10); star.lineTo(-10, 30);
        star.closePath();
        GraphicAttribute starShapeAttr = new ShapeGraphicAttribute(star,
                                        GraphicAttribute.TOP_ALIGNMENT,
                                        false);
        attribString.addAttribute(
                    TextAttribute.CHAR_REPLACEMENT, /* Attribute Key */
                    starShapeAttr, /* Attribute Value */
                    0, /* Begin Index */
                    1); /* End Index */
        attribString.addAttribute(TextAttribute.FOREGROUND,
                        new Color(255, 255, 0),
                        0, 1); // Start and end indexes.


        // 7. Modify the foreground and font attributes of "This is"
        // in the given string text.
        int index = text.indexOf("This is");
```

```
attribString.addAttribute(TextAttribute.FOREGROUND,
                          Color.blue,
                          index, index+7); // Start and end indexes.
Font font = new Font("sanserif", Font.ITALIC, 40);
attribString.addAttribute(TextAttribute.FONT, font, index, index+7);


// 8. Load the specified image and prepare the image attribute
loadImage();
BufferedImage bimage = new BufferedImage(javaImage.getWidth(this),
                               javaImage.getHeight(this),
                               BufferedImage.TYPE_INT_ARGB);
Graphics2D big = bimage.createGraphics();
big.drawImage(javaImage, null, this);
GraphicAttribute javaImageAttr = new ImageGraphicAttribute(bimage,
                          GraphicAttribute.TOP_ALIGNMENT,
                          0, 0);


// 9. Add the image attribute before the "Java" substring
index = text.indexOf("Java");
attribString.addAttribute(TextAttribute.CHAR_REPLACEMENT,
                          javaImageAttr, index-1, index);


// 10. Modify the attributes of the substring "Java"
font = new Font("serif", Font.BOLD, 60);
attribString.addAttribute(TextAttribute.FONT, font, index, index+4);
attribString.addAttribute(TextAttribute.FOREGROUND,
                          new Color(243, 63, 163),
                          index, index+4); // Start and end indexes.

// 11. Underline the substring "2D"
index = text.indexOf("2D");
attribString.addAttribute(TextAttribute.UNDERLINE,
                          TextAttribute.UNDERLINE_ON,
                          index, index+2);

// 12. Modify the font sizes after the substring Java.
index = text.indexOf("2D Text!!!");
font = new Font("sanserif", Font.ITALIC, 40);
attribString.addAttribute(TextAttribute.FONT, font, index, index+10);

// 13. Change the color of "2D" to white and the color of remaining
// text to blue.
attribString.addAttribute(TextAttribute.FOREGROUND,
                          Color.white,
                          index, index+2); // Start and end indexes.
attribString.addAttribute(TextAttribute.FOREGROUND,
```

continues

Listing 6.4   continued

```
                                Color.blue,
                                index+3, index+10); // Start and end indexes.
    }


    // 14. This method loads the specified image.
    public void loadImage() {
        // Create an image object using the specified file
        javaImage = Toolkit.getDefaultToolkit().getImage("images/java.gif");
        MediaTracker mt = new MediaTracker(this);
        mt.addImage(javaImage, 1);
        try {
            mt.waitForAll();
        } catch (Exception e) {
            System.out.println("Exception while loading.");
        }

        // If the image has an unknown width, the image is not created
        // by using the suggested file. Therefore, exit the program.
        if (javaImage.getWidth(this) == -1) {
            System.out.println("*** Make sure you have the suggested image "
                            + "(java.gif) file in the images directory.***");
            System.exit(0);
        }
    }


    // 15. The paintComponent method...
    public void paintComponent(Graphics g) {
        super.paintComponent(g);
        Graphics2D g2 = (Graphics2D) g;

        // Retrieve the character iterator from the attributed string
        attribCharIterator = attribString.getIterator();

        // Create a font render context object and text layout
        FontRenderContext frc = new FontRenderContext(null, false, false);
        TextLayout layout = new TextLayout(attribCharIterator, frc);

        // Draw the string
        layout.draw(g2, 20, 100);
    }
}
```

Code Analysis

The class TAttributes is the main frame. Snippet-1 is the constructor of this class that assigns a title and sets the background color to white. Snippet-2 defines the main method that creates an instance of the main frame. The snippet also registers a window closing listener with the frame, and then displays it at a suitable size.

Snippet-3 defines the display panel class. Inside the constructor, snippet-4 prepares the display panel with a suitable size and background color. Snippet-5 creates the attributed string object using the given text. Snippet-6 creates a star-shaped graphic attribute and adds it to the beginning of the text string. Snippet-7 modifies the foreground color and font of the "This is" portion of the string.

Snippet-8 loads an image, and then prepares an image graphic attribute. Snippet-9 adds the image attribute before the "Java" portion of the string. Snippet-10 modifies the font and foreground colors of the substring "Java". Snippet-11 underlines the "2D" portion of the string. Snippet-12 modifies the font sizes for the portion following the substring "Java". Snippet-13 changes the color of "2D" to white, and the color of the following portion of text to blue.

Snippet-14 is the `loadImage()` method that creates an image object using the specified image file. The method also reports if the image file with the specified name is not available.

Snippet-15 is the `paintComponent()` method that creates a 2D graphics context object. Then the method retrieves the character iterator object from the attributed string, and also creates a font render context object. These objects are used to create a text layout object. Then the `draw()` method is invoked on the text layout object to render the text string with the specified attributes.

Creating Paragraphs by Wrapping Text

This section presents how to break a single line of styled text into different rows to create paragraphs. The styled text can also contain the graphic attributes, such as shapes and images. The line of text is wrapped at the end of a certain width, called the *wrapping width*.

The class `java.awt.font.LineBreakMeasurer` represents the mechanism to break a line of text into multiple lines using the specified wrapping width. An object of this class uses an attributed character iterator of a text string, and a break iterator of type `java.text.BreakIterator`.

Initially, the line break measurer begins with the starting position of the text, and can retrieve the text layout for the wrapping width. The text layout is of type `TextLayout` class and is retrieved by calling the method `nextLayout()` on the line break measurer object. The `nextLayout()` method takes the wrapping width as its argument value. Now you can invoke the `draw()` method on the text layout object to render the text string of the wrapping width.

The complete string of text can be broken into lines and rendered by checking whether the position of the line break measurer is still before the last character in the text. The `getPosition()` method retrieves the current position of the line break measurer. This position can be recursively checked to see whether it is smaller than the length of the string.

Wrapping Text Example

Listing 6.5 shows an example application that demonstrates how to create paragraphs by wrapping text strings. The program displays a display panel with a paragraph of text in window. When the user reduces the width of window, each line of the paragraph is wrapped to the subsequent row to display the text completely. Figure 6.6 shows the output of this program.

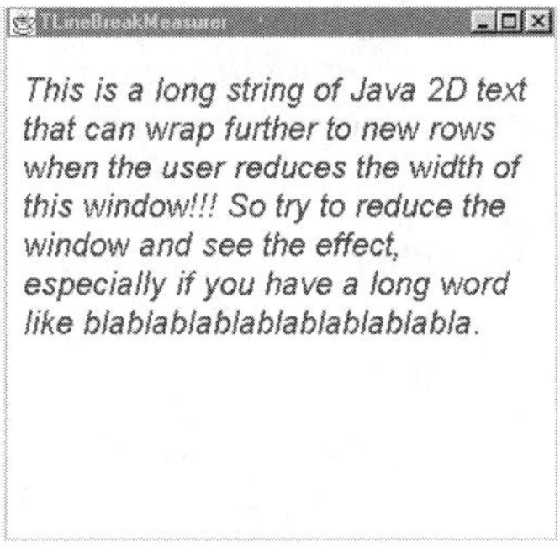

Figure 6.6

An application that wraps the lines of a text string.

Listing 6.5   Using Line Break Measurer to Wrap the Lines of a Text String (TLineBreakMeasurer.java)

```
import java.awt.*;
import java.awt.event.*;
import javax.swing.*;
import java.awt.font.*;
import java.text.*;
import java.awt.geom.*;

public class TLineBreakMeasurer extends JFrame {
    // 1. Constructor
    public TLineBreakMeasurer(String title) {
        super(title);
        setBackground(Color.white);
    }

    // 2. The main method...
    public static void main(String arg[]) {
        TLineBreakMeasurer frame = new TLineBreakMeasurer(
                                "TLineBreakMeasurer");
        frame.addWindowListener(new WindowAdapter() {
            public void windowClosing(WindowEvent e) {System.exit(0);}
        });
        frame.getContentPane().add("Center", new DisplayPanel());
```

```
        frame.pack();
        frame.setSize(new Dimension(350,400));
        frame.show();
    }
}


// 3. Definition of the display panel class
class DisplayPanel extends JPanel {
    String text = "This is a long string of Java 2D text "
                + "that can wrap further to new rows when the "
                + "user reduces the width of this window!!! "
                + "So try to reduce the window and see the effect, "
                + "especially if you have a long word like "
                + "blablablablablablablablabla.";
    AttributedString attribString;
    AttributedCharacterIterator attribCharIterator;

    public DisplayPanel() {
        // 4. Prepare the display panel with suitable size and background
        setBackground(Color.white);
        setSize(350, 400);

        // 5. Create the attributed string object using the given text, and
        // assign a new font and foreground color.
        attribString = new AttributedString(text);
        attribString.addAttribute(TextAttribute.FOREGROUND,
                          Color.blue,
                          0, text.length()); // Start and end indexes.
        Font font = new Font("sanserif", Font.ITALIC, 20);
        attribString.addAttribute(TextAttribute.FONT, font, 0, text.length());
    }

    // 6. The paintComponent method...
    public void paintComponent(Graphics g) {
        super.paintComponent(g);
        Graphics2D g2 = (Graphics2D) g;

        // 7. Retrieve the character iterator from the attributed string
        attribCharIterator = attribString.getIterator();

        // 8. Create a font render context object and line break measurer.
        FontRenderContext frc = new FontRenderContext(null, false, false);
        LineBreakMeasurer lbm = new LineBreakMeasurer(attribCharIterator, frc);


        // 9. Perform the layout using the line break measurer, and
        // draw the text on different rows in a 'while' loop.
```

continues

Listing 6.5 continued

```
        int x = 10, y = 20; // Left and top margins
        int w = getWidth(), h = getHeight(); // Window dimensions
        // Leave 15 pixels before the right edge of the window.
        float wrappingWidth = w - 15;

        while (lbm.getPosition() < text.length()) {
            // Retrieve the text layout for the wrapping width
            TextLayout layout = lbm.nextLayout(wrappingWidth);

            // Compute the base line
            y += layout.getAscent();

            // Draw the string from the layout
            layout.draw(g2, x, y);

            //Go to the line passing through the ascent of characters.
            y += layout.getDescent() + layout.getLeading();
        }
    }
}
```

Code Analysis

The class `TLineBreakMeasurer` is the main frame. Snippet-1 is the constructor of this class that assigns a title and background color. Snippet-2 defines the main method that creates an instance of the main frame. The snippet also registers a window closing listener with the frame, and then displays it with suitable size.

Snippet-3 defines the display panel class. This class defines a long text string, and references to the objects of type `AttributedString` and `AttributedCharacterIterator` classes. Inside the constructor, snippet-4 prepares the display panel with suitable size and background color. Snippet-5 creates the attributed string object by passing the long text string as its argument value. The snippet also modifies the background color and font size of the text string by using the `addAttribute()` method.

Snippet-6 is the `paintComponent()` method that creates a 2D graphics context object. Snippet-7 retrieves the character iterator from the attributed string. Snippet-8 creates a font render context, and then a line break measurer object of type `LineBreakMeasurer`. The remaining code statements draw the text by creating the text layout objects.

The `while` loop checks whether the length of the text is greater than the current position of the line break measurer. If the condition is true, the line break measurer returns the text layout object for the text string with a size equal to the wrapping width. This string is rendered by using the draw method at the specified location. Next, the y coordinate is updated. The sequence of these operations is performed until control exits from the `while` loop.

CHAPTER 7

Buffered Imaging

Working with buffered or off-screen images is not new to Java developers. The Java language first introduced the API for imaging in Version 1.0 of the JDK. To create images in the accessible memory of a computer and to perform various pixel-level image processing operations, Java 2D provides the interfaces and classes based on a new imaging model. The Java 2 Software Development Kit arrives with an imaging model called the *immediate mode* model. Using this model, developers can access the image data at the pixel level, and manipulate it by using a variety of filtering operations.

The first section in this chapter examines the anatomy of a buffered image that is based on the immediate mode model. This section discusses the storage of image data, and the models used to access and interpret image data to arrive at pixel colors. The remaining sections in the chapter will show you how to create and display buffered images. You will also observe the advantage in storing images in a buffer through certain examples that demonstrate image replication and animation.

Processing an image stored in a buffer to blur, sharpen, improve contrast, apply color corrections, and so on deserves a separate chapter of its own. Therefore, the image processing API supported in Java 2D will be discussed in Chapter 8, "Image Processing."

Anatomy of a Buffered Image

A *buffered image* is an image that is directly created in the accessible memory (buffer) of a computer. The buffer of memory can store an actual image that is supplied by an image file or by means of a URL. For storing data, the buffered image retrieves data from the specified image file and holds it in the memory buffer.

The class BufferedImage represents a buffered image. This class extends the abstract class java.awt.Image and is stored in the package java.awt.image. So the BufferedImage class implements the abstract operations and fields for scaling algorithms encapsulated in the class Image. The top-left corner of a buffered image has the coordinates (0, 0).

The class BufferedImage supports a number of fields that represent various types of buffered images (see the quick reference given in Chapter 10, "Inheritance Hierarchies and API Quick Reference"). To create a buffered image object, you can use one of the following constructors:

```
public BufferedImage(int width, int height, int imageType)
public BufferedImage(int width, int height,
                     int imageType, IndexColorModel cm)
public BufferedImage(ColorModel cm,
                     WritableRaster raster,
                     boolean isRasterPremultiplied,
                     Hashtable properties)
```

The first constructor

```
public BufferedImage(int width, int height, int imageType)
```
creates a buffered image with the specified width, height, and image type. The image type is specified by using one of the static fields of the class. The color space of the created image is the default standard RGB (sRGB) space. Note that the values for width and height cannot be zero. The image type must be one of the predefined types given in the BufferedImage class. If these conditions are not satisfied, the constructor throws an exception of type IllegalArgumentException.

```
public BufferedImage(int width, int height,
                     int imageType, IndexColorModel cm)
```
creates a buffered image with the specified size, image type, and color model. The color model object must be of type IndexColorModel, and the image type must be TYPE_BYTE_BINARY or TYPE_BYTE_INDEXED. If the image type is not one of these two fields, the method throws an exception of type IllegalArgumentException.

```
public BufferedImage(ColorModel cm,
                     WritableRaster raster,
                     boolean isRasterPremultiplied,
                     Hashtable properties)
```
creates a buffered image with the specified color model and raster. If the number and types of bands in the sample model of the raster do not match the number and types required by the color model to represent its color and alpha components, the constructor throws a RasterFormatException. The properties of the buffered image can be specified by passing it through a hash table.

Retrieving Data, Image Type, and Color Model

From a buffered image object, you can retrieve the raster of data by calling the following methods.

```
public Raster getData()
```
creates a copy of the raster and returns that object. The raster is returned as a single tile of rectangular shape. To directly access the raster of data, instead of a copy of the buffered image, you must call the following method:

```
public WritableRaster getRaster()
```

```
public Raster getData(Rectangle rect)
```
returns a raster object containing the data. However, the raster represents the specified rectangular portion of the buffered image. The raster object is a copy of the image data, and thus, it is not updated if the image is changed.

To retrieve the image type of the buffered image, you can invoke the method

```
public int getType()
```
which returns the image type as an integer. If the image type is not known, the method returns the field TYPE_CUSTOM.

To obtain the color model of the buffered image, call the following method:

```
public ColorModel getColorModel()
```

Retrieving the Dimensions of a Buffered Image

To retrieve the width of a buffered image, you can invoke one of the following methods:

```
public int getWidth()
public int getWidth(ImageObserver observer)
public int getTileWidth()
```

All these methods essentially return the width of the raster.

```
public int getWidth(ImageObserver observer)
```
takes the image observer as its argument. If the width of the image is not yet known, the ImageObserver is notified later and −1 is returned. Similarly, the following methods retrieve the height of the image:

```
public int getTileHeight()
public int getTileHeight(ImageObserver observer)
public int getTileHeight()
```

Retrieving a Portion of the BufferedImage

You can retrieve the subimage or rectangular portion of a buffered image by invoking the following method:

```
public BufferedImage getSubimage(int x, int y, int w, int h)
```

This method requires the origin (x, y) and width and height (w, h) of the subimage.

Image Data Management Using a Raster

The immediate mode model provides an architecture that can efficiently manage image data. The `BufferedImage` class uses this architecture by encapsulating a raster of data and a color model to interpret pixel colors. The class `Raster` represents a raster, which essentially is a rectangular array of pixels that represent an image. The subclass `WritableRaster` represents a raster that gives permission to write and, thus, allows data manipulations.

A raster encapsulates a data buffer and a sample model. The sample model allows access to samples in the data buffer. The abstract class `DataBuffer` represents a data buffer. A data buffer encloses arrays of data called *banks*. The concrete subclasses of `DataBuffer` called `DataBufferByte`, `DataBufferInt`, `DataBufferShort`, and `DataBufferUShort` represent data buffers with byte, int, short, and unsigned short type data banks, respectively.

The sample model describes a mechanism for extracting sample data from a data buffer. The sample model is represented by the abstract class `SampleModel`. The model does not depend on the type of data storage that exists in the data buffer. The model provides low-level information to directly manipulate samples of pixel values in the data buffer. The `java.awt.image` package supports five sample models, represented by the concrete classes, as follows:

- `ComponentSampleModel`—This class extends `SampleModel` and provides access to image data stored with each pixel sample residing in a separate element of a data buffer.
- `BandedSampleModel`—This class extends `ComponentSampleModel` and provides access to image data stored in separate banks of a data buffer. Each bank of data represents a band of sample pixels.
- `PixelInterleavedSampleModel`—This class extends `ComponentSampleModel` and provides access to data stored with the sample data for each pixel in adjacent elements, or all elements of a data array.
- `SinglePixelPackedSampleModel`—This class extends `SampleModel` and provides access to image data stored with all the samples belonging to an individual pixel stored in an element of a data buffer.
- `MultiPixelPackedSampleModel`—This class extends `SampleModel` and provides access to image data stored with multiple single-sample pixels stored in an element of a data buffer.

Very often you do not have to directly work with a raster; however, a raster helps to access the pixels of an image to support raster-level processing. The BufferedImage constructors allow you to construct buffered images from a raster. You can use any one of the static methods supported in the Raster class to create a raster with the specified data buffer and sample model. (See Chapter 10 for the API quick reference on some of the classes discussed in this section.)

Color Models

A color model is used to interpret pixel data as colors. The sample model in a raster presents the color model with pixel data for interpretation (see Figure 7.1). The abstract class ColorModel represents a color model. There are four color model classes: PackedColorModel, ComponentColorModel, DirectColorModel, and IndexColor-Model. Java 2D introduces the classes PackedColorModel and ComponentColorModel. These classes encapsulate operations to convert pixel data into color values in the relevant color space.

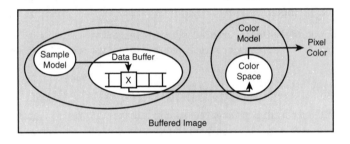

Figure 7.1

Extracting the pixel color from its value in a data buffer.

Working with Buffered Images

In this section, you will study how to create a buffered (off-screen) image, paint graphics elements to it, and finally flip or blit it to the display screen. The following topics will present these concepts.

Creating a Buffered Image

In order to create an off-screen image, you can create an instance of the class BufferedImage with the required dimensions and image type. The class BufferedImage supports a variety of off-screen image types based on the bit size of pixel values, color space, and alpha values. Various image types are encapsulated as the static fields of the BufferedImage class.

For example, to create a buffered image with 8-bit RGB color components along with the effect of alpha value (for transparency control), you can use the field TYPE_INT_ARGB. Similarly, to create a buffered image to store an image of unknown type, the field TYPE_CUSTOM takes care of the input type. See Chapter 10 for a quick reference on the complete list of fields from the BufferedImage class. For information on the constructors and methods supported in the BufferedImage class, see the earlier section "Anatomy of a Buffered Image."

To create a BufferedImage object, you can also use the method createImage() from the Component class. This method returns a BufferedImage object whose graphics attributes are similar to those of the component on which the method has been invoked. Essentially, you must consider whether the image is opaque or transparent. If the image has a transparent background and the component has an opaque background, using the createImage() method can produce a dark background for the image. Therefore, if the image has a transparent background, you should use an appropriate constructor of BufferedImage to consider the argument value of ARGB type.

Creating a buffered image with a compatible format to the graphics device can result in better performance while flipping the image. The class GraphicsConfiguration in the package java.awt supports operations that can create buffered images of suitable type based on the graphics device on which the buffered image is displayed. The following are those methods:

```
public abstract BufferedImage createCompatibleImage(int width, int height)
public abstract BufferedImage createCompatibleImage(int width, int height,
                                            int transparency)
```

The first method

```
public abstract BufferedImage createCompatibleImage(int width, int height)
```
returns an object of BufferedImage with the specified width and height. The data layout and color model are the closest and most compatible with the current GraphicsConfiguration for efficient blitting of the image to the device.

```
public abstract BufferedImage createCompatibleImage(int width, int height,
                                            int transparency)
```
is similar to the first method, but takes care of the transparency effects of colors. Note that the transparency of an image usually affects performance; therefore, it must be used with reservations.

The following code snippet illustrates how to create a buffered image by using its constructor. This code requires the specification of the image dimensions and the image type:

```
public void paint(Graphics g) {
    // Create the graphics context object
    Graphics2D g2D = (Graphics2D) g;

    // Create a buffered image of the size of canvas.
    if (getWidth() != 0 && getHeight() != 0) {
        BufferedImage bi = new BufferedImage(
                        getWidth(), getHeight(),
```

```
                    BufferedImage.TYPE_INT_ARGB);
    }

    // Remaining code follows...
    ...
}
```

The preceding code creates a buffered image that has width and height equal to that of the corresponding component. The buffered image is of type RGB with the effects of alpha value.

NOTE

When creating a buffered image, the dimensions such as width and height cannot be zero. If the component width or height happens to be zero, the program throws an `IllegalArgumentException` at runtime.

Painting on a Buffered Image

After an off-screen buffered image is created, you can easily render various graphics elements onto it by setting up its graphics context. The method `createGraphics()` in the class `BufferedImage` creates a graphics context of the image, and retrieves a reference to it. The graphics context object is of type `Graphics2D`. So, by using this object, you can set the stroke type and draw some text or a geometric shape, apply an affine transform, draw an existing image into the buffer, and so on. Recollect that the buffered image's top-left coordinates are (0, 0).

The following code snippet illustrates the retrieving of a graphics context and drawing an existing image into the buffer:

```
public void paint(Graphics g) {
    // Create the graphics context object
    Graphics2D g2D = (Graphics2D) g;

    // Create a buffered image of the size of canvas.
    if (getWidth() != 0 && getHeight() != 0) {
        BufferedImage bi = new BufferedImage(
                        getWidth(), getHeight(),
                        BufferedImage.TYPE_INT_ARGB);
    }

    // Obtain the graphics context of the buffered image
    Graphics2D big = bi.createGraphics();

    // Draw an existing image into the buffer.
    big.drawImage(existingImage, 0, 0, this);
}
```

The drawImage() method in this code takes four arguments. The argument value existingImage is an image object that has already been created. The argument values (0, 0) represent the x- and y- coordinates of the top-left corner of the buffered image. The remaining argument specifies the image observer.

Displaying a Buffered Image

An image stored into an off-screen buffer of memory can be rendered into the graphics context of a device such as the monitor screen. For example, to display the buffered image, you can draw the image into the 2D context by using the method drawImage() from Graphics2D. The following code snippet illustrates this concept:

```
public void paint(Graphics g) {
    // Create the graphics context object
    Graphics2D g2D = (Graphics2D) g;

    // Create a buffered image of the size of canvas.
    if (getWidth() != 0 && getHeight() != 0) {
        BufferedImage bi = new BufferedImage(
                    getWidth(), getHeight(),
                    BufferedImage.TYPE_INT_ARGB);
    }

    // Obtain the graphics context of the buffered image
    Graphics2D big = bi.createGraphics();

    // Draw an existing image into the buffer.
    big.drawImage(existingImage, 0, 0, this);

    // Now blit the image onto the screen by using
    // its graphics context g2D created previously.
    g2D.drawImage(bi, 0, 0, this);
}
```

In this code, you can notice that the buffered image object bi is specified to the drawImage() method that is invoked on the graphics context object of the monitor screen.

Buffered Image Example

Listing 7.1 provides an example program that demonstrates how to create a buffered image and blit it to the monitor screen. The program also demonstrates the efficiency in blitting the buffered image rather than directly drawing the image to the screen.

The program enables the user to select a buffered or non-buffered option, and then to click the Display button to perform rendering. The Clear button clears the canvas to draw again. By using the options provided while rendering, you can observe the efficiency in displaying an image (or texture, as given in this example) by using the memory buffer. The program output is shown in Figure 7.2.

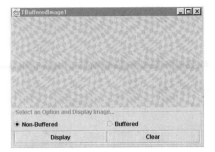

Figure 7.2

A demonstration of using a buffered image.

Listing 7.1   Creating a Buffered Image and Blitting It to the Screen (TBufferedImage1.java)

```java
import javax.swing.*;
import javax.swing.border.*;
import java.awt.*;
import java.awt.event.*;
import java.awt.image.*;

class TBufferedImage1 extends JFrame {
    DisplayCanvas canvas;
    JRadioButton buffButton, nonBuffButton;
    JButton displayButton, clearButton;

    public TBufferedImage1() {
        // 1. Assign a title to the frame and get a handle on
        // the frame's content pane
        super("TBufferedImage1");
        Container container = getContentPane();

        // 2. Define and add a canvas that displays textures.
        canvas = new DisplayCanvas();
        container.add(canvas);

        // 3. Create a panel to add the control buttons. Add the
        // panel to the main frame.
        JPanel panel = new JPanel();
        panel.setLayout(new GridLayout(2, 2)); // 2 rows and 2 cols
        panel.setBorder(new TitledBorder(
            "Select an Option and Display Image..."));

        buffButton = new JRadioButton("Buffered");
        buffButton.addActionListener(new ButtonListener());
```

continues

Listing 7.1   continued

```
nonBuffButton = new JRadioButton("Non-Buffered", true);
nonBuffButton.addActionListener(new ButtonListener());
ButtonGroup group = new ButtonGroup();
group.add(buffButton);
group.add(nonBuffButton);

displayButton = new JButton("Display");
displayButton.addActionListener(new ButtonListener());
clearButton = new JButton("Clear");
clearButton.addActionListener(new ButtonListener());

panel.add(nonBuffButton);
panel.add(buffButton);
panel.add(displayButton);
panel.add(clearButton);

container.add(BorderLayout.SOUTH, panel);

// 4. Add a frame closing listener and display the frame
addWindowListener(new WindowEventHandler());
pack(); // Packs around the contents with suitable size
show(); // Display the frame
}

// 5. Code to handle closing of the frame
class WindowEventHandler extends WindowAdapter {
    public void windowClosing(WindowEvent e) {
        System.exit(0);
    }
}

// 6. The main method...
public static void main(String arg[]) {
    new TBufferedImage1();
}

// 7. Action listener to handle the event fired by radio
// buttons and push type buttons.
class ButtonListener implements ActionListener {
    public void actionPerformed(ActionEvent e) {
        Object obj =  e.getSource();

        if (obj instanceof JRadioButton) {
            JRadioButton button = (JRadioButton) obj;
            if (button.equals(buffButton)) {
                canvas.buffered = true;
            }
            else if (button.equals(nonBuffButton)) {
```

```
                    canvas.buffered = false;
                }
            }

            if (obj instanceof JButton) {
                JButton button = (JButton) obj;
                if (button.equals(displayButton)) {
                    canvas.display = true;
                    canvas.repaint();
                }
                else if (button.equals(clearButton)) {
                    canvas.clear = true;
                    canvas.repaint();
                }
            }
        }
    }
}

// 8. Canvas to display the selected texture
class DisplayCanvas extends Canvas {
    boolean display = false;
    boolean clear = false;
    boolean buffered = false;

    Image displayImage; // for texture image

    // Constructor
    DisplayCanvas() {
        // Create an image object using the specified file
        displayImage = Toolkit.getDefaultToolkit().getImage("texture.jpg");
        MediaTracker mt = new MediaTracker(this);
        mt.addImage(displayImage, 1);
        try {
            mt.waitForAll();
        } catch (Exception e) {
            System.out.println("Exception while loading.");
        }
        // If the image has an unknown width, the image is not created
        // by using the texture file. Therefore, exit the program!
        if (displayImage.getWidth(this) == -1) {
            System.out.println("*** Make sure you have the texture image "
                            + "(*.jpg) file in the same directory.***");
            System.exit(0);
        }

        setBackground(Color.white);  // For canvas background color
```

continues

Listing 7.1 continued

```
      setSize(400, 225);  // Canvas width and height
}

  public void paint(Graphics g) {
      // Create the graphics context object
      Graphics2D g2D = (Graphics2D) g;

      if (display) {
          if (buffered) {
              // Create a buffered image of the size of canvas.
              BufferedImage bi = (BufferedImage) createImage(
                              getWidth(),
                              getHeight());

              // Draw the texture image into the memory buffer.
              for (int i=0; i<getWidth(); i=i+displayImage.getWidth(this)) {
                  for (int j=0;
                          j<getHeight();
                          j=j+displayImage.getHeight(this)) {
                      bi.createGraphics().drawImage(
                          displayImage, i, j, this);
                  }
              }
              // Draw the buffered Image on to the screen
              g2D.drawImage(bi, 0,0, this);
          }
          // This block of code draws the texture directly onto the screen.
          else if (!buffered) {
              for (int i=0; i<getWidth(); i=i+displayImage.getWidth(this)) {
                  for (int j=0;
                          j<getHeight();
                          j=j+displayImage.getHeight(this)) {
                      g2D.drawImage(displayImage, i, j, this);
                  }
              }
          }
          display = false;
      }
      // Clears the canvas.
      else if (clear) {
          // Clear Canvas
          g2D.setColor(Color.white);
          g2D.clearRect(0, 0, getWidth(), getHeight());

          clear = false;
      }
  }
}
```

Code Analysis

The class TBufferedImage1 extends the Swing frame. It declares references as fields for the display canvas, radio buttons to select buffering options, and push buttons to display or clear the canvas. Inside the constructor, snippet-1 assigns a title to the frame and obtains a reference to the content panel of the frame.

Snippet-2 defines a canvas object and adds it to the content pane. Snippet-3 creates a panel to display radio and push type buttons. The panel is added to the main frame. The radio buttons are grouped to make them mutually exclusive. Snippet-4 adds a window event handler to close the frame and display it with proper size. Snippet-5 defines the window event handler class. Snippet-6 is the main method that creates an object of the main frame.

Snippet-7 defines the action listener class that is common to both the radio buttons and push-type buttons. The actionPerformed() method figures out the type of object that fires the action event, and performs the relevant operations. The radio buttons are used to select the buffered or nonbuffered options. The push buttons help to display the image and clear the canvas.

Snippet-8 defines the display canvas. The constructor of this class creates an image object using the specified image file of a texture. The code to assign proper size and background color is also included.

Next, the paint() method creates a 2D graphics context. This method conditionally executes the code to create a buffered image and display it on the monitor screen. This is performed when the Buffered option is selected using the corresponding radio button. If the Non-Buffered option is selected, the image object is directly displayed on the monitor screen. The rendering operation creates a texture using the image file. This step is shown in the for loop. In the Buffered option, the texture is painted on the buffered image and then blitted to the screen. In the Non-Buffered option, the texture is painted directly on the screen. The remaining portion of code in this method is used to clear the canvas when the Clear button is clicked.

Accessing Raster/Data Buffer Example

Listing 7.2 shows a sample program that demonstrates how to access data in the data buffer of a raster. A raster in a buffered image is retrieved by invoking the getRaster() method. The data buffer of a raster is retrieved by calling the getDataBuffer() method.

The program accesses the data buffer in a raster or a buffered image to flip the buffered image. The flipping is performed by rearranging the pixels from the data buffer in the reverse order. The user clicks the Flip the Image button to perform flipping, and flipping the flipped image (that is, showing the image in its initial form). Figure 7.3 shows the output from this program when the image has been flipped.

Figure 7.3

A demonstration of accessing the data buffer in a raster.

Listing 7.2   Displaying an Image and Flipping It (TRaster.java)

```java
import javax.swing.*;
import java.awt.*;
import java.awt.event.*;
import java.awt.image.*;

class TRaster extends JFrame {
    DisplayPanel displayPanel;
    JToggleButton flipButton;

    public TRaster() {
        // 1. Assign a title to the frame and get a handle on
        // the frame's content pane
        super("TRaster");
        Container container = getContentPane();

        // 2. Create and add the display panel
        displayPanel = new DisplayPanel();
        container.add(displayPanel);

        // 3. Create and add the button used to flip the image
        Box box = Box.createHorizontalBox();
        flipButton = new JToggleButton("Flip the Image");
        flipButton.addActionListener(new ButtonListener());
        // Add the button at the center of box using glue components
        box.add(Box.createHorizontalGlue());
        box.add(flipButton);
        box.add(Box.createHorizontalGlue());
        // Add the flip button to the bottom portion of frame
        container.add(box, BorderLayout.SOUTH);
```

```
//  4. Add a frame closing listener and display the frame
addWindowListener(new WindowEventHandler());
setSize(450, 400); // Width and height
show(); // Display the frame
}


// 5. Code to handle closing of the frame
class WindowEventHandler extends WindowAdapter {
    public void windowClosing(WindowEvent e) {
        System.exit(0);
    }
}


// 6. The main method...
public static void main(String arg[]) {
    new TRaster();
}


// 7. Button listener class
class ButtonListener implements ActionListener {
    public void actionPerformed(ActionEvent e) {
        // If the image is not flipped
        if (!displayPanel.flipped) {
            // Flip the image
            displayPanel.flipBufferedImage();
            displayPanel.bi = displayPanel.bi2;
            displayPanel.flipped = true;
        }
        // If the image has already been flipped
        else {
            // Prepare to display the normal image
            displayPanel.bi = displayPanel.bi1;
            displayPanel.flipped = false;
        }
        // Update the display panel
        displayPanel.repaint();
    }
}
}

// 8. Definition of the display panel class
class DisplayPanel extends JPanel {
    BufferedImage bi, bi1, bi2;
    boolean flipped = false;

    // 9. Constructor
    DisplayPanel() {
        setBackground(Color.white);  // For canvas background color
```

continues

Listing 7.2   continued

```
    setSize(450, 400);  // panel width & height

    // Get the image file
    Image image = getToolkit().getImage("car.jpg");

    // Track the image loading
    MediaTracker mt = new MediaTracker(this);
    mt.addImage(image, 1);
    try {
        mt.waitForAll();
    } catch (Exception e) {
        System.out.println("Exception while loading image.");
    }

    // If the image has an unknown width, the image is not created
    // by using the specified file. Therefore exit the program!
    if (image.getWidth(this) == -1) {
        System.out.println("*** Make sure you have the image "
            + "(car.jpg) file in the same directory.***");
        System.exit(0);
    }

    // Create the buffered image
    // NOTE: You need to use the image type ARGB to consider the
    //       effect of alpha value of an image.
    bi1 = new BufferedImage(image.getWidth(this),
                            image.getHeight(this),
                            BufferedImage.TYPE_INT_ARGB);
    Graphics2D big = bi1.createGraphics();
    // Draw the image into the buffer
    big.drawImage(image, 0, 0, this);
    bi = bi1; // Assign bi1 to bi for painting
}


// 10. This method performs flipping of the buffered image
// by accessing the data buffers
public void flipBufferedImage() {
    // Create a buffered image to store the flipped image.
    bi2 = new BufferedImage(bi1.getWidth(), bi1.getHeight(),
                            bi1.getType());

    // Retrieve the data buffers from the rasters of buffered images
    DataBuffer db1 = bi1.getRaster().getDataBuffer();
    DataBuffer db2 = bi2.getRaster().getDataBuffer();

    // Perform flipping by retrieving the pixels from db1 in the
    // reverse order and storing them in db2.
```

```
        for (int i=db1.getSize()-1, j=0; i>=0; —i, j++) {
            db2.setElem(j, db1.getElem(i));
        }
    }


    // 11. The update method...
    public void update(Graphics g) {
        g.clearRect(0, 0, getWidth(), getHeight());
        paintComponent(g);
    }


    // 12. The paint method...
    public void paintComponent(Graphics g) {
        super.paintComponent(g);

        // Create the graphics context object
        Graphics2D g2D = (Graphics2D) g;

        // Display the buffered image bi. bi refers to
        // either bi1 or bi2 depending on the context.
        g2D.drawImage(bi, 0, 0, this);
    }
}
```

Code Analysis

The class TRaster is a Swing frame. This class declares the references to a display panel and a button as its data fields. Inside the constructor of this class, snippet-1 assigns a title to the frame and retrieves its content pane. Snippet-2 creates an instance of the display panel and adds it to the content pane of the frame. Snippet-3 creates a button object and adds it to the content pane. This button will be used to perform flipping of the image; therefore, an action listener has also been registered with the button.

Snippet-4 adds a frame closing listener, and displays the frame with suitable size. Snippet-5 defines the window listener class. Snippet-6 is the main method where an instance of the main frame is created.

Snippet-7 defines the button listener class. The actionPerformed() method implements the code to call the flipping operation and then repaint the display panel. If the flipping has already been done, the method simply prepares the code to display the image before flipping. The respective operations are conditionally performed by changing the value of the boolean variable flipped.

Snippet-8 defines the display panel class. Snippet-9 shows the constructor of this class. Inside the constructor, the panel background color and suitable size are assigned. An image is then loaded into the memory buffer that is created by using the BufferedImage class.

Snippet-10 shows the method that flips the buffered image by accessing the data buffers from the rasters. The pixel values of the image are stored in the data buffer of a separate buffered image in the reverse order.

Snippet-11 is the `update()` method that clears the panel background and calls the `paintComponent()` method. Snippet-12 is the `paintComponent()` method that simply displays the image stored in the data buffer referred by `bi`. The reference `bi` is assigned the references of the normal and flipped images.

Using the Buffered Image

Very often, you might prefer to display an image by first drawing it to the off-screen buffer and then blitting it to the display screen. This approach makes the image rendering smooth, flicker-free, and efficient. The buffered imaging technique is especially effective whenever a graphics element is time-consuming to display, or is recursively displayed. The following topics present situations where buffered imaging produces really satisfying results.

Replicating the Buffered Image: An Example

The efficiency in copying an image that is held in an accessible buffer to the screen has already been observed in the output of the program given in Listing 7.1. Here is another program that demonstrates the efficiency in copying an off-screen image to the screen.

Listing 7.3 shows a program that displays an image (butterfly) over a canvas. The user can drag the mouse to move the butterfly. When the mouse is being dragged, the image stored in the buffer is copied by blitting at each location of the mouse pointer. This technique avoids the inefficient redrawing of the image at each mouse pointer location. Figure 7.4 shows the output of the program.

Figure 7.4

Copying a buffered image to move the corresponding image.

Listing 7.3   Moving an Onscreen Graphic by Blitting the Buffered Image (TBufferedImage2.java)
```
import javax.swing.*;
import javax.swing.border.*;
import java.awt.*;
import java.awt.event.*;
```

```java
import java.awt.image.*;

class TBufferedImage2 extends JFrame {
    DisplayCanvas canvas;

    public TBufferedImage2() {
        // 1. Assign a title to the frame and get a handle on
        // the frame's content pane
        super("TBufferedImage2");
        Container container = getContentPane();

        // 2. Add the canvas
        canvas = new DisplayCanvas();
        TitledBorder border = new TitledBorder(
            "Drag the Butterfly Using the Mouse");
        border.setTitlePosition(TitledBorder.BOTTOM);
        canvas.setBorder(border);
        container.add(canvas);

        //  3. Add a frame closing listener and display the frame
        addWindowListener(new WindowEventHandler());
        setSize(450, 400);
        show(); // Display the frame
    }

    // 4. Code to handle closing of the frame
    class WindowEventHandler extends WindowAdapter {
        public void windowClosing(WindowEvent e) {
            System.exit(0);
        }
    }

    // 5. The main method...
    public static void main(String arg[]) {
        new TBufferedImage2();
    }
}
}

// 6. Canvas to display the butterfly
class DisplayCanvas extends JPanel {
    int x, y; // Location of image.
    BufferedImage bi;

    // Constructor
    DisplayCanvas() {
        setBackground(Color.white);  // For canvas background color
        setSize(450, 400);  // Canvas width=450 height=400
```

continues

Listing 7.3   continued

```
        addMouseMotionListener(new MouseMotionHandler());

        Image image = getToolkit().getImage("butterfly.gif");

        MediaTracker mt = new MediaTracker(this);
        mt.addImage(image, 1);
        try {
            mt.waitForAll();
        } catch (Exception e) {
            System.out.println("Exception while loading image.");
        }

        // If the image has an unknown width, the image is not created
        // by using the specified image file. Therefore exit the program!
        if (image.getWidth(this) == -1) {
            System.out.println("*** Make sure you have the image "
                + "(butterfly.gif) file in the same directory.***");
            System.exit(0);
        }

        // NOTE: You need to use the image type ARGB to consider the
        //       effect of alpha value of an image.
        bi = new BufferedImage(image.getWidth(this),
                                image.getHeight(this),
                                BufferedImage.TYPE_INT_ARGB);
        Graphics2D big = bi.createGraphics();
        big.drawImage(image, 0, 0, this);
    }

    public void paintComponent(Graphics g) {
        super.paintComponent(g);

        // Create the graphics context object
        Graphics2D g2D = (Graphics2D) g;

        g2D.drawImage(bi, x, y, this);
    }

    // 7. Mouse listener class
    class MouseMotionHandler extends MouseMotionAdapter {
        public void mouseDragged(MouseEvent e) {
            x = e.getX(); y = e.getY();
            repaint();
        }
    }
}
```

Code Analysis

The class TBufferedImage2 extends the Swing frame. It declares a display canvas as its field. Inside the constructor, snippet-1 assigns a title to the frame and retrieves its content pane. Snippet-2 defines a canvas object with suitable titled border, and adds it to the frame. Snippet-3 adds a frame closing listener to the frame and then displays it at the appropriate size. Snippet-4 defines the frame closing listener class. Snippet-5 defines the main method that creates an object of the application frame.

Snippet-6 defines the canvas object, which is basically a Swing panel. The canvas is used to display the butterfly image. This class defines as its fields the location coordinates of the image and a reference to the buffered image. The constructor of this class creates the image object by using the image file. This snippet also contains the code to create a buffered image object of the specified ARGB type. The ARGB type allows the effect of alpha values of the pixel colors. Then the butterfly image is drawn in the buffered image by obtaining a reference to its graphics context. Next, the paintComponent() method creates the graphics context of the screen and blits the image stored in the buffer to the screen.

Snippet-7 is the mouse listener class that receives mouse events whenever the mouse is dragged over the canvas. Inside the mouseDragged() method, the current coordinates of the mouse are obtained to update the canvas. This update will move the butterfly to the new location.

Animation Using the Buffered Image: An Example

Images are frequently stored in buffers to perform animation. Doing so improves the speed of rendering significantly. To perform animation, you can store a series of images in memory and display them on the screen at a certain controlled frame rate. If necessary, you can exercise control on the frame rate by allowing the thread to sleep for the specified time. You can also animate a graphics shape by storing it in a buffer and flipping it to the screen after applying a transformation to the buffered image.

Listing 7.4 shows a program that animates a butterfly. The animation involves transforming the size and motion coordinates of the butterfly by applying scaling, translation, and rotation. Thus, you can see the butterfly moving around with changing size, producing the effect of the butterfly moving away from or toward the viewer. You can start or stop the animation by operating the Start Animation or Stop Animation button, respectively. Figure 7.5 shows the output of this program.

Figure 7.5

Animation using a buffered image.

Listing 7.4   Animating a Series of Buffered Images (TBufferedImage3.java)

```
import javax.swing.*;
import java.awt.*;
import java.awt.event.*;
import java.awt.geom.*;
import java.awt.image.*;

class TBufferedImage3 extends JFrame {
    AnimationCanvas canvas;
    JButton startButton, stopButton;

    public TBufferedImage3() {
        // 1. Assign a title to the frame and get a handle on
        // the frame's content pane
        super("TBufferedImage3");
        Container container = getContentPane();

        // 2. Add the canvas with rectangles
        canvas = new AnimationCanvas();
        container.add(canvas);

        // 3. Add buttons to start or stop the animation
        startButton = new JButton("Start Animation");
        startButton.addActionListener(new ButtonListener());
        stopButton = new JButton("Stop Animation");
        stopButton.addActionListener(new ButtonListener());
        JPanel panel = new JPanel();
        panel.add(startButton); panel.add(stopButton);
        container.add(BorderLayout.SOUTH, panel);

        // 4. Add a frame closing listener and display the frame
        addWindowListener(new WindowEventHandler());
        setSize(450, 425);
        show(); // Display the frame
    }
```

```java
// 5. Code to handle closing of the frame
class WindowEventHandler extends WindowAdapter {
    public void windowClosing(WindowEvent e) {
        System.exit(0);
    }
}

// 6. Button listener
class ButtonListener implements ActionListener {
    public void actionPerformed(ActionEvent e) {
        JButton temp = (JButton) e.getSource();

        if (temp.equals(startButton)) {
            canvas.start();
        }
        else if (temp.equals(stopButton)) {
            canvas.stop();
        }
    }
}

// 7. The main method...
public static void main(String arg[]) {
    new TBufferedImage3();
}
}
}

// 8. Definition of the canvas that displays animation.
class AnimationCanvas extends JPanel implements Runnable {
    Thread thread;

    Image image;
    BufferedImage bi;

    double x, y, xi, yi;
    int rotate;
    double scale; int UP = 0; int DOWN = 1;
    int scaleDirection;

    // 9. Constructor
    AnimationCanvas() {
        setBackground(Color.green);  // For canvas background color
        setSize(450, 400);  // Canvas width=450 height=400

        image = getToolkit().getImage("butterfly.gif");

        // Create a media-tracker to monitor image loading.
```

continues

Listing 7.4   continued

```
    MediaTracker mt = new MediaTracker(this);
    mt.addImage(image, 1);
    try {
        mt.waitForAll();
    } catch (Exception e) {
        System.out.println("Exception while loading image.");
    }

    // If the image has an unknown width, the image is not created
    // by using the specified file. Therefore exit the program.
    if (image.getWidth(this) == -1) {
        System.out.println("*** Make sure you have the image "
            + "(butterfly.gif) file in the same directory.***");
        System.exit(0);
    }

    rotate = (int) (Math.random() * 360);
    scale = Math.random() * 1.5;
    scaleDirection = DOWN;

    xi = 50.0; yi = 50.0;

}

// This method computes the step size for animation.
public void step(int w, int h) {
    // upgrade the translation coordinates
    x += xi; y += yi;

    // the x and y exceed the dimensions of canvas
    if (x > w) {
        x = w - 1;
        xi = Math.random() * -w/32;
    }
    if (x < 0) {
        x = 2;
        xi =  Math.random() * w/32;
    }
    if (y > h) {
        y = h - 2;
        yi = Math.random() * -h/32;
    }
    if (y < 0) {
        y = 2;
        yi = Math.random() * h/32;
    }
```

```
    // upgrade the rotation coordinates
    if ((rotate += 5) == 360) {
        rotate = 0;
    }
    // upgrade the scaling coordinates depending on the
    // increase or decrease in size. If the increase in size
    // exceeds a limit of 1.5, decrease the size. If the
    // decrease in size falls below 0.5, increase the size.
    if (scaleDirection == UP) {
        if ((scale += 0.5) > 1.5) {
            scaleDirection = DOWN;
        }
    }
    // upgrade the scaling coordinates.

    else if (scaleDirection == DOWN) {
        if ((scale -= .05) < 0.5) {
            scaleDirection = UP;
        }
    }
}

public void paintComponent(Graphics g) {
    super.paintComponent(g);
    Dimension d = getSize(); // Get the dimensions.

    // Create a buffered image of type ARGB.
    bi = new BufferedImage(d.width, d.height, BufferedImage.TYPE_INT_ARGB);
    // Retrieve its graphics context
    Graphics2D big = bi.createGraphics();

    // Update the coordinates by appropriate step sizes
    step(d.width, d.height);

    AffineTransform at = new AffineTransform();
    at.setToIdentity();
    at.translate(x, y); // Translate the image
    at.rotate(Math.toRadians(rotate)); // Rotate the image
    at.scale(scale, scale); // Scale the image
    big.drawImage(image, at, this); // Draw into the buffered image

    Graphics2D g2D = (Graphics2D) g; // 2D Graphics context of the screen.
    // Draw the buffered image into context.
    g2D.drawImage(bi, 0 , 0, null);

    big.dispose();
}
```

continues

Listing 7.4 continued

```
// Starts the thread
public void start() {
    thread = new Thread(this);
    thread.setPriority(Thread.MIN_PRIORITY);
    thread.start();
}

// Stops the thread
public void stop() {
    if (thread != null)
        thread.interrupt();
    thread = null;
}

// Runs the thread
public void run() {
    Thread me = Thread.currentThread();
    while (thread == me) {
        repaint();
    }
    thread = null;
}
}
```

Code Analysis

The class `TBufferedImage3` extends the Swing frame. This class declares references to the animation canvas and Start Animation and Stop Animation buttons as its fields. Inside the constructor, snippet-1 assigns a title to the frame and gets a handle on the frame's content pane. Snippet-2 defines the canvas object and adds it to the frame. Snippet-3 creates a panel to display the Start Animation and Stop Animation buttons, and adds it to the frame. Snippet-4 registers the frame closing listener to the frame and then displays the frame at a suitable size. Snippet-5 defines the frame event handler class. Snippet-6 defines the action listener object to handle operations when the Start Animation and Stop Animation buttons are operated. Snippet-7 shows the main method, in which an instance of the application frame is created.

Snippet-8 defines the canvas class. Snippet-9 is the constructor where an image object of the butterfly is created. You can also find in this snippet the code to initialize the translation, rotation, and scaling parameters for the affine transformation that is applied on the buffered image.

The `paintComponent()` method initially retrieves the dimensions of the canvas (which is a panel). The buffered image of type ARGB is created and the corresponding context is obtained. Next, the translation, rotation, and scaling parameters are updated to new values by using the appropriate step sizes as defined in the method `step()`. Then the affine transformation is applied to the image that is stored in the buffer. The remaining code statements implement the operations to blit the image to the monitor screen.

The `start()` method creates a new thread for the animation and starts it. The `stop()` method is used to stop the animation by interrupting the thread. The `run()` method is invoked when the `start()` operation is invoked on the animation thread. The `start()` and `stop()` methods of the canvas class are invoked in the action listener class that attends to the operations on Start Animation and Stop Animation buttons.

CHAPTER 8

Image Processing

The immediate mode model introduced in Java 2D provides an efficient architecture to handle image data from buffered images or rasters. In addition to storing images in a buffer, you can perform the processing of information at the pixel level. The Java 2D supports two interfaces, called BufferedImageOp and RasterOp, that define the functionality to create various image processing filters. These interfaces reside in the java.awt.image package.

The package java.awt.image also contains classes called LookupOp, ColorConvertOp, RescaleOp, ConvolveOp, AffineTransformOp, and BandCombineOp that implement the BufferedImageOp and RasterOp interfaces. Note that the class BandCombineOp implements only the interface RasterOp. Thus, it performs the filtering operations on rasters. The remaining classes implement both the BufferedImageOp and RasterOp interfaces and, thus, can filter both rasters and buffered images. The only deficiency with the BufferedImageOp and RasterOp interfaces is their lack of support for inputting more than one source image on which the filtering operation is performed. This limitation prevents you from generating pixel values based on an operation that involves combining two or more images.

The filtering classes support operations, such as

- Using look-up tables for filtering
- Performing color conversions from one color space to another
- Rescaling pixel values to alter their brightness and contrast
- Applying convolution on images to sharpen, blur, and detect edges

- Geometrically transforming pixels for scaling, rotation, translation, and shear
- Combining the bands of rasters using linear transformations

This chapter initially presents information on the `BufferedImageOp` and `RasterOp` interfaces. Sections on various filtering operations will follow, with suitable examples.

Buffered Image and Raster Operations

The buffered image and raster operations are applied to buffered images and rasters, respectively. The interfaces `BufferedImageOp` and `RasterOp` describe operations to be performed on the corresponding sources.

The `BufferedImageOp` and `RasterOp` interfaces describe filtering operations based on the immediate mode imaging model. The interfaces describe operations to be performed on single inputs. The interfaces also describe operations only for single outputs. For filtering operations on raster inputs, the source and destination objects must have the appropriate number of bands for a particular filter.

The filter classes that implement the `BufferedImageOp` interface must provide code for the following methods, which define a filter using buffered images as inputs.

`public BufferedImage filter(BufferedImage src, BufferedImage dest)`
performs a filtering operation on a source image. If the color models for the source and destination images do not match, a color conversion into the destination color model is performed. You may specify the destination image to be `null`. If the destination image is `null`, an object of `BufferedImage` with an appropriate `ColorModel` is created. The method can throw an exception of type `IllegalArgumentException` if the source or destination image is incompatible with the types of images allowed by the filter.

`public Rectangle2D getBounds2D(BufferedImage src)`
simply returns the bounding box of the filtered destination image when the source image is specified.

`public BufferedImage createCompatibleDestImage(BufferedImage src,`
                                                          `ColorModel destCM)`
creates a destination image with the correct size and number of bands when the source image and color model are specified. The created image does not contain pixel intensities.

`public Point2D getPoint2D(Point2D srcPt, Point2D dstPt)`
returns the location of the destination point given a point in the source image. If the destination point specified as `dstPt` is not `null`, this object will be used to hold the return value.

`public RenderingHints getRenderingHints()`
returns the rendering hints for the filter implementing the `BufferedImageOp` interface. The method must return `null` if hints are specified to be `null`.

The RasterOp interface also describes a filtering operation by using a set of methods. The implementation filters must provide code for these methods. The following are the encapsulated methods in the RasterOp interface.

`public WritableRaster filter(Raster src, WritableRaster dest)`
provides code to perform a filtering operation on a source raster. The filter image is stored in the destination raster. If the destination raster is specified to be null, a new raster object will be created. The method throws an exception of type IllegalArgumentException if the source or destination raster is incompatible with the types of rasters allowed by the filter.

`public Rectangle2D getBounds2D(Raster src)`
returns the bounding box of the filtered destination raster.

`public WritableRaster createCompatibleDestRaster(Raster src)`
creates a destination raster with the correct size and number of bands. The destination raster possesses pixels that have zero values.

`public Point2D getPoint2D(Point2D srcPt, Point2D dstPt)`
returns the location of the destination point, given a point in the source raster. If the destination point specified by dstPt is not null, it will be used to hold the return value.

`public RenderingHints getRenderingHints()`
returns the rendering hints from the specified implementation filter. The method returns null if no hints are specified.

Filtering Operations Using Look-Up Tables

A Look-Up Table (LUT) is simply one or more arrays of data that use pixel values in a source image as indices to the array elements. The array elements pointed to by the indices are the new values of the destination image. Figure 8.1 illustrates the concept of a look-up table. Look-up tables are useful to implement filtering operations in a simplified and efficient manner.

The abstract class LookupTable represents an LUT. The concrete classes ByteLookupTable and ShortLookupTable extend this abstract class. These classes represent LUT arrays with the byte and short data types. The LUTs contain arrays representing bands of an image. Each array in an LUT stores the data of the corresponding band.

While computing the destination pixels, the pixel value must be set to 0 if the value falls below 0. Similarly, a value exceeding 255 must be set to 255. The image buffer of the source image can serve as the buffer for the destination image. Each pixel in the source is replaced by a corresponding destination pixel. This enables you to use the source buffer to store the destination image and save memory by eliminating the necessity to allocate memory for one more image.

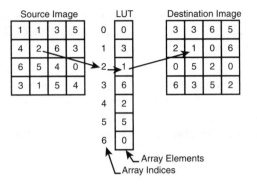

Figure 8.1

This figure illustrates the concept of a look-up table.

Creating Look-Up Tables

The classes `ByteLookupTable` and `ShortLookupTable` define the objects of the `byte` and `short` type look-up tables. For the `byte` type LUT, the arrays for the bands or pixel values contain `byte` data. Similarly, for the `short` type LUT, the arrays contain `short` type data.

You can use the following constructors from the class `ByteLookupTable` to create an object:

```
public ByteLookupTable(int offset, byte[][] array)
public ByteLookupTable(int offset, byte[] array)
```

The first constructor

```
public ByteLookupTable(int offset, byte[][] array)
```

creates a byte look-up table from the specified `array` of `byte` arrays that represent an array of bands. Thus, the length of the array represents the number of bands. The `offset` is used to subtract from the values of input pixels while indexing to the elements of the LUT arrays. The `offset` can be used to reduce the size of the LUT array to make it smaller than the data size of the source image.

```
public ByteLookupTable(int offset, byte[] array)
```
creates a byte look-up table from the `array` of bytes. This array is applied to all the bands in an image.

To create a `short` look-up table, you can use the following constructors:

```
public ShortLookupTable(int offset, short[][] data)
public ShortLookupTable(int offset, short[] data)
```

These constructors are similar to the previous constructors, except that the LUT arrays use the `short` type data.

`public ShortLookupTable(int offset, short[][] data)`
requires an array of `short` type arrays to represent the array of bands. The offset is subtracted from the indexing data.

`public ShortLookupTable(int offset, short[] data)`
uses the band data as an array. This array is applied to all the bands in an image.

Creating and Using a Look-Up Operation Filter

After a look-up table object of type `LookupTable` is created, you can define an LUT operation by using the class `LookupOp`. This class implements the interfaces `BufferedImageOp` and `RasterOp`. Thus, you can filter images by storing them in a buffer, or by using the raster of data. The filtering methods for the respective data inputs are defined in this class. The following constructor can be used to create a look-up operation filter:

`public LookupOp(LookupTable lookupTable, RenderingHints hints)`
This constructor creates a look-up table operation object by specifying an LUT of type `LookupTable`. The remaining argument specifies one of the rendering hints defined in the class `RenderingHints`. (See the quick reference given in Chapter 10, "Inheritance Hierarchies and API Quick Reference," for the fields of this class.)

In order to apply the filter defined by the specified look-up table, the `LookupOp` class supports the following methods.

`public final BufferedImage filter(BufferedImage src, BufferedImage dst)`
receives the source and destination images as argument values. The images must be of type `BufferedImage`; that is, they are created in the accessible memory. The source and destination images can be the same.

If the destination image is specified to be `null`, a buffered image object will be created with a suitable color model. The filtering process does not accept the `IndexColorModel` introduced in the previous release of JDK. If the source image uses the `IndexColorModel`, an exception of type `IllegalArgumentException` is thrown.

`public final WritableRaster filter(Raster src, WritableRaster dst)`
performs the filtering operation based on the LUT specified. The source and destination are objects of type `Raster`. If the destination raster is `null`, a new object will be used to store the filtered bands of the image. The method throws an exception of type `IllegalArgumentException` if the source and destination rasters have different numbers of bands.

Look-Up Table Example

Listing 8.1 shows a sample program that implements LUTs to perform certain filtering operations. The filtering operations will brighten and darken the image, increase and decrease the image contrast, and create a negative. The user can operate the corresponding buttons to change these effects. The user can also reset the image to the original image. Figures 8.2 to 8.6 show the original image and filtered images.

Figure 8.2

The original image that will be subjected to look-up operations.

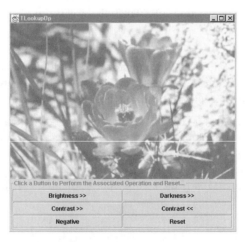

Figure 8.3

The image after its pixels have been brightened.

Figure 8.4

The image after its pixels have been darkened.

Figure 8.5

The image after an increase in contrast.

Figure 8.6

The negative of the original image.

Listing 8.1   Filtering an Image by Using a Look-Up Table (TLookupOp.java)

```java
import javax.swing.*;
import javax.swing.border.*;
import java.awt.*;
import java.awt.event.*;
import java.awt.image.*;

class TLookupOp extends JFrame {
    DisplayPanel displayPanel;
    JButton brightenButton, darkenButton,
            contrastIncButton, contrastDecButton,
            reverseButton, resetButton;

    public TLookupOp() {
        // 1. Assign a title to the frame and get a handle on
        // the frame's content pane
        super("TLookupOp");
        Container container = getContentPane();

        // 2. Create and add a panel to display images.
        displayPanel = new DisplayPanel();
        container.add(displayPanel);

        // 3. Create a control panel and add it to the main frame.
        JPanel panel = new JPanel();
        panel.setLayout(new GridLayout(3, 2));
        panel.setBorder(new TitledBorder(
        "Click a Button to Perform the Associated Operation and Reset..."));
```

```java
brightenButton = new JButton("Brightness >>");
brightenButton.addActionListener(new ButtonListener());
darkenButton = new JButton("Darkness >>");
darkenButton.addActionListener(new ButtonListener());
contrastIncButton = new JButton("Contrast >>");
contrastIncButton.addActionListener(new ButtonListener());
contrastDecButton = new JButton("Contrast <<");
contrastDecButton.addActionListener(new ButtonListener());
reverseButton = new JButton("Negative");
reverseButton.addActionListener(new ButtonListener());
resetButton = new JButton("Reset");
resetButton.addActionListener(new ButtonListener());

panel.add(brightenButton);
panel.add(darkenButton);
panel.add(contrastIncButton);
panel.add(contrastDecButton);
panel.add(reverseButton);
panel.add(resetButton);

container.add(BorderLayout.SOUTH, panel);

// 4. Add a frame closing listener and display the frame
addWindowListener(new WindowEventHandler());
// Assign suitable size. 25 is for the control panel
setSize(displayPanel.getWidth(), displayPanel.getHeight() + 25);
show(); // Display the frame
}

// 5. Code to handle closing of the frame
class WindowEventHandler extends WindowAdapter {
    public void windowClosing(WindowEvent e) {
        System.exit(0);
    }
}

// 6. The main method...
public static void main(String arg[]) {
    new TLookupOp();
}


// 7. Action listener to handle the events fired by buttons.
class ButtonListener implements ActionListener {
    public void actionPerformed(ActionEvent e) {
        JButton button = (JButton) e.getSource();
```

continues

Listing 8.1   continued

```
                 if (button.equals(brightenButton)) {
                     displayPanel.brightenLUT();
                     displayPanel.applyFilter();
                     displayPanel.repaint();
                 }
                 else if (button.equals(darkenButton)) {
                     displayPanel.darkenLUT();
                     displayPanel.applyFilter();
                     displayPanel.repaint();
                 }
                 else if (button.equals(contrastIncButton)) {
                     displayPanel.contrastIncLUT();
                     displayPanel.applyFilter();
                     displayPanel.repaint();
                 }
                 else if (button.equals(contrastDecButton)) {
                     displayPanel.contrastDecLUT();
                     displayPanel.applyFilter();
                     displayPanel.repaint();
                 }
                 else if (button.equals(reverseButton)) {
                     displayPanel.reverseLUT();
                     displayPanel.applyFilter();
                     displayPanel.repaint();
                 }
                 else if (button.equals(resetButton)) {
                     displayPanel.reset();
                     displayPanel.repaint();
                 }
            }
        }
    }
}


// 8. Definition of the display panel.
class DisplayPanel extends JPanel {
    Image displayImage;
    BufferedImage bi;
    Graphics2D big;
    LookupTable LUT;

    // Constructor
    DisplayPanel() {
        setBackground(Color.black);  // panel background color
        loadImage();
        setSize(displayImage.getWidth(this),
                displayImage.getWidth(this));  // panel width and height
```

```
        createBufferedImage();
}


// This method loads the specified image.
public void loadImage() {
    // Create an image object using the specified file
    displayImage = Toolkit.getDefaultToolkit().getImage("images/car.jpg");
    MediaTracker mt = new MediaTracker(this);
    mt.addImage(displayImage, 1);
    try {
        mt.waitForAll();
    } catch (Exception e) {
        System.out.println("Exception while loading.");
    }
    // If the image has an unknown width, the image is not created
    // by using the suggested file. Therefore exit the program.
    if (displayImage.getWidth(this) == -1) {
        System.out.println("*** Make sure you have the image "
                         + "(*.jpg) file in the same directory.***");
        System.exit(0);
    }
}


// This method creates a buffered image.
public void createBufferedImage() {
    // NOTE: Do not use createImage() method here. As the
    // component paint() method is not called, the createImage()
    // returns a null object.
    bi = new BufferedImage(displayImage.getWidth(this),
                           displayImage.getHeight(this),
                           BufferedImage.TYPE_INT_ARGB);

    // Draw the texture image into the memory buffer.
    big = bi.createGraphics();
    big.drawImage(displayImage, 0, 0, this);
}


// Create a look-up table for brightening pixels.
public void brightenLUT() {
    short brighten[] = new short[256];
    for (int i=0; i<256; i++) {
        short pixelValue = (short) (i+10);
        if (pixelValue > 255)
            pixelValue = 255;
        else if (pixelValue < 0)
            pixelValue = 0;
        brighten[i] = pixelValue;
```

continues

Listing 8.1   continued

```
        }
        LUT = new ShortLookupTable(0, brighten);
    }


    // Create a look-up table for darkening pixels.
    public void darkenLUT() {
        short brighten[] = new short[256];
        for (int i=0; i<256; i++) {
            short pixelValue = (short) (i-10);
            if (pixelValue > 255)
                pixelValue = 255;
            else if (pixelValue < 0)
                pixelValue = 0;
            brighten[i] = pixelValue;
        }
        LUT = new ShortLookupTable(0, brighten);
    }


    // Create a look-up table to increase the contrast.
    public void contrastIncLUT() {
        short brighten[] = new short[256];
        for (int i=0; i<256; i++) {
            short pixelValue = (short) (i*1.2);
            if (pixelValue > 255)
                pixelValue = 255;
            else if (pixelValue < 0)
                pixelValue = 0;
            brighten[i] = pixelValue;
        }
        LUT = new ShortLookupTable(0, brighten);
    }


    // Create a look-up table to decrease the contrast.
    public void contrastDecLUT() {
        short brighten[] = new short[256];
        for (int i=0; i<256; i++) {
            short pixelValue = (short) (i/1.2);
            if (pixelValue > 255)
                pixelValue = 255;
            else if (pixelValue < 0)
                pixelValue = 0;
            brighten[i] = pixelValue;
        }
        LUT = new ShortLookupTable(0, brighten);
    }
```

```java
// Create a look-up table to create the negative of an image.
public void reverseLUT() {
    byte reverse[] = new byte[256];
    for (int i=0; i<256; i++) {
        reverse[i] = (byte) (255-i);
    }
    LUT = new ByteLookupTable(0, reverse);
}


// Reset the display panel
public void reset() {
    big.setColor(Color.black);
    big.clearRect(0, 0, bi.getWidth(this), bi.getHeight(this));
    big.drawImage(displayImage, 0, 0, this);
}


// This method creates a look-up filter and applies it to
// the buffered image.
public void applyFilter() {
    LookupOp lop = new LookupOp(LUT, null);
    lop.filter(bi, bi);
}


// The update method
public void update(Graphics g) {
    g.clearRect(0, 0, getWidth(), getHeight());
    paintComponent(g);
}


// The paintComponent method.
public void paintComponent(Graphics g) {
    super.paintComponent(g);
    // Create the graphics context object
    Graphics2D g2D = (Graphics2D) g;

    // Draw the buffered Image on to the screen
    g2D.drawImage(bi, 0,0, this);
}
}
```

Code Analysis

The class TLookupOp represents the main frame. This class declares a reference to the display panel, and references to six buttons as its fields. Snippet-1 assigns a title and retrieves the content pane. Snippet-2 creates and adds the display panel to the main frame. Snippet-3 creates the control panel that contains the buttons, and adds it to the main frame.

Snippet-4 adds a window closing listener, assigns a suitable size to the frame, and displays it. Snippet-5 is the window listener class. Snippet-6 is the main method.

Snippet-7 defines the button listener class. Inside the `actionPerformed()` method, the code to execute the relevant functionality when a specific button is clicked. The last `else if` statement contains the code to be executed when the reset button is clicked. The remaining conditional statements basically call the methods that create the relevant lookup table, apply the lookup operation on the input image, and then repaint the display panel.

Snippet-8 defines the display panel class. Inside the constructor of this class, the background is assigned with suitable color, and then the specified image is loaded by calling `loadImage()`. Then the display panel is suitably sized, and the method `createBufferedImage()`is called to create a buffered image. The methods `brightenLUT()`, `darkenLUT()`, `contrastIncLUT()`, `contrastDecLUT()`, and `reverseLUT()` create the necessary lookup tables used in this program. The `reset()` method clears the background of the panel, and displays the original image. The `applyFilter()` method creates the lookup operation filter using the current lookup table and then performs filtering on the specified buffered image. The `paintComponent()` method displays the buffered image.

Using Rescaling Filters

A *rescaling filter* performs a linear operation on a pixel value using multiplication and addition. The multiplication involves the product of the source pixel with a scaling factor. The addition involves adding an offset to the product of the source pixel value and the scaling factor. The scaling factor and offset are referred to as the *scaling constants*. The following equation represents the rescaling filter:

```
destinationPixelValue = (sourcePixelValue X scaleFactor) +offset
```

According to this equation, two effects can occur when a rescaling filter is applied. The parameter `scaleFactor` in the product can either increase or decrease the contrast of an image. Values of `scaleFactor` that are greater than one can increase contrast, whereas values of `scaleFactor` less than one can decrease the contrast. The contrast of an image is affected because as the `scaleFactor` multiplies pixel values, the intensities of a pixel under consideration and its surrounding pixels change values based on their initial intensities.

The offset basically adds an additional value to all the pixel values in the source image. This addition will uniformly increase the brightness of all pixels if the offset is a positive number. For negative offsets, the values of all the pixels uniformly decrease, resulting in reduced brightness or darkening of the image.

The rescaling operations are encapsulated in a class called `RescaleOp`. This class implements the `BufferedImageOp` and `RasterOp` interfaces. Thus, the class `RescaleOp` supports functionality to filter both buffered images and rasters.

The rescaling operates on each band of a raster. You can specify the scaling constants for all the bands by using arrays. If only one constant is specified for the scaling factor and one constant for the offset, the same constants are applied to all bands in the raster.

The rescaling operates on the color and alpha components of a buffered image. For each component of a color and alpha value, four sets of scaling constants (scale factors and offsets) must be specified: Three sets of scaling constants are applied to the individual color components, and one set is applied to the alpha component.

You can also specify only one set of scaling constants. In this case, the same scaling factor and offset are applied to the three color components. The alpha component will not be changed. You can also specify three sets of scaling constants, which are then applied to the three respective color components. The alpha components will not be changed.

NOTE

Rescale operations are point processes because they operate on only one pixel at a time. This process is repeatedly applied to all the pixels in an image. Therefore, you can use the same source buffer as the destination buffer to store the filtered image.

Creating and Working with a Rescale Filter

The class `RescaleOp` supports two constructors that use scale factors and offsets:

```
public RescaleOp(float[] scaleFactors, float[] offsets,
                RenderingHints hints)
public RescaleOp(float scaleFactor, float offset,
                RenderingHints hints)
```

Following is the discussion of these constructors.

```
public RescaleOp(float[] scaleFactors, float[] offsets,
                RenderingHints hints)
```
creates a `RescaleOp` object with the specified arrays identified by `scaleFactors` and `offsets`. The `scaleFactors` and `offsets` arrays must provide the necessary information for the color components. You may specify the rendering hints to be `null`.

```
public RescaleOp(float scaleFactor, float offset,
                RenderingHints hints)
```
creates a `RescaleOp` object with the specified scale factor and offset. The constructor applies the `scaleFactor` and `offset` to all bands in a source `Raster` and to all color components in a `BufferedImage`. The scaling constants are not applied to the alpha value. You may specify the rendering hints to be `null`.

After an object of the `RescaleOp` filter is created, you can perform filtering by invoking the following methods on the filter object.

`public final BufferedImage filter(BufferedImage src, BufferedImage dst)`
applies the scaling factors to the pixel of the source image. An exception of type `IllegalArgumentException` is thrown if the number of scaling constants is not sufficient, or if the source image has a color model of type `IndexColorModel`.

`public final WritableRaster filter(Raster src, WritableRaster dst)`
applies the scaling factors to the bands of the source raster. You may specify the destination `Raster` to be `null`, in which case a new raster is created. The source and destination rasters must possess the same number of bands. Otherwise, an exception of type `IllegalArgumentException` is thrown.

Rescaling Filter Example

Listing 8.2 shows a program that demonstrates the effects of rescaling the pixels in an image. Rescaling changes the brightness and contrast of an image. You can click the Brightness and Contrast buttons to see their effects. (Also see the example given in Listing 8.2, which implements rescaling using look-up tables.) Figure 8.7 shows the output of this program.

Figure 8.7

This figure demonstrates the brightness and contrast effects due to rescaling.

Listing 8.2   Changing an Image's Brightness and Contrast with Rescaling (TRescaleOp.java)
```
import javax.swing.*;
import javax.swing.border.*;
import java.awt.*;
```

```java
import java.awt.event.*;
import java.awt.image.*;

class TRescaleOp extends JFrame {
    DisplayPanel displayPanel;
    JButton brightenButton, darkenButton,
            contIncButton, contDecButton;

    public TRescaleOp() {
        // 1. Assign a title to the frame and get a handle on
        // the frame's content pane
        super("TRescaleOp");
        Container container = getContentPane();

        // 2. Create the display panel and add it to the main frame.
        displayPanel = new DisplayPanel();
        container.add(displayPanel);

        // 3. Create a panel to add the control buttons. Add the
        // panel to the main frame.
        JPanel panel = new JPanel();
        panel.setLayout(new GridLayout(2, 2));
        panel.setBorder(new TitledBorder(
            "Click a Button to Perform the Associated Operation..."));

        brightenButton = new JButton("Brightness >>");
        brightenButton.addActionListener(new ButtonListener());
        darkenButton = new JButton("Brightness <<");
        darkenButton.addActionListener(new ButtonListener());

        contIncButton = new JButton("Contrast >>");
        contIncButton.addActionListener(new ButtonListener());
        contDecButton = new JButton("Contrast <<");
        contDecButton.addActionListener(new ButtonListener());

        panel.add(brightenButton);
        panel.add(darkenButton);
        panel.add(contIncButton);
        panel.add(contDecButton);

        container.add(BorderLayout.SOUTH, panel);

        // 4. Add a frame closing listener and display the frame
        addWindowListener(new WindowEventHandler());
        // Assign suitable size. 10 is for the control panel
        //setSize(displayPanel.getWidth(), displayPanel.getHeight() + 10);
        pack();
```

continues

Listing 8.2   continued

```
        show(); // Display the frame
    }


    // 5. Code to handle closing of the frame
    class WindowEventHandler extends WindowAdapter {
        public void windowClosing(WindowEvent e) {
            System.exit(0);
        }
    }


    // 6. The main method...
    public static void main(String arg[]) {
        new TRescaleOp();
    }


    // 7. Button listener that handles various control actions
    class ButtonListener implements ActionListener {
        public void actionPerformed(ActionEvent e) {
            JButton temp = (JButton) e.getSource();

            if (temp.equals(brightenButton)) {
                displayPanel.brighten = true;
                displayPanel.changeOffSet();
                System.out.println(displayPanel.offset + "=offset");
                displayPanel.rescale();
                displayPanel.repaint();
            }
            else if (temp.equals(darkenButton)) {
                displayPanel.brighten = false;
                displayPanel.changeOffSet();
                System.out.println(displayPanel.offset + "=offset");
                displayPanel.rescale();
                displayPanel.repaint();
            }
            else if (temp.equals(contIncButton)) {
                displayPanel.contrastInc = true;
                displayPanel.changeScaleFactor();
                System.out.println(displayPanel.scaleFactor + "=scaleF");
                displayPanel.rescale();
                displayPanel.repaint();
            }
            else if (temp.equals(contDecButton)) {
                displayPanel.contrastInc = false;
                displayPanel.changeScaleFactor();
                System.out.println(displayPanel.scaleFactor + "=scaleF");
                displayPanel.rescale();
                displayPanel.repaint();
            }
```

```
        }
    }
}
// 8. Panel to display images
class DisplayPanel extends JPanel {
    Image displayImage;
    BufferedImage biSrc, biDest, bi;
    Graphics2D big;
    RescaleOp rescale;
    float scaleFactor = 1.0f;
    float offset = 10;
    boolean brighten, contrastInc;


    // Constructor
    DisplayPanel() {
        setBackground(Color.black);  // panel background color
        loadImage();
        setSize(displayImage.getWidth(this),
                displayImage.getWidth(this));  // panel width and height
        createBufferedImages();
    }

    // This method loads an image.
    public void loadImage() {
        // Create an image object using the specified file
        displayImage = Toolkit.getDefaultToolkit().getImage("images/car.jpg");
        MediaTracker mt = new MediaTracker(this);
        mt.addImage(displayImage, 1);
        try {
            mt.waitForAll();
        } catch (Exception e) {
            System.out.println("Exception while loading.");
        }
        // If the image has an unknown width, the image is not created
        // by using the suggested file. Therefore exit the program.
        if (displayImage.getWidth(this) == -1) {
            System.out.println("*** Make sure you have the image "
                    + "(*.jpg) file in the same directory.***");
            System.exit(0);
        }
    }

    // This method creates the source and destination images.
    public void createBufferedImages() {
        biSrc = new BufferedImage(displayImage.getWidth(this),
                                  displayImage.getHeight(this),
```

continues

Listing 8.2   continued

```
                                    BufferedImage.TYPE_INT_RGB);

        // Draw the texture image into the memory buffer.
        big = biSrc.createGraphics();
        big.drawImage(displayImage, 0, 0, this);

        biDest = new BufferedImage(displayImage.getWidth(this),
                                   displayImage.getHeight(this),
                                   BufferedImage.TYPE_INT_RGB);
        bi = biSrc;
    }

    // This method changes the offsets.
    public void changeOffSet() {
        if (brighten) {
            if (offset < 255)
                offset = offset+5.0f;
        }
        else {
            if (offset > 0)
                offset = offset-5.0f;
        }
    }

    // This method changes the scaling factors.
    public void changeScaleFactor() {
        if (contrastInc) {
            if (scaleFactor < 2)
                scaleFactor = scaleFactor+0.1f;
        }
        else {
            if (scaleFactor > 0)
                scaleFactor = scaleFactor-0.1f;
        }
    }

    // This method creates a rescaling filter and applies
    // it to the source image.
    public void rescale() {
        rescale = new RescaleOp(scaleFactor, offset, null);
        rescale.filter(biSrc, biDest);
        bi = biDest;
    }

    // The update method
    public void update(Graphics g) {
        g.clearRect(0, 0, getWidth(), getHeight());
```

```
        paintComponent(g);
    }

    // The paintComponent method
    public void paintComponent(Graphics g) {
        super.paintComponent(g);

        // Create the graphics context object
        Graphics2D g2D = (Graphics2D) g;

        // Draw the buffered Image on to the screen
        g2D.drawImage(bi, 0, 0, this);
    }
}
```

Code Analysis

The class TRescaleOp represents the main frame. This class declares a reference to the display panel, and references to four buttons as its fields. Snippet-1 assigns a title to the frame, and retrieves a handle to its content pane. Snippet-2 creates a display panel and adds it to the main frame. Snippet-3 creates the panel that contains control buttons, and then adds the panel to the main frame. Snippet-4 adds a frame closing listener, and then displays the frame with suitable size. Snippet-5 defines the window closing listener. Snippet-6 is the main method.

Snippet-7 defines the button listener class that handles various control actions. You can see the conditional statements to modify the scale factor and offset in the conditional statements. The scale factor changes the contrast, and the offset changes the brightness (or darkness). These parameters are used to create the rescale filter. The conditional statements also execute the filtering operations by calling the rescale() method from the display panel. Next, the canvas is repainted in each case.

Snippet-8 defines the display panel class. Inside the constructor, the specified image is loaded using the loadImage() method, and then the buffered image is created using the createBufferedImages() method. You will also find the statements to assign the background color and suitable size.

The methods changeOffSet() and changeScaleFactor() change the values of the respective parameters. The rescale() method creates the scaling filter using the current values of the scale factor and offset, and then applies the filtering operation on the source image to create the destination image. The update() and paintComponent() methods display the buffered image.

Using Color Conversion Filters

A *color conversion filter* simply converts the colors of pixels in an image from one color space to another. This filter also takes care of adjusting the brightness and contrast of the destination image by rescaling the destination pixels. Color spaces can be specified through an array of color space objects or ICC_Profile objects.

The color conversion operation can be performed by using an object of the class ColorConversionOp. This class implements the interfaces BufferedImageOp and RasterOp. Thus, you can apply the color conversion filter on a buffered image or a raster.

(**NOTE**

When applying color conversion filters, you can use the source buffer as the destination buffer.

Creating and Working with Color Converison Filters

In order to create color conversion filters, the class ColorConvertOp supports four constructors:

```
public ColorConvertOp(RenderingHints hints)
public ColorConvertOp(ColorSpace cspace, RenderingHints hints)
public ColorConvertOp(ColorSpace srcCspace, ColorSpace dstCspace,
                      RenderingHints hints)
public ColorConvertOp(ICC_Profile[] profiles, RenderingHints hints)
```

These constructors use the specified color spaces, ICC_Profile objects, and rendering hints to convert the given source image from one space to another. Following is the discussion of these constructors.

```
public ColorConvertOp(RenderingHints hints)
```
creates a color conversion filter by using the rendering hints. You may also specify the rendering hints to be null. The source and destination images are specified by calling the filter() method on the ColorConvertOp object. The filter converts an image from its color space to the color space of the destination image. Because the constructor requires the destination color space, the destination image object that is specified cannot be null.

```
public ColorConvertOp(ColorSpace cspace, RenderingHints hints)
```
creates a new color conversion filter by using the color space object and rendering hints. You may specify the rendering hints to be null. The color conversion filter can be used only with buffered images and is useful when the filter method is invoked with the destination argument as null. If the destination image is null, the color space defines the destination color space for the destination created by the filter() method. Otherwise, the color space defines an intermediate space to which the source image is converted before being converted to the destination space.

```
public ColorConvertOp(ColorSpace srcCspace, ColorSpace dstCspace,
                      RenderingHints hints)
```

creates a conversion filter object that converts a source image from the specified source color space to the destination color space. You can assign the rendering hints to be null. This constructor is primarily useful for calling the `filter()` method on rasters. The number of bands in the source raster must match the number of components in the source color space. Similarly, the number of bands in the destination raster must match the number of components in the destination color space. If you use buffered images instead of rasters, the two color spaces define intermediate spaces through which the source is converted before being converted to the destination space.

`public ColorConvertOp(ICC_Profile[] profiles, RenderingHints hints)`
creates a conversion filter by using `ICC_Profile` objects and rendering hints. You may specify the rendering hints argument to be null. The array of profiles includes profiles that represent color spaces, profiles that represent effects, and other compatible profiles. If the whole profile sequence in the array does not represent a well-defined color conversion as mentioned, an exception of type `IllegalArgumentException` is thrown.

When a color conversion object of type `ColorConversionOp` is created, you can call the following `filter()` methods to perform filtering of buffered images or rasters.

`public final BufferedImage filter(BufferedImage src, BufferedImage dest)`
operates the filter on the source image to create the destination filter. If the destination image is null, a buffered image with an appropriate color model is created. If the destination is null and the filter is constructed using the constructor that takes only the rendering hints as its argument, an exception of type `IllegalArgumentException` is thrown.

`public final WritableRaster filter(Raster src, WritableRaster dest)`
filters the source raster and stores it in the destination raster. If the destination raster is specified to be null, a new raster is created. If the number of source or destination bands is incorrect, or if the source or destination color spaces are undefined, or if this operation was constructed with one of the constructors that applies only to operations on `BufferedImages`, an exception of type `IllegalArgumentException` is thrown.

Color Conversion Filter Example

Listing 8.3 shows a program that demonstrates how to use a color conversion filter. The program converts the color space of the specified image to a gray scale image. Figure 8.8 shows the destination image after applying the color conversion filter.

Figure 8.8

A gray scale image generated by a color conversion filter.

Listing 8.3   Converting an Image's Color Space Using a Color Conversion Filter (TColorConvertOp.java)

```java
import javax.swing.*;
import javax.swing.border.*;
import java.awt.*;
import java.awt.event.*;
import java.awt.color.*;
import java.awt.image.*;

class TColorConvertOp extends JFrame {
    DisplayPanel displayPanel;
    JButton grayButton, resetButton;

    public TColorConvertOp() {
        // 1. Assign a title to the frame and get a handle on
        // the frame's content pane
        super("TColorConvertOp");
        Container container = getContentPane();

        // 2. Create a display panel and add it to the main frame.
        displayPanel = new DisplayPanel();
        container.add(displayPanel);

        // 3. Create a control panel and add it to the main frame
        JPanel panel = new JPanel();
        panel.setLayout(new GridLayout(1, 2));
        panel.setBorder(new TitledBorder(
            "Click the Gray Scale Button to Create Gray Scale Image..."));

        grayButton = new JButton("Gray Scale");
        grayButton.addActionListener(new ButtonListener());
```

```
        resetButton = new JButton("Reset");
        resetButton.addActionListener(new ButtonListener());

        panel.add(grayButton);
        panel.add(resetButton);

        container.add(BorderLayout.SOUTH, panel);

        // 4. Add a frame closing listener and display the frame
        addWindowListener(new WindowEventHandler());
        // Assign suitable size. 15 is for the control panel
        setSize(displayPanel.getWidth(), displayPanel.getHeight() + 15);
        show(); // Display the frame
    }

    // 5. Code to handle closing of the frame
    class WindowEventHandler extends WindowAdapter {
        public void windowClosing(WindowEvent e) {
            System.exit(0);
        }
    }

    // 6. The main method...
    public static void main(String arg[]) {
        new TColorConvertOp();
    }

    // 7. Action listener to handle the event fired by buttons.
    class ButtonListener implements ActionListener {
        public void actionPerformed(ActionEvent e) {
            JButton button = (JButton) e.getSource();

            if (button.equals(grayButton)) {
                displayPanel.grayOut();
                displayPanel.repaint();
            }
            else if (button.equals(resetButton)) {
                displayPanel.reset();
                displayPanel.repaint();
            }
        }
    }
}

// 8. Definition of the display panel.
class DisplayPanel extends JPanel {
    Image displayImage;
```

continues

Listing 8.3   continued

```
    BufferedImage bi;
    Graphics2D big;

    // Constructor
    DisplayPanel() {
        setBackground(Color.black);  // panel background color
        loadImage();
        setSize(displayImage.getWidth(this),
                displayImage.getWidth(this));  // panel width and height

        createBufferedImage();
    }

    // This method loads the specified image
    public void loadImage() {
        // Create an image object using the specified file
        displayImage = Toolkit.getDefaultToolkit().getImage("images/car.jpg");
        MediaTracker mt = new MediaTracker(this);
        mt.addImage(displayImage, 1);
        try {
            mt.waitForAll();
        } catch (Exception e) {
            System.out.println("Exception while loading.");
        }
        // If the image has an unknown width, the image is not created
        // by using the suggested file. Therefore exit the program.
        if (displayImage.getWidth(this) == -1) {
            System.out.println("*** Make sure you have the image "
                            + "(*.jpg) file in the same directory.***");
            System.exit(0);
        }
    }

    // This method creates a buffered image object.
    public void createBufferedImage() {
        // NOTE: Do not use createImage() method here. As the
        // component paint() method is not called, createImage()
        // returns a null object.
        bi = new BufferedImage(displayImage.getWidth(this),
                               displayImage.getHeight(this),
                               BufferedImage.TYPE_INT_RGB);

        // Draw the texture image into the memory buffer.
        big = bi.createGraphics();
        big.drawImage(displayImage, 0, 0, this);
    }

    // This method creates a color conversion filter and applies
```

```
// the filtering operation on the buffered image.
public void grayOut() {
    ColorConvertOp colorConvert = new ColorConvertOp(
        ColorSpace.getInstance(ColorSpace.CS_GRAY), null);
    colorConvert.filter(bi, bi);
}

// Reset the display panel
public void reset() {
    big.setColor(Color.black);
    big.clearRect(0, 0, bi.getWidth(this), bi.getHeight(this));
    big.drawImage(displayImage, 0, 0, this);
}

// The update method
public void update(Graphics g) {
    g.clearRect(0, 0, getWidth(), getHeight());
    paintComponent(g);
}

// The paintComponent method
public void paintComponent(Graphics g) {
    super.paintComponent(g);
    // Create the graphics context object
    Graphics2D g2D = (Graphics2D) g;

    // Draw the buffered Image on to the screen
    g2D.drawImage(bi, 0,0, this);
}
}
```

Code Analysis

The class TColorConvertOp() represents the main frame. This class declares the references to a display panel and control buttons as its fields. Snippet-1 assigns a title to the frame and obtains a handle on the frame's content pane. Snippet-2 creates a display panel and adds it to the main frame. Snippet-3 creates the panel that contains control buttons, and adds it to the frame. Snippet-4 adds a frame closing listener, and then displays the frame with suitable size. Snippet-5 defines the window closing listener. Snippet-6 is the main method.

Snippet-7 defines the action listener for the button objects. The actionPerformed() method conditionally executes the grayOut() and reset() methods.

Snippet-8 defines the display panel class. The constructor of this class loads the specified image by using the loadImage() method, and creates a buffered image by using the createdBufferedImage() method. The grayOut() method creates a color conversion operation filter, and then applies the filter on the buffered image. The reset() method clears the background and displays the original image. The update() and paintComponent() methods paint the buffered image.

Using Convolution Filters

A *convolution* is the weighted sum of pixels in the neighborhood of a source pixel. A matrix called a *convolution kernel* or *convolution mask* helps to compute the weights of neighboring pixels of an input pixel. Usually, this matrix is considered with a size that has an odd number of rows and columns to determine its center, as shown in Figure 8.9. The center corresponds to the location of the destination pixel. Convolutions are often applied to images for sharpening, blurring, edge detection, and other effects.

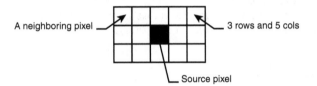

Figure 8.9

A convolution window with an odd number of rows and columns.

A *convolution window* is positioned on each source pixel to generate the corresponding destination pixel. The destination pixel is computed by multiplying the pixel values in the neighborhood with the corresponding weights in the convolution kernel, and then summing the resulting products (see Figure 8.10).

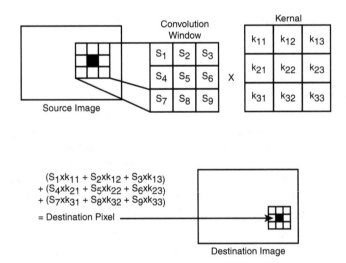

Figure 8.10

Convolving a pixel in an image using the weighted sum.

> **NOTE**
>
> The source image and the destination image cannot be stored in the same buffer. When a new pixel replaces an old pixel, the new value will be used to compute the next new pixel. If the images are stored in the same buffer, this calculation will not produce the expected results.

Creating a Convolution Kernel

The class `java.awt.image.Kernel` represents the convolution kernel or mask. The objects of this class are specified to the convolution filters that operate on an image. You can use the following constructor to create a kernel object.

`public Kernel(int width, int height, float[] data)`
creates a kernel instance from an array of `data` with `float` precision. This array stores the matrix of the convolution mask. The width and height specify the respective parameters of the matrix. The length of the array must not be smaller than the product of the width and height. If the array length is smaller, an exception of type `IllegalArgumentException` is thrown. Here is a sample array that specifies a kernel with three rows and three columns:

```
float data[] = {-1.0f, -1.0f, -1.0f,
                -1.0f,  9.0f, -1.0f,
                -1.0f, -1.0f, -1.0f};
```

The X origin and Y origin indicate the column and row of the element in the kernel that is multiplied by the pixel under consideration. The remaining elements of the kernel are multiplied by the pixels surrounding this pixel.

The X origin and Y origin are computed as

`(width-1)/2`

and

`(height-1)/2`

respectively. You can also retrieve the values of X origin and Y origin by invoking the respective methods `getXorigin()` and `getYorigin()`.

Creating and Working with Convolution Filters

A convolution filter operates by computing the weighted value of each pixel in an image by using the values specified in the convolution mask. The class `ConvolveOp` represents a convolution filter. This class implements `BufferedImageOp` and `RasterOp` interfaces, so you can apply the filter on either buffered images or rasters.

Sometimes there are no pixel values to be multiplied with some kernel elements when you're operating near the edges of the source image. Two different conditions to handle this case are implemented in the class ConvolveOp. The convolution algorithm can simply copy the pixels at the edges of the source image directly to the destination image without altering the pixel values. The static field EDGE_NO_OP specifies this condition to the convolution filter. Another simple solution is to set the pixels at the edge of the destination image to zero. The static field EDGE_ZERO_FILL specifies this condition to the convolution filter.

After a convolution kernel is created, you can construct the objects of the convolution filter by using one of the following constructors:

```
public ConvolveOp(Kernel kernel)
public ConvolveOp(Kernel kernel, int edgeCondition, RenderingHints hints)
```

The first constructor

```
public ConvolveOp(Kernel kernel)
```
creates a convolution filter by using the specified kernel. The filter uses the edge condition to set the pixels in the edges to zeros.

```
public ConvolveOp(Kernel kernel, int edgeCondition, RenderingHints hints)
```
creates a filter by using the specified kernel, edge condition, and rendering hints. The rendering hints argument can take a null value.

The class ConvolveOp supports two different filter() methods to apply the filtering operations on buffered images and rasters:

```
public final BufferedImage filter(BufferedImage src, BufferedImage dst)
public final WritableRaster filter(Raster src, WritableRaster dst)
```

The first method

```
public final BufferedImage filter(BufferedImage src, BufferedImage dst)
```

applies a convolution operation on buffered images that are specified. The transparency components (or alpha values) of the pixels are also convolved. If the destination image is specified to be null, a buffered image will be created with the color model of the source. The method throws an exception of type IllegalArgumentException if the source and destination images happen to be the same.

```
public final WritableRaster filter(Raster src, WritableRaster dst)
```
applies a convolution filter on raster objects. The destination image must be a writable raster to allow storing of the convolved image. The source and destination rasters must have the same number of bands. If the destination object is null, a new object will be created. This method also throws an exception of type IllegalArgumentException if the source and destination rasters happen to be the same.

Convolved Image Example

Listing 8.4 shows a program that demonstrates the effects of convolution filters. The output of the program allows the user to sharpen, blur, or detect edges of the specified image. The user can operate the respective buttons to see these effects. Figure 8.11 shows the original image; Figures 8.12 to 8.14 show the filtered images.

Figure 8.11

The original image that will be subjected to convolution filters.

Figure 8.12

The image after being sharpened by using a convolution filter.

Figure 8.13

The image after being blurred by using a convolution filter.

Figure 8.14

The image after the edge detection (convolution) filter has been applied.

Listing 8.4   Convolving an Image to Sharpen, Blur, and Detect Edges (TConvolveOp.java)

```
import javax.swing.*;
import javax.swing.border.*;
import java.awt.*;
import java.awt.event.*;
import java.awt.image.*;

class TConvolveOp extends JFrame {
```

```
DisplayPanel displayPanel;
JButton sharpenButton, blurringButton,
      edButton, resetButton;

public TConvolveOp() {
    // 1. Assign a title to the frame and get a handle on
    // the frame's content pane
    super("TConvolveOp");
    Container container = getContentPane();

    // 2. Define and add a panel that displays images.
    displayPanel = new DisplayPanel();
    container.add(displayPanel);

    // 3. Create a panel to add the control buttons. Add the
    // panel to the main frame.
    JPanel panel = new JPanel();
    panel.setLayout(new GridLayout(2, 2));
    panel.setBorder(new TitledBorder(
    "Click a Button to Perform the Associated Operation and Reset..."));

    sharpenButton = new JButton("Sharpen");
    sharpenButton.addActionListener(new ButtonListener());
    blurringButton = new JButton("Blur");
    blurringButton.addActionListener(new ButtonListener());
    edButton = new JButton("Edge Detect");
    edButton.addActionListener(new ButtonListener());
    resetButton = new JButton("Reset");
    resetButton.addActionListener(new ButtonListener());

    panel.add(sharpenButton);
    panel.add(blurringButton);
    panel.add(edButton);
    panel.add(resetButton);

    container.add(BorderLayout.SOUTH, panel);

    // 4. Add a frame closing listener and display the frame
    addWindowListener(new WindowEventHandler());
    // Assign suitable size. 10 is for the control panel
    setSize(displayPanel.getWidth(), displayPanel.getHeight() + 10);
    show(); // Display the frame
}

// 5. Code to handle closing of the frame
class WindowEventHandler extends WindowAdapter {
    public void windowClosing(WindowEvent e) {
```

continues

Listing 8.4   continued

```java
            System.exit(0);
        }
    }


    // 6. The main method...
    public static void main(String arg[]) {
        new TConvolveOp();
    }


    // 7. Action listener to handle the events fired by buttons.
    class ButtonListener implements ActionListener {
        public void actionPerformed(ActionEvent e) {
            JButton button = (JButton) e.getSource();

            if (button.equals(sharpenButton)) {
                displayPanel.sharpen();
                displayPanel.repaint();
            }
            else if (button.equals(blurringButton)) {
                displayPanel.blur();
                displayPanel.repaint();
            }
            else if (button.equals(edButton)) {
                displayPanel.edgeDetect();
                displayPanel.repaint();
            }
            else if (button.equals(resetButton)) {
                displayPanel.reset();
                displayPanel.repaint();
            }
        }
    }
}


// 8. Definition of the display panel.
class DisplayPanel extends JPanel {
    Image displayImage;
    BufferedImage biSrc;
    BufferedImage biDest; // Destination image is mandatory.
    BufferedImage bi; // Only an additional reference.
    Graphics2D big;

    // Constructor
    DisplayPanel() {
        setBackground(Color.black);  // panel background color
        loadImage();
        setSize(displayImage.getWidth(this),
                displayImage.getWidth(this));  // panel width and height
```

```
        createBufferedImages();
        bi = biSrc;
}


// This method loads the specified image.
public void loadImage() {
    // Create an image object using the specified file
    displayImage = Toolkit.getDefaultToolkit().getImage("images/car.jpg");
    MediaTracker mt = new MediaTracker(this);
    mt.addImage(displayImage, 1);
    try {
        mt.waitForAll();
    } catch (Exception e) {
        System.out.println("Exception while loading.");
    }
    // If the image has an unknown width, the image is not created
    // by using the suggested file. Therefore exit the program.
    if (displayImage.getWidth(this) == -1) {
        System.out.println("*** Make sure you have the image "
                        + "(*.jpg) file in the same directory.***");
        System.exit(0);
    }
}


// This method creates the source and destination buffers
public void createBufferedImages() {
    // NOTE: Do not use createImage() method here. As the
    // component paint() method is not called, the createImage()
    // returns a null object.
    biSrc = new BufferedImage(displayImage.getWidth(this),
                            displayImage.getHeight(this),
                            BufferedImage.TYPE_INT_RGB);

    // Draw the texture image into the memory buffer.
    big = biSrc.createGraphics();
    big.drawImage(displayImage, 0, 0, this);

    // Create a buffer for the destination image.
    // NOTE: You can not use the source buffer.
    biDest = new BufferedImage(displayImage.getWidth(this),
                            displayImage.getHeight(this),
                            BufferedImage.TYPE_INT_RGB);
}

// This method creates a convolution mask to sharpen the image,
// a convolution filter, and then applies the filter on the
// source image.
```

continues

Listing 8.4   continued

```
public void sharpen() {
    // Define the kernel data which is basically the
    // Sharpening mask.
    float data[] = {-1.0f, -1.0f, -1.0f,
                    -1.0f,  9.0f, -1.0f,
                    -1.0f, -1.0f, -1.0f};
    Kernel kernel = new Kernel(3, 3, data);
    ConvolveOp convolve = new ConvolveOp(kernel,
                                    ConvolveOp.EDGE_NO_OP,
                                    null);

    convolve.filter(biSrc, biDest);
    bi = biDest;
}


// This method creates a convolution mask to blur the image,
// a convolution filter, and then applies the filter on the
// source image.

public void blur() {
    float data[] = {0.0625f, 0.125f, 0.0625f,
                    0.125f,  0.25f,  0.125f,
                    0.0625f, 0.125f, 0.0625f};
    Kernel kernel = new Kernel(3, 3, data);
    ConvolveOp convolve = new ConvolveOp(kernel,
                                    ConvolveOp.EDGE_NO_OP,
                                    null);

    convolve.filter(biSrc, biDest);
    bi = biDest;
}
// This method creates convolution mask to detect the edges in the image,
// a convolution filter, and then applies the filter on the
// source image.

public void edgeDetect() {
    // Prewitt's horizontal convolution mask
    float data[] = {1.0f, 0.0f, -1.0f,
                    1.0f, 0.0f, -1.0f,
                    1.0f, 0.0f, -1.0f};

    Kernel kernel = new Kernel(3, 3, data);
    ConvolveOp convolve = new ConvolveOp(kernel,
                                    ConvolveOp.EDGE_NO_OP,
                                    null);
    convolve.filter(biSrc, biDest);

    bi = biDest;
}
```

```
// Reset the display panel
public void reset() {
    big.setColor(Color.black);
    big.clearRect(0, 0, bi.getWidth(this), bi.getHeight(this));
    big.drawImage(displayImage, 0, 0, this);
    bi = biSrc;
}

// The update method
public void update(Graphics g) {
    g.clearRect(0, 0, getWidth(), getHeight());
    paintComponent(g);
}

// The paintComponent method
public void paintComponent(Graphics g) {
    super.paintComponent(g);
    // Create the graphics context object
    Graphics2D g2D = (Graphics2D) g;

    // Draw the buffered Image on to the screen
    g2D.drawImage(bi, 0,0, this);
}
}
```

Code Analysis

The class TConvolveOp represents the main frame. This class declares references to the display panel and control buttons as its fields. Inside the constructor, snippet-1 assigns a title to the frame and obtains a handle on the frame's content pane. Snippet-2 creates a display panel object and adds it to the frame. Snippet-3 creates a panel that contains control buttons, and adds it to the frame. Snippet-4 adds the window closing listener, and then displays the frame with suitable size. Snippet-5 defines the window closing listener. Snippet-6 is the main method.

Snippet-7 defines the action listener class. The actionPerformed() method implements the conditional statements to invoke the sharpen(), blur(), edgeDetect(), and reset() methods. These methods are called when the relevant control button is clicked.

Snippet-8 defines the display panel class. The constructor of this class loads the specified image by using the loadImage() method and then creates a buffered image by calling the createBufferedImage() method. The sharpen(), blur(), and edgeDetect() methods use appropriate kernels to create the corresponding filters. Then the filtering operation is performed on the source buffer. The resulting image is stored in the destination buffer.

The reset() method clears the background of the display panel, and then displays the original image. The paintComponent() method simply paints the buffered image.

Using Affine Transform Filters

An *affine transform filter* uses an affine transform to perform translation, rotation, scaling, and shearing on a buffered image or raster. Thus, the filter enables you to apply geometric processes on images just as they are performed on various geometric shapes and text.

The class `AffineTransformOp` represents affine transform filters. This class implements the `BufferedImageOp` and `RasterOp` interfaces to allow filtering of buffered images and rasters. While using buffered images, you need to use a separate destination image to store the filtered image. The raster objects that are used as source and destination must possess the same number of bands.

In order to perform the computation of a pixel value, the `AffineTransformOp` class supports two types of interpolation algorithms. You can use either the bilinear interpolation or nearest neighbor interpolation. These interpolation types are specified by the static fields `TYPE_BILINEAR` and `TYPE_NEAREST_NEIGHBOR`.

Bilinear interpolation is commonly used as an interpolation technique for images. Using this algorithm, the value of the newly generated pixel is computed by using the weighted sum of the four nearest pixels. The weight of each pixel is directly proportional to its distance from each existing pixel. Nearest neighbor interpolation assigns the pixel closest to the newly generated address for the source pixel as the output pixel. The fractional address computed is rounded to the nearest valid pixel address.

Creating and Working with an Affine Transform Filter

Before creating an affine transform filter, you must create an object of type `AffineTransform`. This object will enable you to translate, rotate, scale, and shear an image. You can call either the set methods—such as `setToTranslation()`, `setToRotation()`, `setToScale()`, and `setToShear()`—or the concatenation methods—such as `translate()`, `rotate()`, `scale()`, and `shear()`. The set methods assign the affine transform to the respective operations.

The method `setToIdentity()` resets the affine transform object to the `Identity` transform. Then, by using an affine transform object, you can call one of the following constructors to create an instance of `AffineTransformOp`:

```
public AffineTransformOp(AffineTransform af, RenderingHints hints)
public AffineTransformOp(AffineTransform xform, int interpolationType)
```

The first constructor

```
public AffineTransformOp(AffineTransform af, RenderingHints hints)
```

creates an affine transform filter by using the given affine transform. The constructor determines the interpolation algorithm based on the `RenderingHints` object. The rendering hints argument may be `null`, in which case the interpolation type is considered to be `TYPE_NEAREST_NEIGHBOR`.

```
public AffineTransformOp(AffineTransform xform, int interpolationType)
```
is similar to the previous constructor, but it does not require the rendering hints. You must specify the interpolation type, such as TYPE_NEAREST_NEIGHBOR or TYPE_ BILINEAR.

In order to perform the filtering operation, you can use either buffered images or rasters. The following methods from the AffineTransformOp class support the operations:

```
public final BufferedImage filter(BufferedImage src, BufferedImage dst)
public final WritableRaster filter(Raster src, WritableRaster dst)
```

These methods return the transformed objects in each case. The methods require different source and destination objects for images or rasters. If the source and destination objects happen to be the same, the methods throw an exception of type IllegalArgumentException. If the source image cannot be transformed using the specified transform, the filter throws an exception of type ImagingOpException.

Affine Transform Filter Example

Listing 8.5 shows a program that demonstrates how to apply geometric transformations on an image by using the affine transform filter. The geometric transformations scale and shear an image. The transformation parameters are displayed in combo boxes. The user can select scaling or shearing parameters for the X and Y axes. Figures 8.15 to 8.17 illustrate the program's output: Figure 8.15 shows the original image, and Figures 8.16 and 8.17 show the image in scaled and sheared forms.

Figure 8.15

The original image that will undergo scaling and shearing.

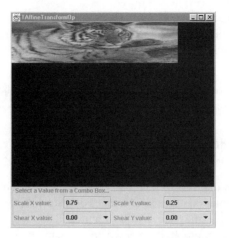

Figure 8.16

An image that has been scaled disproportionately.

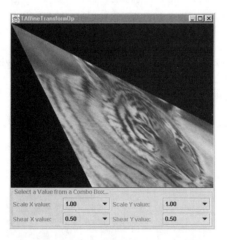

Figure 8.17

An image that has been sheared along its X and Y axes.

*Listing 8.5   Scaling and Shearing an Image by Using Affine Transform Filters
(TAffineTransformOp.java)*

```
import javax.swing.*;
import javax.swing.border.*;
import java.awt.*;
import java.awt.event.*;
import java.awt.image.*;
import java.awt.geom.*;
```

```java
class TAffineTransformOp extends JFrame {
    DisplayPanel displayPanel;
    JComboBox scaleXval, scaleYval, shearXval, shearYval;
    String[] scaleValues = {"0.10", "0.25", "0.50", "0.75", "1.00",
                            "1.25", "1.50", "1.75", "2.00"};
    String[] shearValues = {"0.00", "0.25", "0.50", "0.75", "1.00"};

    public TAffineTransformOp() {
        // 1. Assign a title to the frame and get a handle on
        // the frame's content pane
        super("TAffineTransformOp");
        Container container = getContentPane();

        // 2. Define and add a panel to display images.
        displayPanel = new DisplayPanel();
        container.add(displayPanel);

        // 3. Create a control panel and add the panel to the
        // the main frame.
        JPanel panel = new JPanel();
        panel.setLayout(new GridLayout(2, 4, 5, 5));
        panel.setBorder(new TitledBorder(
            "Click a Button to Perform the Associated Operation..."));

        scaleXval = new JComboBox(scaleValues);
        scaleXval.setSelectedItem("1.00");
        scaleXval.addActionListener(new ComboBoxListener());
        scaleYval = new JComboBox(scaleValues);
        scaleYval.setSelectedItem("1.00");
        scaleYval.addActionListener(new ComboBoxListener());

        shearXval = new JComboBox(shearValues);
        shearXval.setSelectedItem("0.00");
        shearXval.addActionListener(new ComboBoxListener());
        shearYval = new JComboBox(shearValues);
        shearYval.setSelectedItem("0.00");
        shearYval.addActionListener(new ComboBoxListener());

        panel.add(new JLabel("Scale X value:"));
        panel.add(scaleXval);
        panel.add(new JLabel("Scale Y value:"));
        panel.add(scaleYval);
        panel.add(new JLabel("Shear X value:"));
        panel.add(shearXval);
        panel.add(new JLabel("Shear Y value:"));
        panel.add(shearYval);
```

continues

Listing 8.5   continued

```java
        container.add(BorderLayout.SOUTH, panel);

        // 4. Add a frame closing listener and display the frame
        addWindowListener(new WindowEventHandler());
        // Assign suitable size. 10 is for the control panel
        setSize(displayPanel.getWidth(), displayPanel.getHeight() + 10);
        show(); // Display the frame
    }

    // 5. Code to handle closing of the frame
    class WindowEventHandler extends WindowAdapter {
        public void windowClosing(WindowEvent e) {
            System.exit(0);
        }
    }

    // 6. The main method...
    public static void main(String arg[]) {
        new TAffineTransformOp();
    }


    // 7. Action listener to handle the events fired by combo boxes.
    class ComboBoxListener implements ActionListener {
        public void actionPerformed(ActionEvent e) {
            JComboBox temp = (JComboBox) e.getSource();

            if (temp == scaleXval) {
                displayPanel.scalex = Double.parseDouble(
                                    (String)temp.getSelectedItem());
                displayPanel.applyValue(true, false);
                displayPanel.applyFilter();
                displayPanel.repaint();
            }
            else if (temp == scaleYval) {
                displayPanel.scaley = Double.parseDouble(
                                    (String)temp.getSelectedItem());
                displayPanel.applyValue(true, false);
                displayPanel.applyFilter();
                displayPanel.repaint();
            }
            else if (temp == shearXval) {
                displayPanel.shearx = Double.parseDouble(
                                    (String)temp.getSelectedItem());
                displayPanel.applyValue(false, true);
                displayPanel.applyFilter();
                displayPanel.repaint();
            }
```

```
            else if (temp == shearYval) {
                displayPanel.sheary = Double.parseDouble(
                                    (String)temp.getSelectedItem());
                displayPanel.applyValue(false, true);
                displayPanel.applyFilter();
                displayPanel.repaint();
            }
        }
    }
}

// 8. Panel to display images
class DisplayPanel extends JPanel {
    Image displayImage;
    BufferedImage biSrc, biDest; // Source and Destination
    BufferedImage bi; // For reference purpose
    Graphics2D big;

    AffineTransform transform;
    double scalex = 1.0;
    double scaley = 1.0;
    double shearx = 1.0;
    double sheary = 1.0;

    // Constructor
    DisplayPanel() {
        setBackground(Color.black);  // panel background color
        loadImage();
        setSize(displayImage.getWidth(this),
                displayImage.getWidth(this));  // panel width and height

        createBufferedImages();

        // Create the affine transform object.
        transform = new AffineTransform(); // Identity transform
    }

    // This method loads the image.
    public void loadImage() {
        // Create an image object using the specified file
        displayImage = Toolkit.getDefaultToolkit().getImage("images/car.jpg");
        MediaTracker mt = new MediaTracker(this);
        mt.addImage(displayImage, 1);
        try {
            mt.waitForAll();
        } catch (Exception e) {
            System.out.println("Exception while loading.");
```

continues

Listing 8.5   continued

```
        }
        // If the image has an unknown width, the image is not created
        // by using the suggested file. Therefore exit the program.
        if (displayImage.getWidth(this) == -1) {
            System.out.println("*** Make sure you have the image "
                        + "(*.jpg) file in the same directory.***");
            System.exit(0);
        }
    }


    // This method creates the buffered images: source and destination.
    public void createBufferedImages() {
        // NOTE: Do not use createImage() method here. As the
        // component paint() method is not called, the createImage()
        // returns a null object.
        biSrc = new BufferedImage(displayImage.getWidth(this),
                            displayImage.getHeight(this),
                            BufferedImage.TYPE_INT_RGB);

        // Draw the texture image into the memory buffer.
        big = biSrc.createGraphics();
        big.drawImage(displayImage, 0, 0, this);

        // Initially display this image
        bi = biSrc;

        // Create the destination image
        biDest = new BufferedImage(displayImage.getWidth(this),
                            displayImage.getHeight(this),
                            BufferedImage.TYPE_INT_RGB);
    }


    // This method applies the scaling and shearing values to
    // the affine transforms.
    public void applyValue(boolean scale, boolean shear) {
        if (scale) {
            transform.setToScale(scalex, scaley);
            scale = false;
        }
        else if (shear) {
            transform.setToShear(shearx, sheary);
            shear = false;
        }
    }


    // This method applies the affine transform filter to the
    // source image.
```

```
public void applyFilter() {
    AffineTransformOp op = new AffineTransformOp(
                             transform, null);
    Graphics2D biDestG2D = biDest.createGraphics();
    biDestG2D.clearRect(0, 0, biDest.getWidth(this),
                        biDest.getHeight(this));
    op.filter(biSrc, biDest);
    bi = biDest;
}


// Resets the panel to the initial image.
public void reset() {
    big.setColor(Color.black);
    big.clearRect(0, 0, bi.getWidth(this), bi.getHeight(this));
    big.drawImage(displayImage, 0, 0, this);
}


// The update method
public void update(Graphics g) {
    g.clearRect(0, 0, getWidth(), getHeight());
    paintComponent(g);
}


// The paintComponent method
public void paintComponent(Graphics g) {
    super.paintComponent(g);

    // Create the graphics context object
    Graphics2D g2D = (Graphics2D) g;

    // Draw the buffered Image on to the screen
    g2D.drawImage(bi, 0,0, this);
}
}
```

Code Analysis

The class `TAffineTransformOp` represents the main frame. This class declares references to a display panel and a combo box as its references. Inside the constructor of this class, snippet-1 assigns a title to the frame, and obtains a handle to the frame's content pane. Snippet-2 creates the display panel object, and adds it to the main frame. Snippet-3 creates a panel that contains combo boxes, and adds the panel to the frame. Snippet-4 adds a window closing listener to the frame, and then displays it with suitable size. Snippet-5 defines the frame closing listener. Snippet-6 is the main method.

Snippet-7 defines the action listener class that implements the code to apply the affine transform filtering operation with suitable transform. The filtering operations are performed whenever a selection is made in a combo box. The display panel is also updated to apply the effect of the filtering operations.

Snippet-8 defines the display panel. The constructor loads the specified image by using the `loadImage()` method, and then creates a buffered image by calling the `createBufferedImage()` method. The constructor also creates an affine transform object that is used to create the affine transform operation filter.

The `applyValue()` method applies the scaling or shearing values depending on the combo box from which the selection has been made. The `applyFilter()` method creates an affine transform operation filter and performs filtering operation on the source buffer.

The `reset()` method clears the background of display panel, and displays the original image. The `paintComponent()` method paints the buffered image on the display panel.

Using Band Combine Filters

A *band combine filter* linearly combines the bands in a raster. The linear operation is specified by a coefficient matrix. The coefficient matrix of the linear combination is obtained as follows.

If the equations of linear combinations of bands are defined as follows with b_{1new}, b_{2new}, and b_{3new} representing the newly generated bands after filtering, and b_1, b_2, and b_3 are the current bands before filtering

$$b_{1new} = a_{11}*b_1 + a_{12}*b_2 + a_{13}*b_3$$
$$b_{2new} = a_{21}*b_1 + a_{22}*b_2 + a_{23}*b_3$$
$$b_{3new} = a_{31}*b_1 + a_{32}*b_2 + a_{33}*b_3$$

$$\begin{bmatrix} b_{1new} \\ b_{2new} \\ b_{3new} \end{bmatrix} = \begin{bmatrix} a_{11} & a_{12} & a_{13} \\ a_{21} & a_{22} & a_{23} \\ a_{31} & a_{32} & a_{33} \end{bmatrix} * \begin{bmatrix} b1 \\ b2 \\ b3 \end{bmatrix}$$

then the band combine matrix is

$$\begin{bmatrix} a_{11} & a_{12} & a_{13} \\ a_{21} & a_{22} & a_{23} \\ a_{31} & a_{32} & a_{33} \end{bmatrix}$$

If the band combine matrix contains any additional columns for other information, the current bands represented as a vector are appended as additional rows, with each row containing 1.

The class `BandCombineOp` represents a band combine filter. This class implements only the `RasterOp` interface, so you can apply the filtering operations only to rasters. You can use the same raster for the source as well as for the destination.

Creating and Working with Band Combine Filters

The class `BandCombineOp` supports only one constructor to create a band combine filter:

```
public BandCombineOp(float[][] matrix, RenderingHints hints)
```

The constructor requires the band combine `matrix` and the rendering hints. The rendering hints can also take a `null` value.

After the band combine operation object is created, you can call the following `filter()` method on the object to perform filtering of a raster:

```
public WritableRaster filter(Raster src, WritableRaster dst)
```

This method filters the source raster by combining the bands using the band combine matrix. The number of bands in the source and the destination must be the same. Otherwise, the method throws an exception of type `IllegalArgumentException`. The destination may be `null`, in which case a destination raster is created with the number of bands equal to the number of rows in the matrix.

Band Combine Filter Example

Listing 8.6 shows a program that demonstrates the band combine filtering operations. The program displays an image that can be subjected to filtering by clicking the buttons from the control panel. The control panel provides the buttons to display only the red band, or blue band, or green band, or to invert all the bands, or to display only the average of each band. The user can also click the Reset button that brings the original image back to display. Figure 8.18 shows the output of this program.

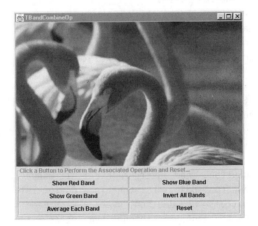

Figure 8.18

The original image that will undergo band combine filtering operations.

Listing 8.6   Performing Band Combine Filtering Operations on an Image (TBandCombineOp.java)

```
import javax.swing.*;
import javax.swing.border.*;
import java.awt.*;
```

continues

Listing 8.6   continued

```java
import java.awt.event.*;
import java.awt.image.*;

class TBandCombineOp extends JFrame {
    DisplayPanel displayPanel;
    JButton redBandButton, greenBandButton, blueBandButton,
            inverseBandButton, middleBandButton,
            resetButton;

    public TBandCombineOp() {
        // 1. Assign a title to the frame and get a handle on
        // the frame's content pane
        super("TBandCombineOp");
        Container container = getContentPane();

        // 2. Define and add a panel that displays images.
        displayPanel = new DisplayPanel();
        container.add(displayPanel);

        // 3. Create a panel to add the control buttons. Add the
        // panel to the main frame.
        JPanel panel = new JPanel();
        panel.setLayout(new GridLayout(3, 2));
        panel.setBorder(new TitledBorder(
        "Click a Button to Perform the Associated Operation and Reset..."));

        redBandButton = new JButton("Show Red Band");
        redBandButton.addActionListener(new ButtonListener());
        greenBandButton = new JButton("Show Green Band");
        greenBandButton.addActionListener(new ButtonListener());
        blueBandButton = new JButton("Show Blue Band");
        blueBandButton.addActionListener(new ButtonListener());
        inverseBandButton = new JButton("Invert All Bands");
        inverseBandButton.addActionListener(new ButtonListener());
        middleBandButton = new JButton("Average Each Band");
        middleBandButton.addActionListener(new ButtonListener());

        resetButton = new JButton("Reset");
        resetButton.addActionListener(new ButtonListener());

        // Add the buttons to the panel.
        panel.add(redBandButton);
        panel.add(blueBandButton);
        panel.add(greenBandButton);
        panel.add(inverseBandButton);
        panel.add(middleBandButton);
        panel.add(resetButton);
```

```
// Add the panel at the bottom portion of the main frame.
container.add(BorderLayout.SOUTH, panel);

// 4. Add a frame closing listener and display the frame
addWindowListener(new WindowEventHandler());
// Assign suitable size.
setSize(displayPanel.getWidth(), displayPanel.getHeight());
show(); // Display the frame
}

// 5. Code to handle closing of the frame
class WindowEventHandler extends WindowAdapter {
    public void windowClosing(WindowEvent e) {
        System.exit(0);
    }
}

// 6. The main method...
public static void main(String arg[]) {
    new TBandCombineOp();
}


// 7. Action listener to handle the events fired by buttons.
class ButtonListener implements ActionListener {
    public void actionPerformed(ActionEvent e) {
        JButton button = (JButton) e.getSource();

        // If the red band button is clicked...
        if (button.equals(redBandButton)) {
            displayPanel.bandCombine(DisplayPanel.RED_BAND_MATRIX);
            displayPanel.repaint();
        }
        // If the green band button is clicked...
        else if (button.equals(greenBandButton)) {
            displayPanel.bandCombine(DisplayPanel.GREEN_BAND_MATRIX);
            displayPanel.repaint();
        }
        // If the blue band button is clicked...
        else if (button.equals(blueBandButton)) {
            displayPanel.bandCombine(DisplayPanel.BLUE_BAND_MATRIX);
            displayPanel.repaint();
        }
        // If the button to invert all bands is clicked...
        else if (button.equals(inverseBandButton)) {
            displayPanel.bandCombine(DisplayPanel.INVERSE_BAND_MATRIX);
            displayPanel.repaint();
        }
```

continues

Listing 8.6   continued

```
            // If the button to consider half of each band intensity
            // is clicked...
            else if (button.equals(middleBandButton)) {
                displayPanel.bandCombine(DisplayPanel.AVERAGE_BAND_MATRIX);
                displayPanel.repaint();
            }
            // If the reset button is clicked...
            else if (button.equals(resetButton)) {
                displayPanel.reset();
                displayPanel.repaint();
            }
        }
    }
}


// 8. Definition of the display panel.
class DisplayPanel extends JPanel {
    // Matrix that shows only the red band
    static final float RED_BAND_MATRIX[][] = {{1.0f, 0.0f, 0.0f},
                                              {0.0f, 0.0f, 0.0f},
                                              {0.0f, 0.0f, 0.0f}};
    // Matrix that shows only the green band
    static final float GREEN_BAND_MATRIX[][] = {{0.0f, 0.0f, 0.0f},
                                                {0.0f, 1.0f, 0.0f},
                                                {0.0f, 0.0f, 0.0f}};
    // Matrix that shows only the blue band
    static final float BLUE_BAND_MATRIX[][] = {{0.0f, 0.0f, 0.0f},
                                               {0.0f, 0.0f, 0.0f},
                                               {0.0f, 0.0f, 1.0f}};
    // Matrix that inverts all the bands
    // That is, this matrix produces the negative of the image.
    static final float INVERSE_BAND_MATRIX[][] = {{-1.0f, 0.0f, 0.0f},
                                                  {0.0f, -1.0f, 0.0f},
                                                  {0.0f, 0.0f, -1.0f}};

    // Matrix that reduces the intensities of all bands
    static final float AVERAGE_BAND_MATRIX[][] = {{0.5f, 0.0f, 0.0f},
                                                  {0.0f, 0.5f, 0.0f},
                                                  {0.0f, 0.0f, 0.5f}};

    // For loading the given image
    Image displayImage;

    // The source and destination images for the display purpose.
    BufferedImage biSrc;
    BufferedImage biDest;
```

```
// The source and destination rasters for the filtering purpose
Raster srcRaster;
WritableRaster dstRaster;

BufferedImage bi; // Only an additional reference.
Graphics2D big;

// 9. Constructor
DisplayPanel() {
    setBackground(Color.black);  // panel background color
    loadImage();
    setSize(displayImage.getWidth(this),
            displayImage.getWidth(this));  // panel width and height

    createBufferedImages();
    bi = biSrc;
}

// 10. This method loads the specified image.
public void loadImage() {
    // Create an image object using the specified file
    displayImage = Toolkit.getDefaultToolkit().getImage(
                    "images/Flamingo.jpg");
    MediaTracker mt = new MediaTracker(this);
    mt.addImage(displayImage, 1);
    try {
        mt.waitForAll();
    } catch (Exception e) {
        System.out.println("Exception while loading.");
    }

    // If the image has an unknown width, the image is not created
    // by using the suggested file. Therefore exit the program.
    if (displayImage.getWidth(this) == -1) {
        System.out.println("*** Make sure you have the image "
                    + "(*.jpg) file in the same directory.***");
        System.exit(0);
    }
}

// 11. This method creates the source and destination buffers
public void createBufferedImages() {
    // NOTE: Do not use createImage() method here. As the
    // component paint() method is not at called, the createImage()
    // returns a null object.
    biSrc = new BufferedImage(displayImage.getWidth(this),
                            displayImage.getHeight(this),
                            BufferedImage.TYPE_INT_RGB);
```

continues

Listing 8.6   continued

```
        // Draw the texture image into the memory buffer.
        big = biSrc.createGraphics();
        big.drawImage(displayImage, 0, 0, this);

        // Retrieve the raster of this image
        srcRaster = biSrc.getRaster();

        // Create a buffer for the destination image.
        // NOTE: You can not use the source buffer.
        biDest = new BufferedImage(displayImage.getWidth(this),
                                   displayImage.getHeight(this),
                                   BufferedImage.TYPE_INT_RGB);

        dstRaster = (WritableRaster) biDest.getRaster();
    }

    // 12. This method creates a band combine operation filter using the
    // specified matrix, and then filters the source image.
    public void bandCombine(float[][] bandCombineMatrix) {
        BandCombineOp bandCombineOp = new BandCombineOp(bandCombineMatrix,
                                                        null);
        bandCombineOp.filter(srcRaster, dstRaster);
        bi = biDest;
    }

    // 13. Reset the display panel
    public void reset() {
        big.setColor(Color.black);
        big.clearRect(0, 0, bi.getWidth(this), bi.getHeight(this));
        big.drawImage(displayImage, 0, 0, this);
        bi = biSrc;
    }

    // 14. The update method...
    public void update(Graphics g) {
        g.clearRect(0, 0, getWidth(), getHeight());
        paintComponent(g);
    }

    // 15. The paintComponent method...
    public void paintComponent(Graphics g) {
        super.paintComponent(g);
        // Create the graphics context object
        Graphics2D g2D = (Graphics2D) g;

        // Draw the buffered Image on to the screen
        g2D.drawImage(bi, 0,0, this);
    }
}
```

Code Analysis

The class TBandCombineOp represents the main frame. The class declares the references to the display panel and control buttons as its fields. Inside the constructor, snippet-1 assigns a title to the frame and obtains a handle on the frame's content pane. Snippet-2 creates the display panel and adds it to the content pane. Snippet-3 creates a panel that contains the control buttons, and adds it to the main frame. Snippet-4 registers a window closing listener, and displays the frame with suitable size. Snippet-5 defines the window closing listener. Snippet-6 is the main method.

Snippet-7 defines the button listener class to handle the events fired by various control buttons. The actionPerformed() method contains the conditional statements that are executed when a relevant button is clicked. The last else if statement is meant for resetting the display panel by displaying the original image. The remaining conditional statements call the bandCombine() method with an appropriate argument value that represents a particular band combine operation. The conditional statements call the bandCombine() method with the argument values to show only the red band, or green band, or blue band, or to invert all bands, or to show the effect of the average of each band. Then the display panel is updated to display the effect of different bandCombine()operations.

Snippet-8 defines the display panel class. This class initially defines the matrices for various band combine operations as its static fields. Snippet-9 is the constructor of this class that loads the image using the loadImage() method (see snippet-10), and then creates a buffered image by using the createdBufferedImages() method (see snippet-11).

Snippet-12 is the bandCombine() method that creates a band combine filter. The filter is then applied to the source raster and the output is stored in the destination raster. These rasters are retrieved from the source and destination buffered images, respectively.

Snippet-13 resets the display panel by clearing the panel background, and then displaying the original image. Snippet-14 is the update() method that calls the paintComponent() method. The paintComponent() method displays the buffered image.

CHAPTER 9

Printing

The Abstract Windowing Toolkit (AWT) in the previous release of the Java Development Kit (JDK1.1) has already introduced the printing capabilities in Java. However, the printing system suffers from certain deficiencies that include lack of support for the following features:

- Setting the page format to portrait, landscape, or reverse landscape, except by using the printer dialog boxes
- Assigning imageable width and height to specify the printing area of paper by excluding the margins
- Selecting paper dimensions

Also, after the creation of printed pages begins, there is no way to abort or cancel printing. The Java 2D API has introduced comprehensive printing capabilities to overcome these deficiencies.

Using the printing framework in Java 2D, various applications can provide device-independent printing features. Now print jobs can control single- as well as multiple-format pages. Applications can provide features that enable the user to select printing with landscape, portrait, and reverse landscape page formats. The Java applications can also display dialog boxes in which the user can manipulate various parameters for page setup and printing. The only feature that's still missing in the Java 2D printing system is an API for previewing the printable content.

This chapter presents the printing concepts introduced by Java 2D, the governing interfaces and classes, and suitable practical examples.

Mechanism of Printing

The mechanism of printing is very similar to that of displaying various graphics shapes on the monitor screen of a computer. In printing, an appropriate graphics context, called the *printer graphics context*, sends the output to a different target device, which is a printer. Figure 9.1 shows a comparison of how the information content is directed to different target devices: computer screen and printer.

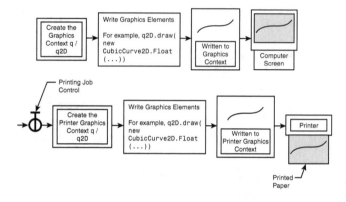

Figure 9.1

The mechanism of screen and printer outputs.

The approach to implementing printing in a Java 2D application (or applet) is to create a printable object with a suitable format such as portrait, landscape, or reverse landscape for printing pages. Then the pages containing the printable content are registered with a job control system.

A *job control system* is an object that supports operations to activate or abort a print job and display necessary dialog boxes to modify the printing parameters (such as the format). Once the printable content is given to the job control, you can invoke different printing operations from the job control system. Figure 9.2 depicts the printing operation from the job control system.

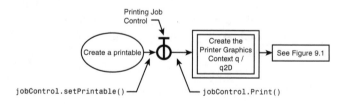

Figure 9.2

A printing operation using the job control system.

The following sections will tell you how to create a printer graphics context, write graphics elements to the graphics context, and harness the operations from the job control system. The package java.awt.print contains the interfaces and classes that govern the printing process in Java 2D. Because the process of printing might not always be completely smooth, the package also supports the necessary classes to deal with exceptional situations.

Creating the Printer Graphics Context

In Java 2D, an intermediate object, called a *printable* object, serves as a medium to create the printer graphics context and write the graphics content to it. A class that implements the interface Printable represents the printable object. The implementation class must define the body of the following method from this interface:

```
public int print (Graphics graphicsContext,
                  PageFormat pageFormat,
                  int pageIndex)
                  throws PrinterException
```

The first argument, graphicsContext, is the printer graphics context object that sends graphics content to the printer with a suitable page format (pageFormat) for the page indicated by the index (pageIndex). The pageFormat object contains the information such as the paper size, dimensions of imageable area, and orientation. You must also note that the page index begins with the value zero.

This method returns the integer constant PAGE_EXISTS when the rendering of the page is successful; it returns the integer constant NO_SUCH_PAGE if the page index does not indicate a valid existing page. These constants are static fields of the interface Printable. If the print job is terminated due to any exceptional reason, the method throws an exception of type PrinterException.

The body of the print() method contains certain rendering operations to write the content to the graphics context. That is, the output from these operations will eventually appear on the printing paper. To write graphics elements to the printer graphics context, you can invoke the relevant draw...() method from the graphics context. For example, to draw the text string "Java 2D" to the printer graphics context, you can use the following code:

```
public int print(Graphics g, PageFormat pageFormat, int pageIndex)
                  throws PrinterException {
    // Create the 2D printer graphics context
    Graphics2D g2D = (Graphics2D) g;

    // Draw the text string 'Java 2D'
    g2D.drawString("Java 2D", 100, 200); // location x = 100, y = 200.

    // Return this field on successful printing of the page
    return Printable.PAGE_EXISTS;
}
```

In case a modification is required in the final printout, the printer graphics context is a point at which you can modify the attributes of the graphics elements. For example, you can change the fill color or stroke type of a geometric shape, or convert an image to gray scale. For applications with preview support, the preview component must display the content exactly as written to the printer graphics context.

Working with Page Formats

Two classes—PageFormat and Paper—deal with the page formats in printing. You can create a PageFormat object by calling its constructor public PageFormat(). An object of PageFormat represents a portrait page format by default. This class encapsulates other page format constants as its static fields. Following is a list of these constants (also see the program given in Listing 9.2):

```
public static final int PORTRAIT
public static final int LANDSCAPE
public static final int REVERSE_LANDSCAPE
```

In the portrait format, the origin is at the top-left corner of the paper. The X axis runs from left to right, and the Y axis runs from top to bottom of the paper. In the landscape format, the origin is at the bottom-left corner of the paper. The X axis points from bottom to top, and the Y axis points from left to right. In the reverse landscape format, the origin is at the top-right corner of the paper with the X axis running from top to bottom and the Y axis running right to left.

You can alter the format of printing by calling the following method on the PageFormat object:

```
public void setOrientation(int orientation)
                 throws IllegalArgumentException
```

This method takes one of the format constants shown previously as its argument value. The method throws an illegal argument exception in case an argument that does not represent any format is fed into the method.

You can specify the properties of the printing paper to the job control system through the PageFormat object. The following method specifies a paper object to be used for the page format:

```
public void setPaper(Paper paper)
```

The paper object represents a sheet of printing paper by encapsulating its physical properties. You can create a paper object by calling its constructor public Paper(). This paper object represents letter-size paper with one-inch margins around its boundaries.

You can change the size of the printing paper and its imageable area by invoking the following methods on the paper object:

```
public void setSize(double width, double height)
public void setImageableArea(double x, double y,
                             double width, double height)
```

The first method

```
public void setSize(double width, double height)
```

assigns the values for the width and height of the paper (see Figure 9.3). These values are measured in points (1/72 of an inch).

```
public void setImageableArea(double x, double y,
                             double width, double height)
```

specifies the imageable area of the Paper object. This method requires the (x, y) coordinates of the top-left corner of the imageable area, and the width and height of the imageable area (see Figure 9.3).

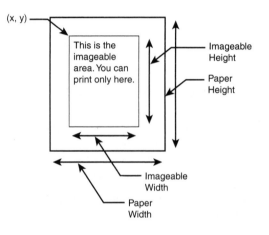

Figure 9.3

Actual and imageable dimensions of paper.

Controlling a Printing Job

Once a printable object is prepared, you can perform printing by assigning this object to a printing job control object. The job control object provides a handle to perform actions such as printing, canceling printing, or modifying the parameters of the print format or page setup to change the dimensions of the paper and imageable area.

The class PrinterJob represents a job control object; it encapsulates a number of operations to control the printing process. Initially, you can create a job control object by calling the following static method:

```
public static PrinterJob getPrinterJob()
```

The following methods from the `PrinterJob` class enable you to register a printable object with a job control object:

```
public abstract void setPrintable(Printable painter)
public abstract void setPrintable(Printable painter, PageFormat format)
```

These methods take the printable object that implements the interface `Printable` as an argument value. The second method additionally requires a specified page format, whereas the first one uses the default page format.

The following methods support the format requirements while assigning formats to a printable page:

```
public PageFormat defaultPage()
public abstract PageFormat defaultPage(PageFormat page)
```

The first method

```
public PageFormat defaultPage()
```

creates and returns a page format object that contains the default size and orientation.

```
public abstract PageFormat defaultPage(PageFormat page)
```
takes the specified page format, creates a clone or copy of it, and then returns the clone as the default format.

```
public abstract PageFormat validatePage(PageFormat page)
```
sets the current page format of the printer job to the specified page format. The specified page format will then be used for printing. This method returns a page format object that is copied from the specified page format object passed as its argument value.

The following methods from the `PrinterJob` class pop up dialog boxes to modify the printer setup and page setup:

```
public abstract boolean printDialog()
public abstract PageFormat pageDialog(PageFormat page)
```

The first method

```
public abstract boolean printDialog()
```

pops up a dialog box to change the parameters of the print job. The method returns true if the user clicks the OK or approval button; otherwise, it returns false if the user clicks the Cancel button.

```
public abstract PageFormat pageDialog(PageFormat page)
```
pops up a dialog box to change the page setup, especially to change the paper size and margins of the imageable area. This method takes a page format as its argument value. The available page format values are displayed in the dialog box. The user can modify the format values and click the OK or Cancel button. The method returns the modified

page format object with modified or new values when the user clicks OK; otherwise, the method returns the initial page format passed as the argument value.

In addition to these methods, the following methods enable you to add to an application the functionality to assign a job name and the number of copies to print:

```
public abstract void setJobName(String jobName)
public abstract void setCopies(int copies)
```

After a printable object is assigned to a job control object, you can call the following methods to initiate or abort the printing of pages:

```
public abstract void print() throws PrinterException
public abstract void cancel()
```

Note that the `print()` method throws a printer exception in case any problem aborts the printing process.

The `cancel()` method tells the printing system to cancel printing as soon as it gets a chance. The method simply does nothing if no printing jobs are in progress. If you want to test whether a print job is going to be canceled shortly, you can invoke the following method:

```
public abstract boolean isCancelled()
```

This method returns true if a print job is in progress, but will be canceled at the immediate opportunity; otherwise, it returns false.

A Single-Format Printing Example

Listing 9.1 shows a sample program that demonstrates the concepts of printing. The program uses an implementation object of the interface type `Printable`.

NOTE

The implementation in Listing 9.1 can use only a single format for printing pages. For printing pages with different page formats, you must use book-type documents, as discussed later in the chapter.

This program also demonstrates how to call the Print and Page Setup dialog boxes and initiate and cancel printing. An important feature of this program is that the printable content is proportionally positioned in the application frame as well as on the printed paper, irrespective of their dimensions. To achieve this result, the program uses a separate method (`paintContent()` in the `DrawingCanvas` class) for rendering or printing the graphics content. This method specifies the location and sizes of graphics elements in terms of the dimensions (w, h) of the container or paper. When different graphics contexts for rendering on the computer screen or printing to a printer invoke this method, the dimensions of the corresponding target device are used.

For example, when the print() method from the Printable object invokes the method paintContent(), it supplies the imageable width and height of the printing paper to compute the location and size of graphics elements. Similarly, when the paintComponent() method from the drawing canvas invokes the paintContent() method, it supplies the width and height of the canvas to render the graphics elements appropriately.

The output of this program is shown in Figure 9.4. The user can click the Page Setup button to pop up the Page Setup dialog box and alter such aspects of the page format as the paper size and imageable dimensions. Figure 9.5 shows the Page Setup dialog box in Windows 95. The modified values of the parameters are then used for printing the content.

Figure 9.4

An application frame to demonstrate printing.

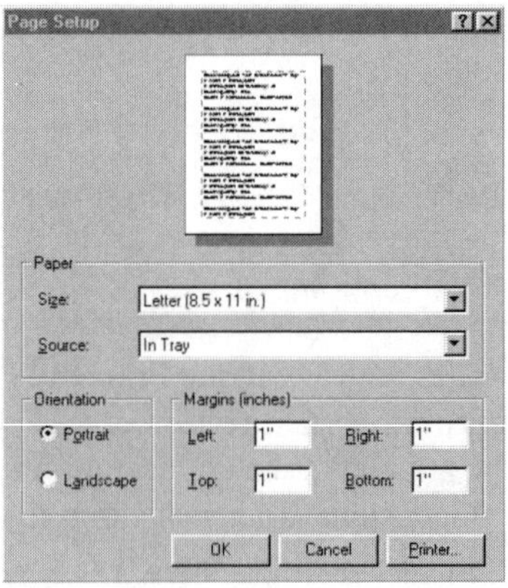

Figure 9.5

The Page Setup dialog box displayed in Windows 95.

When the user clicks the Print button, a Print dialog box opens, as shown in Figure 9.6. After performing the necessary modifications, the user can click the OK button to validate the modifications to the print parameters. Following this, the Print dialog box closes and the pages are printed out. The user can also click the Cancel button displayed on the application frame at any time during the printing process to cancel printing as soon as possible.

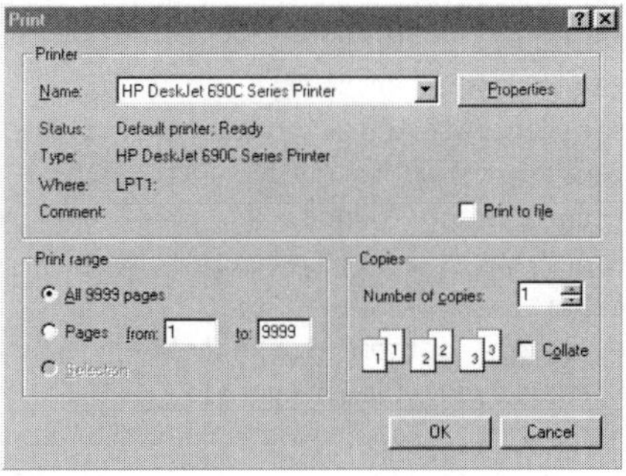

Figure 9.6

The Print dialog box displayed in Windows 95.

Listing 9.1   Single-Format Printing Example (TPrinting1.java)

```
import javax.swing.*;
import javax.swing.event.*;
import javax.swing.border.*;
import java.awt.*;
import java.awt.event.*;
import java.awt.geom.*;
import java.awt.font.*;
import java.awt.print.*;

class TPrinting1 extends JFrame {
    DrawingCanvas canvas;
    JButton setUpButton, printButton, cancelButton;

    public TPrinting1() {
        // 1. Assign a name to the frame and retrieve its content pane
        super("TPrinting1");
        Container container = getContentPane();

        // 2. Add the canvas
        canvas = new DrawingCanvas();
        container.add(canvas);
```

continues

Listing 9.1   continued

```
// 3. Create the buttons panel
JPanel panel = new JPanel();
panel.setLayout(new GridLayout(1,3));

setUpButton = new JButton("Page Setup");
ButtonListener buttonListener = new ButtonListener();
setUpButton.addActionListener(buttonListener);
panel.add(setUpButton);
printButton = new JButton("Print");
printButton.addActionListener(buttonListener);
panel.add(printButton);
cancelButton = new JButton("Cancel");
cancelButton.addActionListener(buttonListener);
panel.add(cancelButton);
// Add the panel at the bottom of the frame
container.add(BorderLayout.SOUTH, panel);

// 4. Add a frame closing listener and display the frame
addWindowListener(new WindowEventHandler());
setSize(400, 275); // Frame size
show(); // Display the frame
}

// 5. Button listener to handle action events
class ButtonListener implements ActionListener {
    PrinterJob printJob;
    PageFormat pageFormat;
    PrintableCanvas printableCanvas;

    ButtonListener() {
        // 6. Create a printer job
        printJob = PrinterJob.getPrinterJob();

        // 7. Obtain a default page format object
        pageFormat = printJob.defaultPage();
    }

    // 8. Action code for button objects
    public void actionPerformed(ActionEvent e) {
        JButton tempButton = (JButton) e.getSource();

        if (tempButton.equals(setUpButton)) {
            pageFormat = printJob.pageDialog(pageFormat);
            printJob.validatePage(pageFormat);
        }
        else if (tempButton.equals(printButton)) {
            printableCanvas = new PrintableCanvas(pageFormat);
```

```java
            printJob.setPrintable(printableCanvas);

            boolean ok = printJob.printDialog();
            if (ok) {
                try {
                    printJob.print();
                } catch (Exception pe) {
                    System.out.println("Printing Exception Occured!");
                    pe.printStackTrace();
                }
            }
        }
        else if (tempButton.equals(cancelButton)) {
            printJob.cancel();
        }
    }
}


// 9. Code to handle closing of the frame
class WindowEventHandler extends WindowAdapter {
    public void windowClosing(WindowEvent e) {
        System.exit(0);
    }
}


// 10. The main method...
public static void main(String arg[]) {
    new TPrinting1();
}
}


// 11. The display canvas
class DrawingCanvas extends JPanel {
    Font font;
    FontMetrics fontMetrics;
    int w, h;

    // 12. Constructor
    DrawingCanvas() {
        setBackground(Color.white);
        setSize(400, 275);

        // Obtain the canvas dimensions to display graphics
        // elements appropriately.
        w = this.getWidth();
        h = this.getHeight();
```

continues

Listing 9.1   continued

```
    // Font used for text, and its font metrics
    font = new Font("Dialog", Font.BOLD, 50);
    fontMetrics = getFontMetrics(font);
}


// 13. Overridden paint component method
public void paintComponent(Graphics g) {
    super.paintComponent(g); // important for proper behavior of
            // containers, especially for assigning background color.

    // Set up the 2D graphics context
    Graphics2D g2D = (Graphics2D) g;

    // Paint the contents of this canvas
    paintContent(g2D, w, h);
}

// 14. Write graphics content to the printer graphics context using the
// dimensions of the imageable area.
public void paintContent(Graphics2D g2D, int w, int h) {
    // Assign the font object
    g2D.setFont(font);

    // Create a gradient paint object
    GradientPaint gp = new GradientPaint(
            (float)(0.5*(w-fontMetrics.stringWidth("Java 2D"))),
            (float)(0.5*h+fontMetrics.getHeight()-10.0),
            Color.blue,
            (float)(0.5*w+0.5*fontMetrics.stringWidth("Java 2D")),
            (float)(0.5*h+fontMetrics.getHeight()-10.0),
            Color.red);
    g2D.setPaint(gp);  // Assign the gradient paint to the graphics context

    // Draw the string Java 2D
    g2D.drawString("Java 2D",
            (float)(0.5*(w-fontMetrics.stringWidth("Java 2D"))),
            (float)(0.5*h-1.25*fontMetrics.getHeight()));

    // Draw the string "Printing Demo"
    AffineTransform at = new AffineTransform();
    at.setToTranslation(
        0.5*(w-fontMetrics.stringWidth("Printing Demo")),
        0.5*h-0.25*fontMetrics.getHeight());
    at.shear(-0.5, 0.0);
    FontRenderContext frc = new FontRenderContext(at, false, false);
    TextLayout tl = new TextLayout("Printing Demo", font, frc);
    Shape outline = tl.getOutline(null);
```

```
        BasicStroke wideStroke = new BasicStroke(2.0f);
        g2D.setStroke(wideStroke);
        g2D.draw(outline);
    }
}


// 15. Encapsulation for the printable object
class PrintableCanvas implements Printable {
    DrawingCanvas canvas;
    PageFormat pageFormat;

    public PrintableCanvas(PageFormat pf) {
        pageFormat = pf;
    }

    // 16. Implementation method from the Printable interface
    public int print(Graphics g, PageFormat pageFormat, int pageIndex)
                throws PrinterException {
        if (pageIndex >= 1) {
            return Printable.NO_SUCH_PAGE;
        }

        // Setup the 2D graphics context for printing
        Graphics2D g2D = (Graphics2D) g;

        canvas = new DrawingCanvas();

        // Use the current format for printing
        canvas.paintContent(g2D,
                            (int) pageFormat.getImageableWidth(),
                            (int) pageFormat.getImageableHeight());

        // Notify on successful printing of the page
        return Printable.PAGE_EXISTS;
    }
}
```

Code Analysis

The class TPrinting1 is a Swing frame. This class declares a drawing canvas object and a set of buttons as its fields. The buttons are meant for invoking the Page Setup dialog box, printing, and canceling printing. Inside the constructor of this class, snippet-1 assigns a name to the frame and retrieves its content pane. Snippet-2 defines a drawing canvas and attaches it to the frame. Snippet-3 defines the set of control buttons and adds them to a panel. The panel is added to the bottom portion of the frame. Snippet-4 registers a window listener object with the frame. The snippet also displays the frame with suitable dimensions.

Snippet-5 defines an action listener that is registered with the buttons created in snippet-3. Inside this class, a printer job control object, a page format object, and a printable canvas are declared as fields. The constructor of this class defines the printer job object by calling the getPrinterJob() method, as shown in snippet-6. Snippet-7 defines the page format object by invoking the defaultPage() method on the printer job object.

Snippet-8 shows the actionPerformed() method. When the user clicks the Page Setup button, this method pops up the Page Setup dialog box that displays the current page format information at any given time. When the user clicks the OK button in the dialog box, the format is validated with the printer job object so that the format information is used from then on. When the user clicks the Print button, the governing code creates an instance of the printable canvas and assigns it to the printer job control object. Next, the Print setup dialog box is displayed. When the user clicks the OK button on this dialog box, the print() method is invoked from the job control object. If the Cancel button is clicked, the snippet executes the cancel() method from the job control object.

Snippet-9 shows the code for the window listener class. Snippet-10 is the main method in which an instance of the TPrinting1 is created.

Snippet-11 defines the drawing canvas class with its constructor defined in snippet-12. This class implements the overridden paintComponent() method as shown in snippet-13. This method calls the method paintContent() (see snippet-14) to perform rendering of graphics elements. This method takes the dimensions of the component, on which the graphics elements are rendered or printed, as its arguments.

Snippet-15 defines the class PrintableCanvas that implements the interface Printable. This class implements the print() method (see snippet-16) in which you can find the paintContent() method being called again—but this time, by passing the imageable width and height of the paper. The paint() method finally returns the constant PAGE_EXISTS on successful printing.

Printing a Book (Multi-Format) Document

A *book* is a document that can possess several printable pages. That is, each page of a book implements the Printable interface. The pages can have their own print() methods containing the corresponding code for writing graphics elements to the respective printer graphics contexts. This approach allows each page to format the printable content differently. The result is a multi-page document in which each page possesses a format of its own.

NOTE

Book-type documents can support multi-format printable pages.

A book-type document is represented by the class Book. This class implements the Pageable interface that represents a set of pages to be printed. The interface encapsulates the following three methods:

```
public Printable getPrintable(int pageIndex)
                throws IndexOutOfBoundsException
public PageFormat getPageFormat(int pageIndex)
                throws IndexOutOfBoundsException
public int getNumberOfPages()
```

The first method

```
public Printable getPrintable(int pageIndex)
                throws IndexOutOfBoundsException
```
retrieves the printable page of the specified index.

```
public PageFormat getPageFormat(int pageIndex)
                throws IndexOutOfBoundsException
```
returns the page format object for the page at the specified index.

```
public int getNumberOfPages()
```
returns the count of the total number of pages in the set of printable pages. A constant called UNKNOWN_NUMBER_OF_PAGES is returned by this method if the page count is unknown for some reason. Note that these methods will be overridden by the corresponding methods from the Book class.

Creating and Working with Books

In order to print a Book-type document, you must create an instance of the class Book by using the following constructor:

```
public Book()
```

Next, you can compile the printable pages that implement the interface Printable and provide code for the corresponding print() methods. These pages can either be added or appended to the Book-type object. The following method from the Book class enables you to add a printable page to a book with the specified page index and page format:

```
public void setPage(int pageIndex,
                Printable printablePage,
                PageFormat pageFormat)
                throws IndexOutOfBoundsException
```

Note that the page index begins at zero. The method throws an IndexOutOfBoundsException if the specified page does not exist in the book. The arguments printablePage and pageFormat cannot be null.

You can append a single page or a specified number of pages to a book by invoking the following methods, respectively:

```
public void append (Printable printablePage, PageFormat pageFormat)
public void append (Printable printablePage, PageFormat pageFormat,
                int numPages)
```

The arguments `printablePage` and `pageFormat` represent the printable object and its specified format, and neither value can be `null`. The `numPages` argument in the second method specifies the number of pages to be appended to the book.

Assigning a Book to a Printer Job Control

In order to perform various printing operations on a `Book`-type document, you must register it with a job control system. The job control system is an object of type `PrinterJob`, as discussed in the previous sections on how to control the printing process of single page documents.

The following method from the class `PrinterJob` enables you to assign a document of type `Pageable` to a job control object:

```
public abstract void setPageable (Pageable book)
                       throws NullPointerException
```

The argument `book` is of the class type `Book` and cannot be `null`. Note that the class `Book` implements the `Pageable` interface. This method analyzes the `book` object to retrieve its printable pages (along with the pages' formats) and the total page count. This information can be requested by invoking the methods `getPrintable()`, `getPageFormat()`, and `getNumberOfPages()` on the book object.

An Interactive Drawing Book Example

Listing 9.2 shows a program that enables you to draw on a canvas, and then assign the page to a book document with suitable page format. A page format can be selected by clicking one of the radio buttons. You can create any number of drawing pages and then add them to the book.

Next, you can print the book by clicking a button. You can also clear the canvas after each drawing on a page. Figure 9.7 shows the output of this program.

Figure 9.7

An application frame that demonstrates printing a book document in different formats.

Listing 9.2   A Multi-Format (Book) Printing Example (TPrinting2.java)

```java
import javax.swing.*;
import javax.swing.border.*;
import java.awt.*;
import java.awt.event.*;
import java.awt.geom.*;
import java.awt.print.*;
import java.util.Vector;


class TPrinting2 extends JFrame {
    DrawingCanvas canvas;
    JRadioButton portraitButton, landscapeButton, rLandscapeButton;
    JButton addButton, printButton, clearButton;

    public TPrinting2() {
        // 1. Assign a name to the frame and retrieve its content pane
        super("TPrinting2");
        Container container = getContentPane();

        // 2. Add the drawing canvas
        canvas = new DrawingCanvas();
        container.add(canvas);

        // 3. Create and add a control panel
        JPanel panel = new JPanel();
        panel.setBorder(new TitledBorder(
            "Select Suitable Format, "
          +"Add the Drawing Pages to Book and Print..."));
        // Add the panel to the main frame
        container.add(panel, BorderLayout.SOUTH);


        // 4. Assign grid layout to the panel
        panel.setLayout(new GridLayout(2,6)); // 2 rows and 6 cols

        // 5. Create radio buttons to select a format
        portraitButton = new JRadioButton("Portrait", true);
        landscapeButton = new JRadioButton("Landscape");
        rLandscapeButton = new JRadioButton("Reverse Landscape");

        // Prepare the radio buttons as a mutually exclusive group
        ButtonGroup exclusiveGroup = new ButtonGroup();
        exclusiveGroup.add(portraitButton);
        exclusiveGroup.add(landscapeButton);
        exclusiveGroup.add(rLandscapeButton);
```

continues

Listing 9.2   continued

```
// 6. Register an action listener with radio buttons
ActionListener buttonListener = new ButtonListener();
portraitButton.addActionListener(buttonListener);
landscapeButton.addActionListener(buttonListener);
rLandscapeButton.addActionListener(buttonListener);

// 7. Add the radio buttons to the panel
panel.add(portraitButton);
panel.add(landscapeButton);
panel.add(rLandscapeButton);

// 8. Create push buttons and add them to the panel
addButton = new JButton("Add to Book");
printButton = new JButton("Print");
clearButton = new JButton("Clear");

// 9. Register the action listener with the push buttons
addButton.addActionListener(buttonListener);
printButton.addActionListener(buttonListener);
clearButton.addActionListener(buttonListener);

// 10. Add the push buttons to the panel
panel.add(addButton);
panel.add(printButton);
panel.add(clearButton);


// 11. Add a frame closing listener and display the frame
addWindowListener(new WindowEventHandler());
setSize(450, 425); // Frame size
show(); // Display the frame
}

// 12. Code to handle closing of the frame
class WindowEventHandler extends WindowAdapter {
    public void windowClosing(WindowEvent e) {
        System.exit(0);
    }
}

// 13. The main method...
public static void main(String arg[]) {
    new TPrinting2();
}
```

```
// 14. Definition of button listener class
class ButtonListener implements ActionListener {
    PrinterJob jobControl;  // print job control object
    PageFormat pageFormat;
    Book book;  // A reference to multi-page document

    ButtonListener() {
        jobControl = PrinterJob.getPrinterJob();
        pageFormat = jobControl.defaultPage();
        book = new Book();
    }

    // 15. Handling actions method...
    public void actionPerformed(ActionEvent e) {
        // Retrieve the source object that fires action events
        Object obj = e.getSource();

        // When the source objects are radio buttons, assign
        // relevant print formats.
        if (obj instanceof JRadioButton) {
            JRadioButton tempButton = (JRadioButton) obj;

            if (tempButton.equals(portraitButton)) {
                pageFormat.setOrientation(PageFormat.PORTRAIT);
            }

            // NOTE: With JDK1.2, the landscape format does not
            // work properly.
            // But it works with Java 2 SDK1.2.2. This is a bug!
            else if (tempButton.equals(landscapeButton)) {
                pageFormat.setOrientation(PageFormat.LANDSCAPE);
            }

            // NOTE: Believed to be a bug in versions
            // JDK 1.2 —> Java 2 SDK 1.2.2. Tested on Windows 95.
            // The reverse landscape does not function.
            else if (tempButton.equals(rLandscapeButton)){
                pageFormat.setOrientation(
                    PageFormat.REVERSE_LANDSCAPE);
            }
        }

        // When the source objects are push-type buttons, execute
        // the relevant operation.
        else if (obj instanceof JButton) {
            JButton tempButton = (JButton) obj;
```

continues

Listing 9.2 continued

```
                if (tempButton.equals(addButton)) {
                    // Append a page to the book with the selected format
                    book.append(
                        new PrintableCanvas(canvas.getShapesVector()),
                        (PageFormat) pageFormat.clone());
                }
                else if (tempButton.equals(printButton)) {
                    // Assign book to the job control system
                    jobControl.setPageable(book);

                    // If the OK button is clicked on print dialog,
                    // continue printing
                    if (jobControl.printDialog()) {
                        try {
                            jobControl.print();
                        } catch (Exception pe) {
                            System.out.println("Printing Exception!");
                            pe.printStackTrace();
                        }
                    }
                }

                // To clear the canvas
                else if (tempButton.equals(clearButton)) {
                    canvas.shapesVector.clear();
                    canvas.clear = true;
                    canvas.repaint();
                }
            }
        }
    }
}


// 16. Canvas for drawing
class DrawingCanvas extends Canvas {
    private Vector shapesVector;
    Point2D currPoint, newPoint;
    Line2D line;
    boolean clear = false;

    // 17. Constructor
    DrawingCanvas() {
        // Initialize the shapes vector
        shapesVector = new Vector();

        // Register the mouse and mouse-motion listeners
        addMouseListener(new MouseHandler());
        addMouseMotionListener(new MouseMotionHandler());
```

```
        setBackground(Color.white);
        setSize(450, 400);  // canvas width & height
}


// 18. Retrieves the shapes vector
public Vector getShapesVector() {
    return shapesVector;
}


// 19. The update() method...
public void update(Graphics g) {
    // Set up the 2D graphics context
    Graphics2D g2D = (Graphics2D) g;

    g2D.setColor(Color.black);

    // Draw the lines on the canvas
    if (currPoint != null && newPoint != null) {
        line = new Line2D.Float(currPoint, newPoint);
        g2D.draw(line);

        // Store the lines in the shapes vector.
        shapesVector.addElement(line);
    }
    currPoint = newPoint;  // update the current point

    // Clear the background when the Clear button is clicked.
    if (clear) {
        g2D.setColor(Color.white);
        g2D.fillRect(0, 0, getWidth(), getHeight());
        clear = false;
    }
}


// 20. The paint() method...
public void paint(Graphics g) {
    // Set up the 2D graphics context
    Graphics2D g2D = (Graphics2D) g;

    g2D.setColor(Color.black);

    // Draw the lines whenever the canvas is resized.
    for (int i=0; i<shapesVector.size(); i++) {
        Line2D.Float line2D = (Line2D.Float) shapesVector.elementAt(i);
        g2D.draw(line2D);
    }
}
```

continues

Listing 9.2   continued

```
// 21. Mouse handler
class MouseHandler extends MouseAdapter {
    public void mousePressed(MouseEvent e) {
        currPoint = newPoint = e.getPoint();
        repaint();
    }
}


// 22. Mouse motion handler
class MouseMotionHandler extends MouseMotionAdapter {
    public void mouseDragged(MouseEvent e) {
        newPoint = e.getPoint();
        repaint();
    }
}
}


// 23. Printable canvas class
class PrintableCanvas implements Printable {
    // Stores the line objects drawn on the drawing canvas.
    private Vector linesVector;

    // Constructor: Pass the lines (shapes) drawn over the
    // drawing canvas.
    public PrintableCanvas(Vector vector) {
        linesVector = (Vector) vector.clone();
    }

    // The print() method...
    public int print(Graphics pg, PageFormat pf, int pi)
                                throws PrinterException {
        // Set up the 2D printer graphics context
        Graphics2D pg2D = (Graphics2D) pg;

        // Translate the origin of printer graphics context
        // to the origin of imageable area.
        pg2D.translate(pf.getImageableX(), pf.getImageableY());

        // Bug Alert!: The versions of JDK1.2 or Java 2 SDK 1.2.2 are
        // believed to have a bug. Tested on Windows 95
        // Bug Description: Assign a color to the printer context
        // and draw something to it to be printed on the first page,
        // and then assign the same color once again and
        // draw something to be printed on the second page. Then
        // the system does not print anything on the second page
        // (and remaining pages, if any).
```

```
// Solution: Hack the print system!!!
// Assign an arbitrary color, then you need to draw something.
pg2D.setPaint(Color.green);
pg2D.drawString(" ", 100, 100);// Draw some invisible thing!

// Now the regular code comes here; this code assigns black color
// to the context, and then prints the lines stored in the
// lines vector.
pg2D.setPaint(Color.black);
for (int i=0; i<linesVector.size(); i++) {
    Line2D.Float line2D = (Line2D.Float) linesVector.elementAt(i);
    pg2D.draw(line2D);
}

// On successfully printing the page
return Printable.PAGE_EXISTS;
        }
    }
}
```

Code Analysis

The class TPrinting2 defines the application frame. Inside the constructor, snippet-1 assigns a name to the frame, and retrieves its content pane. Snippet-2 creates a drawing canvas and adds it to the frame. Snippet-3 creates a control panel and adds it to the frame. Snippet-4 assigns a grid layout with two columns and six rows.

Snippet-5 creates a mutually exclusive set of radio buttons to allow the selection of a page format. Snippet-6 creates an action listener object, and registers the same object with all the radio buttons. Snippet-7 adds the radio buttons to the control panel.

Snippet-8 creates three pushbuttons that add a drawing page to the book document, activate printing, and clear the canvas. Snippet-9 registers the action listener created in snippet-6 with the button objects. Snippet-10 adds these buttons to the control panel.

Snippet-11 adds a frame closing listener to the frame, and then displays the frame at a suitable size. Snippet-12 defines the frame closing listener. Snippet-13 is the main method where the constructor of TPrinting2 is called.

Snippet-14 defines the action listener class whose object is registered with the radio buttons and pushbuttons. This class declares the object references of PrinterJob, PageFormat and Book as its fields. Inside the constructor of this class, the fields are initialized to the respective objects. Snippet-15 shows the actionPerformed() method. This method identifies the radio buttons and pushbuttons, and then executes the associated functionality. If the source object (that fires the events) is a radio button, it sets the appropriate page format to the page format object. This object will later be used while assigning a page to the book.

NOTE

> With JDK1.2, the landscape and reverse landscape formats do not function prop-
> erly. However, the landscape format works fine with the later version Java 2,
> SDK1.2.2. The reverse landscape still doesn't work, however.

If Add To Book button is clicked, a printable canvas object is appended to the book
object. The printable canvas stores the vector of drawing lines as its field. The lines
vector is initialized through its constructor. The constructor takes the shapes vector
from the drawing canvas and stores a copy of it in the lines vector. If the Print button
is clicked, the book object is assigned to the job control object. Next, the Print dialog
is displayed. If the user clicks the OK button, the print() method is called on the job
control object. If the Clear button is clicked, the drawing canvas is cleared so that the
user can perform another drawing operation.

Snippet-16 shows the class definition of DrawingCanvas. This class allows interactive
drawing over the canvas, stores the drawing shapes in a vector, and presents the vector
to the interested objects. Snippet-17 is the constructor of the class where the mouse listeners that help the drawing process are registered. Snippets-18 and 19 implement the
responsibilities of the class: presenting the shapes vector and drawing over the canvas.
Snippet-20 is the paint() method that displays the drawing whenever the canvas is
resized. Snippets-21 and 22 show the mouse and mouse motion listeners.

Snippet-23 shows the printable canvas class. This class implements the Printable
interface and provides the body for the print() method. The class declares the lines
vector as its field. The class has the responsibility to obtain the drawing shapes from
the drawing canvas object, and then draw the shapes over the printer graphics context.
The constructor of the class receives the lines vector from the drawing canvas and then
assigns a copy to its field linesVector.

The print() method initially creates a 2D graphics context of the printer and then
draws the contents of the lines vector for each page of the book. Then it returns a flag
indicating the success of printing.

NOTE

> The versions of JDK1.2 and Java 2 SDK 1.2.2 are believed to have a bug while
> assigning a color inside the print() method. If you assign a color to the printer
> context, the first page is printed properly. However, from the second page (of the
> book) onwards, it doesn't print anything. Note that the second and other pages
> must also use the same code inside the print() method, but with different data
> values. See the complete bug description in the code. This has been tested on
> Windows 95. To overcome this bug, you can use the hacking statements in the
> print() method of snippet-23.

CHAPTER 10

Inheritance Hierarchies and API Quick Reference

This chapter initially presents the inheritance hierarchies of classes and interfaces from various Java 2D packages. The chapter also provides a quick reference for selected classes (such as Graphics and Font) and interfaces from the java.awt package that are important for Java 2D programming work.

Most often, you will find the operations (or method) from a class have already been discussed in the previous chapters of this book. For those operations that are not clear from its method name, a brief description of the method will be presented.

NOTE

The members of a class or interface, such as fields, constructors, methods, and inner classes, are declared by using access control modifiers. An access control modifier is one of the Java keywords: public, private, protected, or package. In case a class or interface member is not declared by using one of the access control modifiers, you can assume that the member is declared to be public.

Inheritance Hierarchy Diagrams

This section provides the diagrams for inheritance hierarchies of various Java 2D classes and interfaces. The notations used for presenting the relationships are based on the graphical notations provided by the Unified Modeling Language (UML), as illustrated in Figure 10.1. Each inheritance diagram depicts interfaces and classes from a Java 2D package.

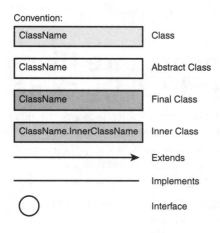

Figure 10.1

The inheritance hierarchy diagrams use this notation.

Important Note About the Inheritance Hierarchy Diagrams

Due to a printing error, Figure 10.1 and the inheritance hierarchy diagrams on pages 299–304 are inaccurate. For a complete set of replacement diagrams, please visit our Web site at

`http://www.samspublishing.com/product_support/`

and type in the ISBN of this book: **0672316692**.

We apologize for the error and hope that the value of having 100% accurate information outweighs the inconvenience of downloading the correct diagrams from our Web site. We will fix this problem in future reprints of the book.

Package Name: java.awt

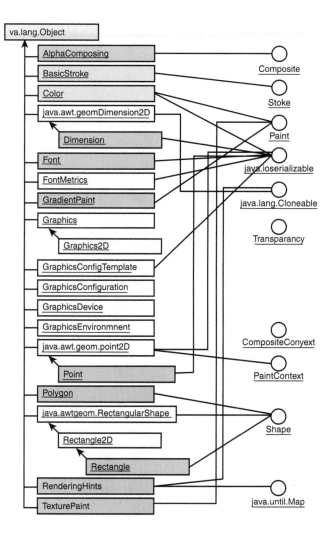

Package Name: java.awt.color

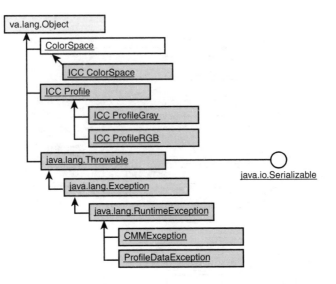

Package Name: java.awt.geom

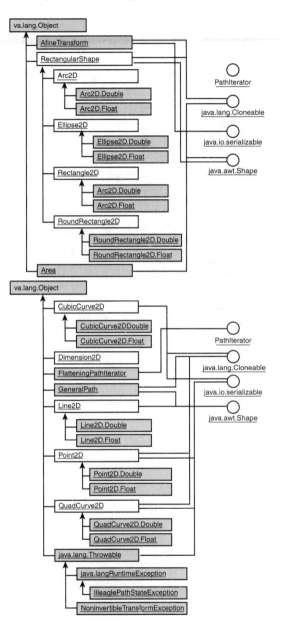

Package Name: java.awt.font

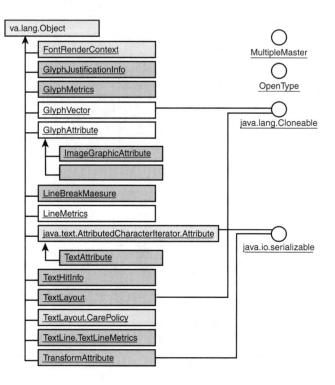

Package Name: java.awt.image

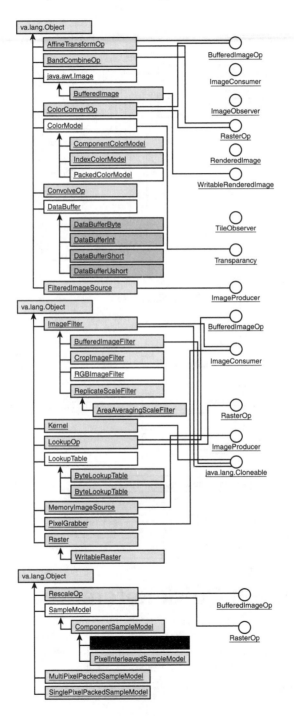

Package Name: java.awt.image.renderable

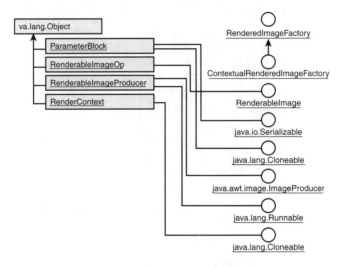

Package Name: java.awt.print

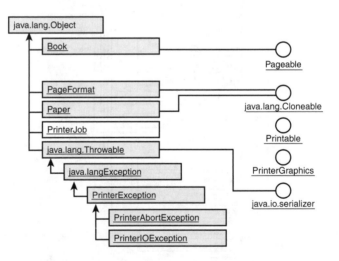

Selected API Quick Reference

This section provides a quick reference for the interfaces and classes in Java 2D. Note that you will not find a reference for every interface and class from every package. I have judiciously considered the necessary encapsulations (those that are important and most often used) to include in this reference.

You will find all the classes that are useful to change the graphics context attributes included. From the package java.awt.geom, all of the graphics primitive classes are included; however, the lower-precision classes, such as Arc.Float, are not included. You will find only the double-precision classes that represent various geometric shapes.

From the java.awt.image package, the interfaces BufferedImageOp and RasterOp are very important for building image processing operation filters. The methods from these interfaces are observed in the implementing classes. Thus, the quick reference for the processing operation classes is unnecessary. Out of all the Java 2D, the contents of the package java.awt.image.renderable have been dropped. However, you will find the selected classes from the java.awt.font package. And the java.awt.print package contains a number of important classes and interfaces that are included in the reference.

Package Name: java.awt

This package stores a number of encapsulations for creating user interfaces and graphics. In the perspective of Java 2D, the package stores various useful interfaces and classes to control rendering quality and compositing of colors, and different color fillings such as gradient and texture paints.

The package also stores the interface Shape that describes various geometric shapes, and the Stroke interface for rendering the outline of a shape with the specified stroke types. The Graphics2D graphics context class in Java 2D is also stored in this package. You can also find the enhanced Font class residing here.

public abstract interface Shape

This interface describes geometric shapes such as lines, rectangular shapes, polygons, areas, general paths, quadratic curves, and cubic curves. The classes for the geometric primitives are regarded as 2D shapes because they implement this interface. Points in Java 2D do not implement this interface and, therefore, are not considered 2D shapes.

Methods

```
boolean      contains(double x, double y)
boolean      contains(double x, double y, double w, double h)
boolean      contains(Point2D p)
boolean      contains(Rectangle2D r)
Rectangle    getBounds()
Rectangle2D  getBounds2D()
PathIterator getPathIterator(AffineTransform at)
PathIterator getPathIterator(AffineTransform at, double flatness)
boolean      intersects(double x, double y, double w, double h)
boolean      intersects(Rectangle2D r)
```

public final class AlphaComposite

```
extends Object
implements Composite
```

This class implements the basic alpha compositing rules for combining source and destination pixels of graphic shapes and images to achieve blending of colors and transparency effects. The color and alpha (transparency) components produced by the compositing operation are calculated as follows:

```
Cd = Cs*Fs + Cd*Fd
Ad = As*Fs + Ad*Fd
```

where `Fs` and `Fd` are specified by a rule represented by the fields of this class.

Fields

```
static AlphaComposite  Clear
static AlphaComposite  DstIn
static AlphaComposite  DstOut
static AlphaComposite  DstOver
static AlphaComposite  Src
static AlphaComposite  SrcIn
static AlphaComposite  SrcOut
static AlphaComposite  SrcOver
static int             CLEAR
static int             DST_IN
static int             DST_OUT
static int             DST_OVER
static int             SRC
static int             SRC_IN
static int             SRC_OUT
static int             SRC_OVER
```

Methods

```
CompositeContext       createContext(ColorModel srcColorModel,
                                     ColorModel dstColorModel,
                                     RenderingHints hints)
boolean                equals(Object obj)
float                  getAlpha()
static AlphaComposite  getInstance(int rule)
static AlphaComposite  getInstance(int rule, float alpha)
int                    getRule()
int                    hashCode()
```

public class BasicStroke

```
extends Object
implements Stroke
```

This class defines rendering attributes for the outlines of graphics primitives. Various stroke types with different pen widths, stroke endcaps, and join types are created by using the constructors and functionality from this class.

Fields

```
static int CAP_BUTT
static int CAP_ROUND
static int CAP_SQUARE
static int JOIN_BEVEL
static int JOIN_MITER
static int JOIN_ROUND
```

Constructors

```
BasicStroke()
BasicStroke(float width)
BasicStroke(float width, int cap, int join)
BasicStroke(float width, int cap, int join, float miterlimit)
BasicStroke(float width, int cap, int join, float miterlimit,
            float[] dash, float dash_phase)
```

Methods

```
Shape    createStrokedShape(Shape s)
boolean  equals(Object obj)
float[]  getDashArray()
float    getDashPhase()
int      getEndCap()
int      getLineJoin()
float    getLineWidth()
float    getMiterLimit()
int      hashCode()
```

public class Color

```
extends Object
implements Paint, Serializable
```

This class encapsulates colors in the default sRGB color space or colors in any arbitrary color spaces that are of type ColorSpace. See the ColorSpace class provided in the java.awt.color package.

Fields

```
static Color black
static Color blue
static Color cyan
static Color darkGray
static Color gray
static Color green
static Color lightGray
static Color magenta
static Color orange
static Color pink
static Color red
static Color white
static Color yellow
```

Constructors

```
Color(ColorSpace cspace, float[] components, float alpha)
Color(float r, float g, float b)
Color(float r, float g, float b, float a)
Color(int rgb)
Color(int rgba, boolean hasalpha)
Color(int r, int g, int b)
Color(int r, int g, int b, int a)
```

Methods

Color	**brighter**()
PaintContext	**createContext**(ColorModel cm, Rectangle r, Rectangle2D r2d, AffineTransform xform, RenderingHints hints)
Color	**darker**()
static Color	**decode**(String nm)
boolean	**equals**(Object obj)
int	**getAlpha**()
int	**getBlue**()
static Color	**getColor**(String nm)
static Color	**getColor**(String nm, Color v)
static Color	**getColor**(String nm, int v)
float[]	**getColorComponents**(ColorSpace cspace, float[] compArray)
float[]	**getColorComponents**(float[] compArray)
ColorSpace	**getColorSpace**()
float[]	**getComponents**(ColorSpace cspace, float[] compArray)
float[]	**getComponents**(float[] compArray)
int	**getGreen**()
static Color	**getHSBColor**(float h, float s, float b)
int	**getRed**()
int	**getRGB**()
float[]	**getRGBColorComponents**(float[] compArray)
float[]	**getRGBComponents**(float[] compArray)
int	**getTransparency**()

```
int            hashCode()
static int     HSBtoRGB(float hue, float saturation, float brightness)
static float[] RGBtoHSB(int r, int g, int b, float[] hsbvals)
String         toString()
```

public class Font

extends Object
implements Serializable

This class represents fonts. The functionality of this class has been enhanced in Java 2D to provide the ability to utilize more sophisticated typographic features. See Chapter 6, "Platform Fonts and Text Layout," for more details.

Fields

```
static int        BOLD
static int        CENTER_BASELINE
static int        HANGING_BASELINE
static int        ITALIC
protected String  name
static int        PLAIN
protected float   pointSize
static int        ROMAN_BASELINE
protected int     size
protected int     style
```

Constructors

```
Font(Map attributes)
Font(String name, int style, int size)
```

Methods

```
boolean          canDisplay(char c)
int              canDisplayUpTo(char[] text,
                 int start, int limit)
int              canDisplayUpTo(CharacterIterator
                 iter, int start, int limit)
int              canDisplayUpTo(String str)
GlyphVector      createGlyphVector(FontRenderContext
                 frc, char[] chars)
GlyphVector      createGlyphVector(FontRenderContext
                 frc, CharacterIterator ci)
GlyphVector      createGlyphVector(FontRenderContext
                 frc, int[] glyphCodes)
GlyphVector      createGlyphVector(FontRenderContext
                 frc, String str)
static Font      decode(String str)
Font             deriveFont(AffineTransform trans)
Font             deriveFont(float size)
Font             deriveFont(int style)
```

Font	**deriveFont**(int style, AffineTransform trans)
Font	**deriveFont**(int style, float size)
Font	**deriveFont**(Map attributes)
boolean	**equals**(Object obj)
protected void	**finalize**()
Map	**getAttributes**()
AttributedCharacterIterator.Attribute[]	**getAvailableAttributes**()
byte	**getBaselineFor**(char c)
String	**getFamily**()
String	**getFamily**(Locale l)
static Font	**getFont**(Map attributes)
static Font	**getFont**(String nm)
static Font	**getFont**(String nm, Font font)
String	**getFontName**()
String	**getFontName**(Locale l)
float	**getItalicAngle**()
LineMetrics	**getLineMetrics**(char[] chars, int beginIndex, int limit, FontRenderContext frc)
LineMetrics	**getLineMetrics**(CharacterIterator ci, int beginIndex, int limit, FontRenderContext frc)
LineMetrics	**getLineMetrics**(String str, FontRenderContext frc)
LineMetrics	**getLineMetrics**(String str, int beginIndex, int limit, FontRenderContext frc)
Rectangle2D	**getMaxCharBounds**(FontRenderContext frc)
int	**getMissingGlyphCode**()
String	**getName**()
int	**getNumGlyphs**()
java.awt.peer.FontPeer	**getPeer**()
String	**getPSName**()
int	**getSize**()
float	**getSize2D**()
Rectangle2D	**getStringBounds**(char[] chars, int beginIndex, int limit, FontRenderContext frc)
Rectangle2D	**getStringBounds**(CharacterIterator ci, int beginIndex, int limit, FontRenderContext frc)
Rectangle2D	**getStringBounds**(String str, FontRenderContext frc)
Rectangle2D	**getStringBounds**(String str, int beginIndex, int limit, FontRenderContext frc)
int	**getStyle**()

AffineTransform	**getTransform**()
int	**hashCode**()
boolean	**hasUniformLineMetrics**()
boolean	**isBold**()
boolean	**isItalic**()
boolean	**isPlain**()
String	**toString**()

public class GradientPaint

extends Object
implements Paint

This class fills a geometric shape with a color pattern that changes from one color to another in a linear style. See Chapter 2, "Color Handling," for the related text.

Constructors

GradientPaint(float x1, float y1, Color color1, float x2, float y2, Color color2)
GradientPaint(float x1, float y1, Color color1, float x2, float y2, Color color2, boolean cyclic)
GradientPaint(Point2D pt1, Color color1, Point2D pt2, Color color2)
GradientPaint(Point2D pt1, Color color1, Point2D pt2, Color color2, boolean cyclic)

Methods

PaintContext	**createContext**(ColorModel cm, Rectangle deviceBounds, Rectangle2D userBounds, AffineTransform xform, RenderingHints hints)
Color	**getColor1**()
Color	**getColor2**()
Point2D	**getPoint1**()
Point2D	**getPoint2**()
	intgetTransparency()
boolean	**isCyclic**()

public abstract class Graphics2D

extends Graphics

This is the graphics context class in Java 2D that extends the Graphics class to provide more sophisticated control over geometry, coordinate transformations, color management, and text layout. The class basically represents the graphics context for a device.

Constructors

protected **Graphics2D**()

Methods

abstract void	**addRenderingHints**(Map hints)
abstract void	**clip**(Shape s)
abstract void	**draw**(Shape s)
void	**draw3DRect**(int x, int y, int width, int height, boolean raised)
abstract void	**drawGlyphVector**(GlyphVector g, float x, float y)
abstract void	**drawImage**(BufferedImage img, BufferedImageOp op, int x, int y)
abstract boolean	**drawImage**(Image img, AffineTransform xform, ImageObserver obs)
abstract void	**drawRenderableImage**(RenderableImage img, AffineTransform xform)
abstract void	**drawRenderedImage**(RenderedImage img, AffineTransform xform)
abstract void	**drawString**(AttributedCharacterIterator iterator, float x, float y)
abstract void	**drawString**(AttributedCharacterIterator iterator, int x, int y)
abstract void	**drawString**(String s, float x, float y)
abstract void	**drawString**(String str, int x, int y)
abstract void	**fill**(Shape s)
void	**fill3DRect**(int x, int y, int width, int height, boolean raised)
abstract Color	**getBackground**()
abstract Composite	**getComposite**()
abstract GraphicsConfiguration	**getDeviceConfiguration**()
abstract FontRenderContext	**getFontRenderContext**()
abstract Paint	**getPaint**()
	getRenderingHint(RenderingHints.Key hintKey)
abstract	**RenderingHints** getRenderingHints()
abstract Stroke	**getStroke**()
abstract AffineTransform	**getTransform**()
abstract boolean	**hit**(Rectangle rect, Shape s, boolean onStroke)
abstract void	**rotate**(double theta)
abstract void	**rotate**(double theta, double x, double y)
abstract void	**scale**(double sx, double sy)
abstract void	**setBackground**(Color color)
abstract void	**setComposite**(Composite comp)
abstract void	**setPaint**(Paint paint)
abstract void	**setRenderingHint**(RenderingHints.Key hintKey, Object hintValue)
abstract void	**setRenderingHints**(Map hints)
abstract void	**setStroke**(Stroke s)
abstract void	**setTransform**(AffineTransform Tx)
abstract void	**shear**(double shx, double shy)

abstract void	**transform**(AffineTransform Tx)
abstract void	**translate**(double tx, double ty)
abstract void	**translate**(int x, int y)

public abstract class GraphicsEnvironment

extends Object

This class describes the collection of GraphicsDevice objects and Font objects available to a Java program on a given platform. The resources can be on the local machine or on a remote machine connected through a network.

Constructors

protected **GraphicsEnvironment**()

Methods

abstract Graphics2D	**createGraphics**(BufferedImage img)
abstract Font[]	**getAllFonts**()
abstract String[]	**getAvailableFontFamilyNames**()
abstract String[]	**getAvailableFontFamilyNames**(Locale l)
abstract GraphicsDevice	**getDefaultScreenDevice**()
static GraphicsEnvironment	**getLocalGraphicsEnvironment**()
abstract GraphicsDevice[]	**getScreenDevices**()

public class RenderingHints

extends Object
implements Map, Cloneable

This class encapsulates rendering hints that can be used by the Graphics2D class, and classes that implement BufferedImageOp and Raster. See Chapters 1, "Fundamentals of Java 2D," and 8, "Image Processing," for more details.

Inner Classes

static class **RenderingHints.Key**

Fields

static RenderingHints.Key **KEY_ALPHA_INTERPOLATION**
static RenderingHints.Key **KEY_ANTIALIASING**
static RenderingHints.Key **KEY_COLOR_RENDERING**
static RenderingHints.Key **KEY_DITHERING**
static RenderingHints.Key **KEY_FRACTIONALMETRICS**
static RenderingHints.Key **KEY_INTERPOLATION**
static RenderingHints.Key **KEY_RENDERING**
static RenderingHints.Key **KEY_TEXT_ANTIALIASING**
static Object **VALUE_ALPHA_INTERPOLATION_DEFAULT**
static Object **VALUE_ALPHA_INTERPOLATION_QUALITY**
static Object **VALUE_ALPHA_INTERPOLATION_SPEED**
static Object **VALUE_ANTIALIAS_DEFAULT**

```
static Object VALUE_ANTIALIAS_OFF
static Object VALUE_ANTIALIAS_ON
static Object VALUE_COLOR_RENDER_DEFAULT
static Object VALUE_COLOR_RENDER_QUALITY
static Object VALUE_COLOR_RENDER_SPEED
static Object VALUE_DITHER_DEFAULT
static Object VALUE_DITHER_DISABLE
static Object VALUE_DITHER_ENABLE
static Object VALUE_FRACTIONALMETRICS_DEFAULT
static Object VALUE_FRACTIONALMETRICS_OFF
static Object VALUE_FRACTIONALMETRICS_ON
static Object VALUE_INTERPOLATION_BICUBIC
static Object VALUE_INTERPOLATION_BILINEAR
static Object VALUE_INTERPOLATION_NEAREST_NEIGHBOR
static Object VALUE_RENDER_DEFAULT
static Object VALUE_RENDER_QUALITY
static Object VALUE_RENDER_SPEED
static Object VALUE_TEXT_ANTIALIAS_DEFAULT
static Object VALUE_TEXT_ANTIALIAS_OFF
static Object VALUE_TEXT_ANTIALIAS_ON
```

Constructors

```
RenderingHints(Map init)
RenderingHints(RenderingHints.Key key, Object value)
```

Methods

```
void        add(RenderingHints hints)
void        clear()
Object      clone()
boolean     containsKey(Object key)
boolean     containsValue(Object value)
Set         entrySet()
boolean     equals(Object o)
Object      get(Object key)
int         hashCode()
boolean     isEmpty()
Set         keySet()
Object      put(Object key, Object value)
void        putAll(Map m)
Object      remove(Object key)
int         size()
String      toString()
Collection  values()
```

public class TexturePaint

```
extends Object
implements Paint
```

Objects of this class fill a geometric shape with a texture that is specified by a BufferedImage object. See Chapter 2 for details on how to use the corresponding objects.

Constructors

TexturePaint(BufferedImage txtr, Rectangle2D anchor)

Methods

```
PaintContext    createContext(ColorModel cm, Rectangle deviceBounds,
                Rectangle2D userBounds, AffineTransform xform,
                RenderingHints hints)
Rectangle2D     getAnchorRect()
BufferedImage   getImage()
int             getTransparency()
```

Package Name: java.awt.color

This package contains encapsulations for color spaces and color profiles based on International Color Consortium (ICC) specifications. Chapter 2 presents the related text. You can also refer to Chapter 8 to see how to transform colors from one space to another using the ColorConvertOp filter.

public abstract class ColorSpace

```
extends Object
```

This is an abstract class that represents a color space. The concrete color space classes extend this class. Note the conversion methods for the RGB and CIEXYZ spaces.

Fields

```
static int  CS_CIEXYZ
static int  CS_GRAY
static int  CS_LINEAR_RGB
static int  CS_PYCC
static int  CS_sRGB
static int  TYPE_2CLR
static int  TYPE_3CLR
static int  TYPE_4CLR
static int  TYPE_5CLR
static int  TYPE_6CLR
static int  TYPE_7CLR
static int  TYPE_8CLR
static int  TYPE_9CLR
static int  TYPE_ACLR
static int  TYPE_BCLR
```

```
static int TYPE_CCLR
static int TYPE_CMY
static int TYPE_CMYK
static int TYPE_DCLR
static int TYPE_ECLR
static int TYPE_FCLR
static int TYPE_GRAY
static int TYPE_HLS
static int TYPE_HSV
static int TYPE_Lab
static int TYPE_Luv
static int TYPE_RGB
static int TYPE_XYZ
static int TYPE_YCbCr
static int TYPE_Yxy
```

Constructor

```
protected ColorSpace(int type, int numcomponents)
```

Methods

```
abstract float[]   fromCIEXYZ(float[] colorvalue)
abstract float[]   fromRGB(float[] rgbvalue)
static ColorSpace getInstance(int colorspace)
String             getName(int idx)
int                getNumComponents()
int                getType()
boolean  isCS    _sRGB()
abstract float[]  toCIEXYZ(float[] colorvalue)
abstract  float[] toRGB(float[] colorvalue)
```

public class ICC_ColorSpace

```
extends ColorSpace
```

This is a concrete class that extends the abstract ColorSpace class. The color space is an implementation based on the ICC Profile Format Specification.

Constructor

```
ICC_ColorSpace(ICC_Profile profile)
```

Methods

```
float[]     fromCIEXYZ(float[] colorvalue)
float[]     fromRGB(float[] rgbvalue)
ICC_Profile getProfile()
float[]     toCIEXYZ(float[] colorvalue)
float[]     toRGB(float[] colorvalue)
```

public class ICC_Profile

extends Object

This class represents a color profile data for device-independent and device-dependent color spaces based on the ICC Profile Format Specification.

Fields

static int **CLASS_ABSTRACT**
static int **CLASS_COLORSPACECONVERSION**
static int **CLASS_DEVICELINK**
static int **CLASS_DISPLAY**
static int **CLASS_INPUT**
static int **CLASS_NAMEDCOLOR**
static int **CLASS_OUTPUT**
static int **icAbsoluteColorimetric**
static int **icCurveCount**
static int **icCurveData**
static int **icHdrAttributes**
static int **icHdrCmmId**
static int **icHdrColorSpace**
static int **icHdrCreator**
static int **icHdrDate**
static int **icHdrDeviceClass**
static int **icHdrFlags**
static int **icHdrIlluminant**
static int **icHdrMagic**
static int **icHdrManufacturer**
static int **icHdrModel**
static int **icHdrPcs static int icHdrPlatform**
static int **icHdrRenderingIntent**
static int **icHdrSize**
static int **icHdrVersion**
static int **icPerceptual**
static int **icRelativeColorimetric**
static int **icSaturation**
static int **icSigAbstractClass**
static int **icSigAToB0Tag**
static int **icSigAToB1Tag**
static int **icSigAToB2Tag**
static int **icSigBlueColorantTag**
static int **icSigBlueTRCTag**
static int **icSigBToA0Tag**
static int **icSigBToA1Tag**
static int **icSigBToA2Tag**
static int **icSigCalibrationDateTimeTag**
static int **icSigCharTargetTag**
static int **icSigCmyData**
static int **icSigCmykData**

```
static int icSigColorSpaceClass
static int icSigCopyrightTag
static int icSigDeviceMfgDescTag
static int icSigDeviceModelDescTag
static int icSigDisplayClass
static int icSigGamutTag
static int icSigGrayData
static int icSigGrayTRCTag
static int icSigGreenColorantTag
static int icSigGreenTRCTag
static int icSigHead
static int icSigHlsData
static int icSigHsvData
static int icSigInputClass
static int icSigLabData
static int icSigLinkClass
static int icSigLuminanceTag
static int icSigLuvData
static int icSigMeasurementTag
static int icSigMediaBlackPointTag
static int icSigMediaWhitePointTag
static int icSigNamedColor2Tag
static int icSigNamedColorClass
static int icSigOutputClass
static int icSigPreview0Tag
static int icSigPreview1Tag
static int icSigPreview2Tag
static int icSigProfileDescriptionTag
static int icSigProfileSequenceDescTag
static int icSigPs2CRD0Tag
static int icSigPs2CRD1Tag
static int icSigPs2CRD2Tag
static int icSigPs2CRD3Tag
static int icSigPs2CSATag
static int icSigPs2RenderingIntentTag
static int icSigRedColorantTag
static int icSigRedTRCTag
static int icSigRgbData
static int icSigScreeningDescTag
static int icSigScreeningTag
static int icSigSpace2CLR
static int icSigSpace3CLR
static int icSigSpace4CLR
static int icSigSpace5CLR
static int icSigSpace6CLR
static int icSigSpace7CLR
static int icSigSpace8CLR
static int icSigSpace9CLR
static int icSigSpaceACLR
```

```
static int icSigSpaceBCLR
static int icSigSpaceCCLR
static int icSigSpaceDCLR
static int icSigSpaceECLR
static int icSigSpaceFCLR
static int icSigTechnologyTag
static int icSigUcrBgTag
static int icSigViewingCondDescTag
static int icSigViewingConditionsTag
static int icSigXYZData
static int icSigYCbCrData
static int icSigYxyData
static int icTagReserved
static int icTagType
static int icXYZNumberX
```

Methods

```
protected void     finalize()
int                getColorSpaceType()
byte[]             getData()
byte[]             getData(int tagSignature)
static ICC_Profile getInstance(byte[] data)
static ICC_Profile getInstance(InputStream s)
static ICC_Profile getInstance(int cspace)
static ICC_Profile getInstance(String fileName)
int                getMajorVersion()
int                getMinorVersion()
int                getNumComponents()
int                getPCSType()
int                getProfileClass()
void               setData(int tagSignature, byte[] tagData)
void               write(OutputStream s)
void               write(String fileName)
```

Package Name: java.awt.geom

This package stores the Java 2D classes for creating and working with two-dimensional geometric primitives. You will also find the affine transformation and area classes in this package. Chapters 3, "Geometric Shapes: Lines and Rectangles," 4, "Geometric Shapes: Curves, Arcs, and Ellipses," and 5, "General Paths and Composite Shapes," present the related text.

public abstract interface PathIterator

This interface describes the mechanism to retrieve the numerical data of the boundary of a geometric shape. The numerical data is computed based on the iteration process along the boundary. The interface retrieves the path of a shape's boundary by using lines, quadratic, or cubic Bézier splines.

Fields

```
static int SEG_CLOSE
static int SEG_CUBICTO
static int SEG_LINETO
static int SEG_MOVETO
static int SEG_QUADTO
static int WIND_EVEN_ODD
static int WIND_NON_ZERO
```

Methods

```
int      currentSegment(double[] coords)
int      currentSegment(float[] coords)
int      getWindingRule()
boolean  isDone()
void     next()
```

public class AffineTransform

```
extends Object
implements Cloneable, Serializable
```

This class represents an affine transform that performs a linear mapping on a pair of 2D coordinates to transform to another pair of 2D coordinates. An important property of this transfromation is to retain the "straightness" and "parallelism" of lines. An affine transformation object can be applied on a geometric shape to perform translation, scaling, flipping, rotation, and shear of the shape.

Fields

```
static int TYPE_FLIP
static int TYPE_GENERAL_ROTATION
static int TYPE_GENERAL_TRANSFORM
static int TYPE_IDENTITY
static int TYPE_MASK_ROTATION
static int TYPE_MASK_SCALE
static int TYPE_QUADRANT_ROTATION
static int TYPE_TRANSLATION
static int TYPE_UNIFORM_SCALE
```

Constructors

```
AffineTransform()
AffineTransform(AffineTransform Tx)
AffineTransform(double[] flatmatrix)
AffineTransform(double m00, double m10, double m01, double m11,
                double m02, double m12)
AffineTransform(float[] flatmatrix)
AffineTransform(float m00, float m10, float m01, float m11,
                float m02, float m12)
```

Methods

Object	**clone**()
void	**concatenate**(AffineTransform Tx)
AffineTransform	**createInverse**()
Shape	**createTransformedShape**(Shape pSrc)
void	**deltaTransform**(double[] srcPts, int srcOff, double[] dstPts, int dstOff, int numPts)
Point2D	**deltaTransform**(Point2D ptSrc, Point2D ptDst)
boolean	**equals**(Object obj)
double	**getDeterminant**()
void	**getMatrix**(double[] flatmatrix)
static AffineTransform	**getRotateInstance**(double theta)
static AffineTransform	**getRotateInstance**(double theta, double x, double y)
static AffineTransform	**getScaleInstance**(double sx, double sy)
double	**getScaleX**()
double	**getScaleY**()
static AffineTransform	**getShearInstance**(double shx, double shy)
double	**getShearX**()
double	**getShearY**()
static AffineTransform	**getTranslateInstance**(double tx, double ty)
double	**getTranslateX**()
double	**getTranslateY**()
int	**getType**()
int	**hashCode**()
void	**inverseTransform**(double[] srcPts, int srcOff, double[] dstPts, int dstOff, int numPts)
Point2D	**inverseTransform**(Point2D ptSrc, Point2D ptDst)
boolean	**isIdentity**()
void	**preConcatenate**(AffineTransform Tx)
void	**rotate**(double theta)
void	**rotate**(double theta, double x, double y)
void	**scale**(double sx, double sy)
void	**setToIdentity**()
void	**setToRotation**(double theta)
void	**setToRotation**(double theta, double x, double y)
void	**setToScale**(double sx, double sy)
void	**setToShear**(double shx, double shy)
void	**setToTranslation**(double tx, double ty)
void	**setTransform**(AffineTransform Tx)
void	**setTransform**(double m00, double m10, double m01, double m11, double m02, double m12)
void	**shear**(double shx, double shy)
String	**toString**()
void	**transform**(double[] srcPts, int srcOff, double[] dstPts, int dstOff, int numPts)
void	**transform**(double[] srcPts, int srcOff, float[] dstPts, int dstOff, int numPts)

void	**transform**(float[] srcPts, int srcOff, double[] dstPts, int dstOff, int numPts)
void	**transform**(float[] srcPts, int srcOff, float[] dstPts, int dstOff, int numPts)
void	**transform**(Point2D[] ptSrc, int srcOff, Point2D[] ptDst, int dstOff, int numPts)
Point2D	**transform**(Point2D ptSrc, Point2D ptDst)
void	**translate**(double tx, double ty)

public abstract class Arc2D

extends RectangularShape

This is an abstract class that serves as the parent for the concrete arc classes Arc2D.Float and Arc2D.Double. The concrete arc classes (inner classes) represent a 2D arc defined by a bounding rectangle, start angle, angular extent, and one of the closure types as OPEN, CHORD, or PIE. The actual storage representation of the coordinates is handled by the concrete subclasses.

Inner Classes

static class **Arc2D.Double**
static class **Arc2D.Float**

Fields

static int **CHORD**
static int **OPEN**
static int **PIE**

Constructor

protected **Arc2D**(int type)

Methods

boolean	**contains**(double x, double y)
boolean	**contains**(double x, double y, double w, double h)
boolean	**contains**(Rectangle2D r)
boolean	**containsAngle**(double angle)
abstract double	**getAngleExtent**()
abstract double	**getAngleStart**()
int	**getArcType**()
Rectangle2D	**getBounds2D**()
Point2D	**getEndPoint**()
PathIterator	**getPathIterator**(AffineTransform at)
Point2D	**getStartPoint**()
boolean	**intersects**(double x, double y, double w, double h)

```
protected abstract Rectangle2D  makeBounds(double x, double y,
                                    double w, double h)
abstract void                   setAngleExtent(double angExt)
void                            setAngles(double x1, double y1, double x2,
                                    double y2)
void                            setAngles(Point2D p1, Point2D p2)
abstract void                   setAngleStart(double angSt)
void                            setAngleStart(Point2D p)
void                            setArc(Arc2D a)
abstract void                   setArc(double x, double y, double w,
                                    double h, double angSt,
                                    double angExt, int closure)
void                            setArc(Point2D loc, Dimension2D size,
                                    double angSt, double angExt, int closure)
void                            setArc(Rectangle2D rect, double angSt,
                                    double angExt, int closure)
void                            setArcByCenter(double x, double y,
                                    double radius, double angSt,
                                    double angExt, int closure)
void                            setArcByTangent(Point2D p1, Point2D p2,
                                    Point2D p3, double radius)
void                            setArcType(int type)
void                            setFrame(double x, double y, double w, double h)
```

public static class Arc2D.Double

extends Arc2D

This is a concrete subclass of Arc that is specified in double precision. This is an inner class of Arc2D.

Fields

```
double extent
double height
double start
double width
double x
double y
```

Constructors

```
Arc2D.Double()
Arc2D.Double(double x, double y, double w, double h, double start,
     double extent, int type)
Arc2D.Double(int type)
Arc2D.Double(Rectangle2D ellipseBounds, double start, double extent,
     int type)
```

Methods

double	**getAngleExtent**()
double	**getAngleStart**()
double	**getHeight**()
double	**getWidth**()
double	**getX**()
double	**getY**()
boolean	**isEmpty**()
protected Rectangle2D	**makeBounds**(double x, double y, double w, double h)
void	**setAngleExtent**(double angExt)
void	**setAngleStart**(double angSt)
void	**setArc**(double x, double y, double w, double h, double angSt, double angExt, int closure)

public class Area

extends Object
implements Shape, Cloneable

This class represents an arbitrarily shaped area. An object of this class is helpful to perform CAG (Constructive Area Geometry) operations on other area-enclosing geometries to create new shapes. The CAG operations are add (union), subtract, intersect, and exclusiveOR.

Constructors

Area()
Area(Shape g)

Methods

void	**add**(Area rhs)
Object	**clone**()
boolean	**contains**(double x, double y)
boolean	**contains**(double x, double y, double w, double h)
boolean	**contains**(Point2D p)
boolean	**contains**(Rectangle2D r)
Area	**createTransformedArea**(AffineTransform t)
boolean	**equals**(Area rhs)
void	**exclusiveOr**(Area rhs)
Rectangle	**getBounds**()
Rectangle2D	**getBounds2D**()
PathIterator	**getPathIterator**(AffineTransform t)
PathIterator	**getPathIterator**(AffineTransform t, double f)
void	**intersect**(Area rhs)
boolean	**intersects**(double x, double y, double w, double h)
boolean	**intersects**(Rectangle2D r)
boolean	**isEmpty**()
boolean	**isPolygonal**()
boolean	**isRectangular**()
boolean	**isSingular**()

```
void       reset()
void       subtract(Area rhs)
void       transform(AffineTransform t)
```

public abstract class CubicCurve2D

extends Object
implements Shape, Cloneable

This abstract class represents a cubic parametric curve segment in 2D space. The concrete classes CubicCurve2D.Float and CubicCurve2D.Double represent the actual implementations.

Inner Classes

```
static class CubicCurve2D.Double
static class CubicCurve2D.Float
```

Constructors

```
protected CubicCurve2D()
```

Methods

```
Object           clone()
boolean          contains(double x, double y)
boolean          contains(double x, double y, double w, double h)
boolean          contains(Point2D p)
boolean          contains(Rectangle2D r)
Rectangle        getBounds()
abstract Point2D getCtrlP1()
abstract Point2D getCtrlP2()
abstract double  getCtrlX1()
abstract double  getCtrlX2()
abstract double  getCtrlY1()
abstract double  getCtrlY2()
double           getFlatness()
static double    getFlatness(double[] coords, int offset)
static double    getFlatness(double x1, double y1,
                 double ctrlx1, double ctrly1, double ctrlx2,
                 double ctrly2, double x2, double y2)
double           getFlatnessSq()
static double    getFlatnessSq(double[] coords, int offset)
static double    getFlatnessSq(double x1, double y1,
                 double ctrlx1, double ctrly1, double ctrlx2,
                 double ctrly2, double x2, double y2)
abstract Point2D getP1()
abstract Point2D getP2()
PathIterator     getPathIterator(AffineTransform at)
PathIterator     getPathIterator(AffineTransform at, double flatness)
abstract double  getX1()
abstract double  getX2()
```

```
abstract double    getY1()
abstract double    getY2()
boolean            intersects(double x, double y, double w, double h)
boolean            intersects(Rectangle2D r)
void               setCurve(CubicCurve2D c)
void               setCurve(double[] coords, int offset)
abstract void      setCurve(double x1, double y1,
                       double ctrlx1, double ctrly1,
                       double ctrlx2, double ctrly2,
                       double x2, double y2)
void               setCurve(Point2D[] pts, int offset)
void               setCurve(Point2D p1, Point2D cp1, Point2D cp2, Point2D p2)
static int         solveCubic(double[] eqn)
void               subdivide(CubicCurve2D left, CubicCurve2D right)
static void        subdivide(CubicCurve2D src, CubicCurve2D left,
                       CubicCurve2D right)
static void        subdivide(double[] src, int srcoff, double[] left,
                       int leftoff, double[] right, int rightoff)
```

public static class CubicCurve2D.Double

extends CubicCurve2D

This is an abstract class that represents a cubic curve in double-precision coordinates.

Fields

```
double ctrlx1
double ctrlx2
double ctrly1
double ctrly2
double x1
double x2
double y1
double y2
```

Constructors

```
CubicCurve2D.Double()
CubicCurve2D.Double(double x1, double y1, double ctrlx1, double ctrly1,
double ctrlx2, double ctrly2, double x2, double y2)
```

Methods

```
Rectangle2D getBounds2D()
Point2D     getCtrlP1()
Point2D     getCtrlP2()
double      getCtrlX1()
double      getCtrlX2()
double      getCtrlY1()
double      getCtrlY2()
Point2D     getP1()
```

Point2D	**getP2**()
double	**getX1**()
double	**getX2**()
double	**getY1**()
double	**getY2**()
void	**setCurve**(double x1, double y1, double ctrlx1, double ctrly1, double ctrlx2, double ctrly2, double x2, double y2)

public abstract class Ellipse2D

extends RectangularShape

This abstract class represents an ellipse that is defined by a bounding rectangle. The concrete subclasses Ellipse2D.Float and Ellipse2D.Double provide the actual storage representation.

Inner Classes

static class **Ellipse2D.Double**
static class **Ellipse2D.Float**

Constructor

protected **Ellipse2D**()

Methods

boolean	**contains**(double x, double y)
boolean	**contains**(double x, double y, double w, double h)
PathIterator	**getPathIterator**(AffineTransform at)
boolean	**intersects**(double x, double y, double w, double h)

public static class Ellipse2D.Double

extends Ellipse2D

This is a concrete class that represents an ellipse in double precision. This is an inner class of Ellipse2D.

Fields

double **height**
double **width**
double **x**
double **y**

Constructors

Ellipse2D.**Double**()
Ellipse2D.**Double**(double x, double y, double w, double h)

Methods

Rectangle2D	**getBounds2D**()
double	**getHeight**()
double	**getWidth**()
double	**getX**()
double	**getY**()
boolean	**isEmpty**()
void	**setFrame**(double x, double y, double w, double h)

public final class GeneralPath

extends Object
implements Shape, Cloneable

This class represents a geometric path constructed from straight lines and quadratic and cubic (Bézier) curves.

Fields

static int **WIND_EVEN_ODD**
static int **WIND_NON_ZERO**

Constructors

GeneralPath()
GeneralPath(int rule)
GeneralPath(int rule, int initialCapacity)
GeneralPath(Shape s)

Methods

void	**append**(PathIterator pi, boolean connect)
void	**append**(Shape s, boolean connect)
Object	**clone**()
void	**closePath**()
boolean	**contains**(double x, double y)
boolean	**contains**(double x, double y, double w, double h)
boolean	**contains**(Point2D p)
boolean	**contains**(Rectangle2D r)
Shape	**createTransformedShape**(AffineTransform at)
void	**curveTo**(float x1, float y1, float x2, float y2, float x3, float y3)
Rectangle	**getBounds**()
Rectangle2D	**getBounds2D**()
Point2D	**getCurrentPoint**()
PathIterator	**getPathIterator**(AffineTransform at)
PathIterator	**getPathIterator**(AffineTransform at, double flatness)
int	**getWindingRule**()
boolean	**intersects**(double x, double y, double w, double h)
boolean	**intersects**(Rectangle2D r)
void	**lineTo**(float x, float y)
void	**moveTo**(float x, float y)

```
void        quadTo(float x1, float y1, float x2, float y2)
void        reset()
void        setWindingRule(int rule)
void        transform(AffineTransform at)
```

public abstract class Line2D

```
extends Object
implements Shape, Cloneable
```

This abstract class represents a line segment in 2D-coordinate space. The concrete sub-classes Line2D.Float and Line2D.Double represent the actual implementations.

Inner Classes

```
static class Line2D.Double
static class Line2D.Float
```

Constructor

```
protected Line2D()
```

Methods

```
Object              clone()
boolean             contains(double x, double y)
boolean             contains(double x, double y, double w, double h)
boolean             contains(Point2D p)
boolean             contains(Rectangle2D r)
Rectangle           getBounds()
abstract Point2D    getP1()
abstract Point2D    getP2()
PathIterator        getPathIterator(AffineTransform at)
PathIterator        getPathIterator(AffineTransform at, double flatness)
abstract double     getX1()
abstract double     getX2()
abstract double     getY1()
abstract double     getY2()
boolean             intersects(double x, double y, double w, double h)
boolean             intersects(Rectangle2D r)
boolean             intersectsLine(double X1, double Y1, double X2, double Y2)
boolean             intersectsLine(Line2D l)
static boolean      linesIntersect(double X1, double Y1, double X2, double Y2,
                      double X3, double Y3, double X4, double Y4)
double              ptLineDist(double PX, double PY)
static double       ptLineDist(double X1, double Y1, double X2, double Y2,
                      double PX, double PY)
double              ptLineDist(Point2D pt)
double              ptLineDistSq(double PX, double PY)
static double       ptLineDistSq(double X1, double Y1, double X2, double Y2,
                      double PX, double PY)
double              ptLineDistSq(Point2D pt)
double              ptSegDist(double PX, double PY)
```

static double	**ptSegDist**(double X1, double Y1, double X2, double Y2, double PX, double PY)
double	**ptSegDist**(Point2D pt)
double	**ptSegDistSq**(double PX, double PY)
static double	**ptSegDistSq**(double X1, double Y1, double X2, double Y2, double PX, double PY)
double	**ptSegDistSq**(Point2D pt)
int	**relativeCCW**(double PX, double PY)
static int	**relativeCCW**(double X1, double Y1, double X2, double Y2, double PX, double PY)
int	**relativeCCW**(Point2D p)
abstract void	**setLine**(double X1, double Y1, double X2, double Y2)
void	**setLine**(Line2D l)
void	**setLine**(Point2D p1, Point2D p2)

public static class Line2D.Double

extends Line2D

This class represents a line object in double precision.

Fields

double **x1**
double **x2**
double **y1**
double **y2**

Constructors

Line2D.**Double**()
Line2D.**Double**(double X1, double Y1, double X2, double Y2)
Line2D.**Double**(Point2D p1, Point2D p2)

Methods

Rectangle2D	**getBounds2D**()
Point2D	**getP1**()
Point2D	**getP2**()
double	**getX1**()
double	**getX2**()
double	**getY1**()
double	**getY2**()
void	**setLine**(double X1, double Y1, double X2, double Y2)

public abstract class Point2D

extends Object
implements Cloneable

This is an abstract class for defining a point in 2D space. Note that this class does not implement the Shape interface; therefore, a point is not considered to be a geometric shape. The subclasses Point2D.Float and Point2D.Double are used for actual implementations.

Inner Classes

```
static class Point2D.Double
static class Point2D.Float
```

Constructor

```
protected Point2D()
```

Methods

```
Object          clone()
double          distance(double PX, double PY)
static double   distance(double X1, double Y1, double X2, double Y2)
double          distance(Point2D pt)
double          distanceSq(double PX, double PY)
static double   distanceSq(double X1, double Y1, double X2, double Y2)
double          distanceSq(Point2D pt)
boolean         equals(Object obj)
abstract double getX()
abstract double getY()
int             hashCode()
abstract void   setLocation(double x, double y)
void            setLocation(Point2D p)
```

public static class Point2D.Double

```
extends Point2D
```

This is a concrete subclass of the Point2D class. You can use this class to define a point object in double precision.

Fields

```
double x
double y
```

Constructors

```
Point2D.Double()
Point2D.Double(double x, double y)
```

Methods

```
double getX()
double getY()
void   setLocation(double x, double y)
String toString()
```

public abstract class QuadCurve2D

extends Object
implements Shape, Cloneable

This abstract class represents a quadratic parametric curve segment in 2D space. The concrete classes QuadraticCurve2D.Float and QuadraticCurve2D.Double represent the actual implementations.

Inner Classes

static class **QuadCurve2D.Double**
static class **QuadCurve2D.Float**

Constructor

protected **QuadCurve2D**()

Methods

Object	**clone**()
boolean	**contains**(double x, double y)
boolean	**contains**(double x, double y, double w, double h)
boolean	**contains**(Point2D p)
boolean	**contains**(Rectangle2D r)
Rectangle	**getBounds**()
abstract Point2D	**getCtrlPt**()
abstract double	**getCtrlX**()
abstract double	**getCtrlY**()
double	**getFlatness**()
static double	**getFlatness**(double[] coords, int offset)
static double	**getFlatness**(double x1, double y1, double ctrlx, double ctrly, double x2, double y2)
double	**getFlatnessSq**()
static double	**getFlatnessSq**(double[] coords, int offset)
static double	**getFlatnessSq**(double x1, double y1, double ctrlx, double ctrly, double x2, double y2)
abstract Point2D	**getP1**()
abstract Point2D	**getP2**()
PathIterator	**getPathIterator**(AffineTransform at)
PathIterator	**getPathIterator**(AffineTransform at, double flatness)
abstract double	**getX1**()
abstract double	**getX2**()
abstract double	**getY1**()
abstract double	**getY2**()
boolean	**intersects**(double x, double y, double w, double h)
boolean	**intersects**(Rectangle2D r)
void	**setCurve**(double[] coords, int offset)
abstract void	**setCurve**(double x1, double y1, double ctrlx, double ctrly, double x2, double y2)
void	**setCurve**(Point2D[] pts, int offset)
void	**setCurve**(Point2D p1, Point2D cp, Point2D p2)

void	**setCurve**(QuadCurve2D c)
static int	**solveQuadratic**(double[] eqn)
static void	**subdivide**(double[] src, int srcoff, double[] left, int leftoff, double[] right, int rightoff)
void	**subdivide**(QuadCurve2D left, QuadCurve2D right)
static void	**subdivide**(QuadCurve2D src, QuadCurve2D left, QuadCurve2D right)

public static class QuadCurve2D.Double

extends QuadCurve2D

This is a concrete class that represents quadratic parametric curves. The objects are specified in double precision.

Fields

double **ctrlx**
double **ctrly**
double **x1**
double **x2**
double **y1**
double **y2**

Constructors

QuadCurve2D.**Double**()
QuadCurve2D.**Double**(double x1, double y1, double ctrlx, double ctrly, double x2, double y2) Methods
Rectangle2D **getBounds2D**()
Point2D **getCtrlPt**()
double **getCtrlX**()
double **getCtrlY**()
Point2D **getP1**()
Point2D **getP2**()
double **getX1**()
double **getX2**()
double **getY1**()
double **getY2**()
voidsetCurve(double x1, double y1, double ctrlx, double ctrly, double x2, double y2)

public abstract class Rectangle2D

extends RectangularShape

This abstract class describes a rectangle defined by a location (x, y) and dimension (w, x, h). The concrete classes Rectangle2D.Float and Rectangle2D.Double represent the actual implementations.

Inner Classes

```
static class Rectangle2D.Double
static class Rectangle2D.Float
```

Fields

```
static int OUT_BOTTOM
static int OUT_LEFT
static int OUT_RIGHT
static int OUT_TOP
```

Constructor

```
protected Rectangle2D()
```

Methods

void	**add**(double newx, double newy)
void	**add**(Point2D pt)
void	**add**(Rectangle2D r)
boolean	**contains**(double x, double y)
boolean	**contains**(double x, double y, double w, double h)
abstract Rectangle2D	**createIntersection**(Rectangle2D r)
abstract Rectangle2D	**createUnion**(Rectangle2D r)
boolean	**equals**(Object obj)
Rectangle2D	**getBounds2D**()
PathIterator	**getPathIterator**(AffineTransform at)
PathIterator	**getPathIterator**(AffineTransform at, double flatness)
int	**hashCode**()
static void	**intersect**(Rectangle2D src1, Rectangle2D src2, Rectangle2D dest)
boolean	**intersects**(double x, double y, double w, double h)
boolean	**intersectsLine**(double x1, double y1, double x2, double y2)
boolean	**intersectsLine**(Line2D l)
abstract int	**outcode**(double x, double y)
int	**outcode**(Point2D p)
void	**setFrame**(double x, double y, double w, double h)
abstract void	**setRect**(double x, double y, double w, double h)
void	**setRect**(Rectangle2D r)
static void	**union**(Rectangle2D src1, Rectangle2D src2, Rectangle2D dest)

public static class Rectangle2D.Double

```
extends Rectangle2D
```

This is a concrete class that is used to create double-precision rectangles in 2D space.

Fields

```
double height
double width
```

```
double x
double y
```

Constructors

```
Rectangle2D.Double()
Rectangle2D.Double(double x, double y, double w, double h)
```

Methods

```
Rectangle2D  createIntersection(Rectangle2D r)
Rectangle2D  createUnion(Rectangle2D r)
Rectangle2D  getBounds2D()
double       getHeight()
double       getWidth()
double       getX()
double       getY()
boolean      isEmpty()
int          outcode(double x, double y)
void         setRect(double x, double y, double w, double h)
void         setRect(Rectangle2D r)
String       toString()
```

public abstract class RectangularShape

```
extends Object
implements Shape, Cloneable
```

This abstract class serves as the base class for objects whose geometry is defined by a rectangular frame as in arcs, ellipses, rectangles, and round rectangles.

Constructor

```
protected RectangularShape()
```

Methods

```
Object           clone()
boolean          contains(Point2D p)
boolean          contains(Rectangle2D r)
Rectangle        getBounds()
double           getCenterX()
double           getCenterY()
Rectangle2D      getFrame()
abstract double  getHeight()
double           getMaxX()
double           getMaxY()
double           getMinX()
double           getMinY()
PathIterator     getPathIterator(AffineTransform at, double flatness)
abstract double  getWidth()
abstract double  getX()
abstract double  getY()
```

boolean	**intersects**(Rectangle2D r)
abstract boolean	**isEmpty**()
abstract void	**setFrame**(double x, double y, double w, double h)
void	**setFrame**(Point2D loc, Dimension2D size)
void	**setFrame**(Rectangle2D r)
void	**setFrameFromCenter**(double centerX, double centerY, double cornerX, double cornerY)
void	**setFrameFromCenter**(Point2D center, Point2D corner)
void	**setFrameFromDiagonal**(double x1, double y1, double x2, double y2)
void	**setFrameFromDiagonal**(Point2D p1, Point2D p2)

public abstract class RoundRectangle2D

extends RectangularShape

This abstract class represents rectangles with rounded corners. The shape requires the parameters such as the location (x, y), dimension (w, x, h), and the width and height of the arc with which to round the corners. The concrete classes RoundRectangle2D.- Float and RoundRectangle2D.Double represent the actual implementations.

Inner Classes

static class **RoundRectangle2D.Double**
static class **RoundRectangle2D.Float**

Constructor

protected **RoundRectangle2D**()

Methods

boolean	**contains**(double x, double y)
boolean	**contains**(double x, double y, double w, double h)
abstract double	**getArcHeight**()
abstract double	**getArcWidth**()
PathIterator	**getPathIterator**(AffineTransform at)
boolean	**intersects**(double x, double y, double w, double h)
void	**setFrame**(double x, double y, double w, double h)
abstract void	**setRoundRect**(double x, double y, double w, double h, double arcWidth, double arcHeight)
void	**setRoundRect**(RoundRectangle2D rr)

public static class RoundRectangle2D.Double

extends RoundRectangle2D

This class defines a rectangle with rounded corners that is specified in double-precision values.

Fields

```
double  archeight
double  arcwidth
double  height
double  width
double  x
double  y
```

Constructors

```
RoundRectangle2D.Double()
RoundRectangle2D.Double(double x, double y, double w, double h,
double arcw, double arch)
```

Methods

```
double       getArcHeight()
double       getArcWidth()
Rectangle2D  getBounds2D()
double       getHeight()
double       getWidth()
double       getX()
double       getY()
boolean      isEmpty()
void         setRoundRect(double x, double y, double w, double h,
             double arcw, double arch)
void         setRoundRect(RoundRectangle2D rr)
```

Package Name: java.awt.font

This package stores the classes and interfaces relating to fonts and text layout in Java 2D. You can consult Chapter 6 for the related text.

public final class LineBreakMeasurer

```
extends Object
```

This class allows styled text to be broken into one or more lines that fit within a particular visual advance. This mechanism is useful to display a paragraph of text that fits within a specific width. The specified width is called the wrapping width.

Constructors

```
LineBreakMeasurer(AttributedCharacterIterator text,
                  BreakIterator breakIter,
                  FontRenderContext frc)
LineBreakMeasurer(AttributedCharacterIterator text,
                  FontRenderContext frc)
```

Methods

void	**deleteChar**(AttributedCharacterIterator newParagraph, int deletePos)
int	**getPosition**()
void	**insertChar**(AttributedCharacterIterator newParagraph, int insertPos)
TextLayout	**nextLayout**(float maxAdvance)
TextLayout	**nextLayout**(float wrappingWidth, int offsetLimit, boolean requireNextWord)
int	**nextOffset**(float maxAdvance)
int	**nextOffset**(float wrappingWidth, int offsetLimit, boolean requireNextWord)
void	**setPosition**(int newPosition)

public final class TextAttribute

extends AttributedCharacterIterator.Attribute

This class defines attribute keys and attribute values used for text rendering.

Fields

static	TextAttribute	**BACKGROUND**
static	TextAttribute	**BIDI_EMBEDDING**
static	TextAttribute	**CHAR_REPLACEMENT**
static	TextAttribute	**FAMILY**
static	TextAttribute	**FONT**
static	TextAttribute	**FOREGROUND**
static	TextAttribute	**INPUT_METHOD_HIGHLIGHT**
static	TextAttribute	**JUSTIFICATION**
static	Float	**JUSTIFICATION_FULL**
static	Float	**JUSTIFICATION_NONE**
static	TextAttribute	**POSTURE**
static	Float	**POSTURE_OBLIQUE**
static	Float	**POSTURE_REGULAR**
static	TextAttribute	**RUN_DIRECTION**
static	Boolean	**RUN_DIRECTION_LTR**
static	Boolean	**RUN_DIRECTION_RTL**
static	TextAttribute	**SIZE**
static	TextAttribute	**STRIKETHROUGH**
static	Boolean	**STRIKETHROUGH_ON**
static	TextAttribute	**SUPERSCRIPT**
static	Integer	**SUPERSCRIPT_SUB**
static	Integer	**SUPERSCRIPT_SUPER**
static	TextAttribute	**SWAP_COLORS**
static	Boolean	**SWAP_COLORS_ON**
static	TextAttribute	**TRANSFORM**
static	TextAttribute	**UNDERLINE**
static	Integer	**UNDERLINE_ON**
static	TextAttribute	**WEIGHT**

```
static Float WEIGHT_BOLD
static Float WEIGHT_DEMIBOLD
static Float WEIGHT_DEMILIGHT
static Float WEIGHT_EXTRA_LIGHT
static Float WEIGHT_EXTRABOLD
static Float WEIGHT_HEAVY
static Float WEIGHT_LIGHT
static Float WEIGHT_MEDIUM
static Float WEIGHT_REGULAR
static Float WEIGHT_SEMIBOLD
static Float WEIGHT_ULTRABOLD
static TextAttribute WIDTH
static Float WIDTH_CONDENSED
static Float WIDTH_EXTENDED
static Float WIDTH_REGULAR
static Float WIDTH_SEMI_CONDENSED
static Float WIDTH_SEMI_EXTENDED
```

Constructor

```
protected TextAttribute(String name)
```

Methods

```
protected Object readResolve()
```

public final class TextHitInfo

```
extends Object
```

The objects of this class help to retrieve the information when the user inputs a hit over text. See the methods of this class to know the related operations.

Methods

```
static TextHitInfo afterOffset(int offset)
static TextHitInfo beforeOffset(int offset)
boolean           equals(Object obj)
boolean           equals(TextHitInfo hitInfo)
int               getCharIndex()
                  intgetInsertionIndex()
TextHitInfo       getOffsetHit(int delta)
TextHitInfo       getOtherHit()
int               hashCode()
boolean           isLeadingEdge()
static TextHitInfo leading(int charIndex)
String            toString()
static TextHitInfo trailing(int charIndex)
```

public final class TextLayout

```
extends Object
implements Cloneable
```

This class represents a mechanism to handle layout out of styled text in Java 2D. This class supports a number of important features to laying out text. See Chapter 6 for detailed information on this class.

Inner Class

```
static class TextLayout.CaretPolicy
```

Fields

```
static TextLayout.CaretPolicy DEFAULT_CARET_POLICY
```

Constructors

```
TextLayout(AttributedCharacterIterator text, FontRenderContext frc)
TextLayout(String string, Font font, FontRenderContext frc)
TextLayout(String string, Map attributes, FontRenderContext frc)
```

Methods

protected Object	**clone**()
void	**draw**(Graphics2D g2, float x, float y)
boolean	**equals**(Object obj)
boolean	**equals**(TextLayout rhs)
float	**getAdvance**()
float	**getAscent**()
byte	**getBaseline**()
float[]	**getBaselineOffsets**()
Shape	**getBlackBoxBounds**(int firstEndpoint, int secondEndpoint)
Rectangle2D	**getBounds**()
float[]	**getCaretInfo**(TextHitInfo hit)
float[]	**getCaretInfo**(TextHitInfo hit, Rectangle2D bounds)
Shape	**getCaretShape**(TextHitInfo hit)
Shape	**getCaretShape**(TextHitInfo hit, Rectangle2D bounds)
Shape[]	**getCaretShapes**(int offset)
Shape[]	**getCaretShapes**(int offset, Rectangle2D bounds)
Shape[]	**getCaretShapes**(int offset, Rectangle2D bounds, TextLayout.CaretPolicy policy)
int	**getCharacterCount**()
byte	**getCharacterLevel**(int index)
float	**getDescent**()
TextLayout	**getJustifiedLayout**(float justificationWidth)
float	**getLeading**()
Shape	**getLogicalHighlightShape**(int firstEndpoint, int secondEndpoint)
Shape	**getLogicalHighlightShape**(int firstEndpoint, int secondEndpoint, Rectangle2D bounds)

int[]	**getLogicalRangesForVisualSelection**(TextHitInfo firstEndpoint, TextHitInfo secondEndpoint)
TextHitInfo	**getNextLeftHit**(int offset)
TextHitInfo	**getNextLeftHit**(int offset, TextLayout.CaretPolicy policy)
TextHitInfo	**getNextLeftHit**(TextHitInfo hit)
TextHitInfo	**getNextRightHit**(int offset)
TextHitInfo	**getNextRightHit**(int offset, TextLayout.CaretPolicy policy)
TextHitInfo	**getNextRightHit**(TextHitInfo hit)
Shape	**getOutline**(AffineTransform tx)
float	**getVisibleAdvance**()
Shape	**getVisualHighlightShape**(TextHitInfo firstEndpoint, TextHitInfo secondEndpoint)
Shape	**getVisualHighlightShape**(TextHitInfo firstEndpoint, TextHitInfo secondEndpoint, Rectangle2D bounds)
TextHitInfo	**getVisualOtherHit**(TextHitInfo hit)
protected void	**handleJustify**(float justificationWidth)
int	**hashCode**()
TextHitInfo	**hitTestChar**(float x, float y)
TextHitInfo	**hitTestChar**(float x, float y, Rectangle2D bounds)
boolean	**isLeftToRight**()
boolean	**isVertical**()
String	**toString**()

Package Name: java.awt.image

This package stores the image processing operations supported in Java 2D. The package contains two very important interfaces: BufferedImageOp and RasterOp. The classes that represent various filtering operations implement these interfaces. Therefore, the methods from these interfaces appear in the implementation classes. See the text presented in Chapter 8, "Image Processing," for details of various filtering operations that implement these interfaces. Chapter 7, "Buffered Imaging," presents the topics on buffered imaging.

public abstract interface BufferedImageOp

This is a design-level interface that describes single-input/single-output filtering operations performed on objects of type BufferedImage. The implementation classes will specify whether an in-place filtering operation is allowed. In-place filtering operations allow the source buffer to be used by the destination image to avoid unnecessary memory usage. The filtering classes LookupOp, RescaleOp, ColorConvertOp, ConvolveOp, and AffineTransformOp implement this interface.

Methods

BufferedImage	**createCompatibleDestImage**(BufferedImage src, ColorModel destCM)
BufferedImage	**filter**(BufferedImage src, BufferedImage dest)
Rectangle2D	**getBounds2D**(BufferedImage src)
Point2D	**getPoint2D**(Point2D srcPt, Point2D dstPt)
RenderingHints	**getRenderingHints**()

public abstract interface RasterOp

This is a design-level interface that describes single-input/single-output operations performed on `Raster` objects. The filter classes `LookupOp`, `RescaleOp`, `ColorConvertOp`, `BandCombineOp`, `ConvolveOp`, and `AffineTransformOp` implement this interface.

Methods

```
WritableRaster createCompatibleDestRaster(Raster src)
WritableRaster filter(Raster src, WritableRaster dest)
Rectangle2D    getBounds2D(Raster src)
Point2D        getPoint2D(Point2D srcPt, Point2D dstPt)
RenderingHints getRenderingHints()
```

public class BufferedImage

```
extends Image
implements WritableRenderedImage
```

This class represents an image stored in the accessible memory of a computer. This class consists of a `ColorModel` and a `Raster` of image data. The buffered image objects have the top-left corner coordinates (0, 0). See Chapter 7 to learn about imaging using `BufferedImage` objects.

Fields

```
static int TYPE_3BYTE_BGR
static int TYPE_4BYTE_ABGR
static int TYPE_4BYTE_ABGR_PRE
static int TYPE_BYTE_BINARY
static int TYPE_BYTE_GRAY
static int TYPE_BYTE_INDEXED
static int TYPE_CUSTOM
static int TYPE_INT_ARGB
static int TYPE_INT_ARGB_PRE
static int TYPE_INT_BGR
static int TYPE_INT_RGB
static int TYPE_USHORT_555_RGB
static int TYPE_USHORT_565_RGB
static int TYPE_USHORT_GRAY
```

Constructors

```
BufferedImage(ColorModel cm, WritableRaster raster,
              boolean isRasterPremultiplied, Hashtable properties)
BufferedImage(int width, int height, int imageType)
BufferedImage(int width, int height, int imageType, IndexColorModel cm)
```

Methods

```
void           addTileObserver(TileObserver to)
void           coerceData(boolean isAlphaPremultiplied)
WritableRaster copyData(WritableRaster outRaster)
```

```
Graphics2D      createGraphics()
void            flush()
WritableRaster  getAlphaRaster()
ColorModel      getColorModel()
Raster          getData()
Raster          getData(Rectangle rect)
Graphics        getGraphics()
int             getHeight()
int             getHeight(ImageObserver observer)
int             getMinTileX()
int             getMinTileY()
int             getMinX()
int             getMinY()
int             getNumXTiles()
int             getNumYTiles()
Object          getProperty(String name)
Object          getProperty(String name, ImageObserver observer)
String[]        getPropertyNames()
WritableRaster  getRaster()
int             getRGB(int x, int y)
int[]           getRGB(int startX, int startY, int w, int h, int[] rgbArray,
                int offset, int scansize)
SampleModel     getSampleModel()
ImageProducer   getSource()
Vector          getSources()
BufferedImage   getSubimage(int x, int y, int w, int h)
Raster          getTile(int tileX, int tileY)
int             getTileGridXOffset()
int             getTileGridYOffset()
int             getTileHeight()
int             getTileWidth()
int             getType()
int             getWidth()
int             getWidth(ImageObserver observer)
WritableRaster  getWritableTile(int tileX, int tileY)
Point[]         getWritableTileIndices()
boolean         hasTileWriters()
boolean         isAlphaPremultiplied()
boolean         isTileWritable(int tileX, int tileY)
void            releaseWritableTile(int tileX, int tileY)
void            removeTileObserver(TileObserver to)
void            setData(Raster r)
void            setRGB(int x, int y, int rgb)
void            setRGB(int startX, int startY, int w, int h, int[] rgbArray,
                int offset, int scansize)
String          toString()
```

public class Raster

extends Object

This class represents a rectangular array of pixels, which is called a raster. The class encapsulates a DataBuffer that stores the sample values and a SampleModel that describes how to locate a given sample value in a DataBuffer. See Chapter 7 to learn how to use a raster.

Fields

```
protected DataBuffer dataBuffer
protected int height
protected int minX
protected int minY
protected int numBands
protected int numDataElements
protected Raster parent
protected SampleModel sampleModel
protected int sampleModelTranslateX
protected int sampleModelTranslateY
protected int width
```

Constructors

```
protected Raster(SampleModel sampleModel, DataBuffer dataBuffer,
                 Point origin)
protected Raster(SampleModel sampleModel, DataBuffer dataBuffer,
                 Rectangle aRegion, Point sampleModelTranslate,
                 Raster parent)
protected Raster(SampleModel sampleModel, Point origin)
```

Methods

```
static WritableRaster  createBandedRaster(DataBuffer dataBuffer, int w,
                          int h, int scanlineStride, int[] bankIndices,
                          int[] bandOffsets, Point location)
static WritableRaster  createBandedRaster(int dataType, int w, int h,
                          int scanlineStride, int[] bankIndices,
                          int[] bandOffsets, Point location)
static WritableRaster  createBandedRaster(int dataType, int w, int h,
                          int bands, Point location)
Raster                 createChild(int parentX, int parentY, int width,
                          int height, int childMinX, int childMinY,
                          int[] bandList)
WritableRaster         createCompatibleWritableRaster()
WritableRaster         createCompatibleWritableRaster(int w, int h)
WritableRaster         createCompatibleWritableRaster(int x, int y, int w,
                          int h)
WritableRaster         createCompatibleWritableRaster(Rectangle rect)
```

```
static WritableRaster  createInterleavedRaster(DataBuffer dataBuffer,
                            int w, int h, int scanlineStride, int pixelStride,
                            int[] bandOffsets, Point location)
static WritableRaster  createInterleavedRaster(int dataType, int w, int h,
                            int scanlineStride, int pixelStride,
                            int[] bandOffsets, Point location)
static WritableRaster  createInterleavedRaster(int dataType, int w, int h,
                            int bands, Point location)
static WritableRaster  createPackedRaster(DataBuffer dataBuffer, int w,
                            int h, int scanlineStride, int[] bandMasks,
                            Point location)
static WritableRaster  createPackedRaster(DataBuffer dataBuffer, int w,
                            int h, int bitsPerPixel, Point location)
static WritableRaster  createPackedRaster(int dataType, int w, int h,
                            int[] bandMasks, Point location)
static WritableRaster  createPackedRaster(int dataType, int w, int h,
                            int bands, int bitsPerBand, Point location)
static Raster          createRaster(SampleModel sm, DataBuffer db,
                            Point location)
Raster                 createTranslatedChild(int childMinX, int childMinY)
static WritableRaster  createWritableRaster(SampleModel sm, DataBuffer db,
                            Point location)
static WritableRaster  createWritableRaster(SampleModel sm, Point location)
Rectangle              getBounds()
DataBuffer             getDataBuffer()
Object                 getDataElements(int x, int y, int w, int h,
                            Object outData)
Object                 getDataElements(int x, int y, Object outData)
int                    getHeight()
int                    getMinX()
int                    getMinY()
int                    getNumBands()
int                    getNumDataElements()
Raster                 getParent()
double[]               getPixel(int x, int y, double[] dArray)
float[]                getPixel(int x, int y, float[] fArray)
int[]                  getPixel(int x, int y, int[] iArray)
double[]               getPixels(int x, int y, int w, int h,
                            double[] dArray)
float[]                getPixels(int x, int y, int w, int h, float[] fArray)
int[]                  getPixels(int x, int y, int w, int h, int[] iArray)
int                    getSample(int x, int y, int b)
double                 getSampleDouble(int x, int y, int b)
float                  getSampleFloat(int x, int y, int b)
SampleModel            getSampleModel()
int                    getSampleModelTranslateX()
int                    getSampleModelTranslateY()
double[]               getSamples(int x, int y, int w, int h, int b,
                            double[] dArray)
```

float[]	**getSamples**(int x, int y, int w, int h, int b, float[] fArray)
int[]	**getSamples**(int x, int y, int w, int h, int b, int[] iArray)
int	**getTransferType**()
int	**getWidth**()

Package Name: java.awt.print

This package contains very important classes and interfaces for implementing print capabilities in an application. For the related text, you can consult Chapter 9, "Printing."

public abstract interface Pageable

This interface represents a set of pages to be printed. The implementation object can return the total number of pages in the set as well as the page format and the printable object for a specified page.

Field

static int **UNKNOWN_NUMBER_OF_PAGES**

Methods

int	**getNumberOfPages**()
PageFormat	**getPageFormat**(int pageIndex)
Printable	**getPrintable**(int pageIndex)

public abstract interface Printable

This interface must be implemented by the classes that send output to a printer. The implementation classes provide code for the print() method. The print() method is similar to the paint() method used for the display graphics context. The printing system calls the print method of the current page painter to render a page. See Chapter 9 for more details.

Fields

static int **NO_SUCH_PAGE**
static int **PAGE_EXISTS**

Method

int **print**(Graphics graphics, PageFormat pageFormat, int pageIndex)

public class Book

extends Object
implements Pageable

This class represents a multipage document in which pages can have different page formats and page painters. This class implements the Pageable interface to interact with a PrinterJob.

Constructor

Book()

Methods

void	**append**(Printable painter, PageFormat page)
void	**append**(Printable painter, PageFormat page, int numPages)
int	**getNumberOfPages**()
PageFormat	**getPageFormat**(int pageIndex)
Printable	**getPrintable**(int pageIndex)
void	**setPage**(int pageIndex, Printable painter, PageFormat page)

public class PageFormat

extends **Object**
implements **Cloneable**

This class represents the page format by encapsulating the properties such as the size and orientation of the page to be printed.

Fields

static int **LANDSCAPE**
static int **PORTRAIT**
static int **REVERSE_LANDSCAPE**

Constructor

PageFormat()

Methods

Object	**clone**()
double	**getHeight**()
double	**getImageableWidth**()
double	**getImageableX**()
double	**getImageableY**()
double[]	**getMatrix**()
int	**getOrientation**()
Paper	**getPaper**()
double	**getWidth**()
void	**setOrientation**(int orientation)
void	**setPaper**(Paper paper)

public class Paper

extends Object
implements Cloneable

This class represents the actual paper used for printing. It encapsulates the physical characteristics of the paper.

Constructor

```
Paper()
```

Methods

```
Object   clone()
double   getHeight()
double   getImageableHeight()
double   getImageableWidth()
double   getImageableX()
double   getImageableY()
double   getWidth()
void     setImageableArea(double x, double y, double width, double height)
void     setSize(double width, double height)
```

public abstract class PrinterJob

```
extends Object
```

This class is represents the control mechanism to control the printing process. The class encapsulates operations to prepare a print job, optionally to invoke a print dialog box for the user, and then to print the pages of the job. See Chapter 9 for details.

Constructor

```
PrinterJob()
```

Methods

```
abstract void       cancel()
PageFormat          defaultPage()
abstract PageFormat defaultPage(PageFormat page)
abstract int        getCopies()
abstract String     getJobName()
static PrinterJob   getPrinterJob()
abstract String     getUserName()
abstract boolean    isCancelled()
abstract PageFormat pageDialog(PageFormat page)
abstract void       print()
abstract boolean    printDialog()
abstract void       setCopies(int copies)
abstract void       setJobName(String jobName)
abstract void       setPageable(Pageable document)
abstract void       setPrintable(Printable painter)
abstract void       setPrintable(Printable painter, PageFormat format)
abstract PageFormat validatePage(PageFormat page)
```

INDEX

A

abstract classes
abstract interfaces
Abstract Windowing Toolkit. *See* **AWT**
addition operation, CAG and, 145
affine transform filter, 256-264
affine transforms, 13
AffineTransform class, 13, 320-322
AffineTransformOp class, 256
alpha value, color, 29
AlphaComposite class, 306
animation, buffered images and, 211-217
API quick reference, 304-348

Personal Bookshelf

Get FREE books and more...when you register this book online for our Personal Bookshelf Program

http://register.samspublishing.com/

SAMS

 Register online and you can sign up for our *FREE Personal Bookshelf Program*...unlimited access to the electronic version of more than 200 complete computer books—immediately! That means you'll have 100,000 pages of valuable information onscreen, at your fingertips!

 Plus, you can access product support, including complimentary downloads, technical support files, book-focused links, companion Web sites, author sites, and more!

 And you'll be automatically registered to receive a *FREE subscription to a weekly email newsletter* to help you stay current with news, announcements, sample book chapters, and special events, including sweepstakes, contests, and various product giveaways!

 We value your comments! Best of all, the entire registration process takes only a few minutes to complete, so go online and get the greatest value going—absolutely FREE!

Don't Miss Out On This Great Opportunity!

Sams is a brand of Macmillan Computer Publishing USA.

For more information, please visit *www.mcp.com*

Copyright ©1999 Macmillan Computer Publishing USA

It's
Here!

The IT site
you asked for...

InformIT™

InformIT is a complete online library
delivering information, technology,
reference, training, news, and opinion to IT
professionals, students, and corporate users.

Find IT Solutions Here!

www.informit.com

InformIT is a trademark of Macmillan USA, Inc.
Copyright © 1999 Macmillan USA, Inc.